Gender and Inequalities

Praise for this book

'*Gender and Inequalities* is a timely and multi-faceted engagement with urgent issues of development. Its key message, 'economic growth, if pursued without strategies to curb widening inequalities in society, is fundamentally fragile and precarious' needs to be heard urgently to challenge the mainstream reductive reasoning on development.'

Professor Shirin M. Rai, Phd, FAcSS,
Department of Politics and International Studies, University of Warwick

Gender and Inequalities

Edited by
Naila Kabeer and Caroline Sweetman

Published by Practical Action Publishing in association with Oxfam GB

Practical Action Publishing Ltd
Rugby, Warwickshire, UK
www.practicalactionpublishing.org

A catalogue record for this book is available from the British Library.
A catalogue record for this book has been requested from the Library of Congress.

ISBN 978-1-78853-013-2 Paperback
ISBN 978-1-78853-012-5 Hardback
ISBN 978-1-78044-728-5 Ebook
ISBN 978-1-78044-727-8 Library PDF

Citation: Kabeer, N. and Sweetman, C. (eds) (2018) *Gender and Inequalities*, Rugby, UK: Practical Action Publishing and Oxford: Oxfam GB. <http://dx.doi.org/10.3362/9781780447278>

Since 1974, Practical Action Publishing has published and disseminated books and information in support of international development work throughout the world.

Practical Action Publishing is a trading name of Practical Action Publishing Ltd (Company Reg. No. 1159018), the wholly owned publishing company of Practical Action. Practical Action Publishing trades only in support of its parent charity objectives and any profits are covenanted back to Practical Action (Charity Reg. No.247257, Group VAT Registration No. 880 9924 76).

Oxfam is a registered charity in England and Wales (no 202918) and Scotland (SC039042). Oxfam GB is a member of Oxfam International.

Oxfam GB,
Oxfam House, John Smith Drive,
Oxford, OX4 2JY, UK
www.oxfam.org.uk

Cover photo shows: a tribal woman watering the cement during road construction in Pune, India.
Credit: Nita Jatar Kulkarni

Printed in the United Kingdom

Contents

http://dx.doi.org/10.3362/9781780447278.000

About the editors

Naila Kabeer is co-editor of the Inequalities issue in the international journal *Gender & Development*. She is Professor of Gender and Development at the Gender Institute, London School of Economics.

Caroline Sweetman is Editor of the international journal *Gender & Development* and works for Oxfam GB.

Working in Gender and Development

The *Working in Gender and Development series* brings together themed selections of the best articles from the journal *Gender & Development* and other Oxfam publications for development practitioners and policy makers, students, and academics. Titles in the series present the theory and practice of gender-oriented development in a way that records experience, describes good practice, and shares information about resources. Books in the series will contribute to and review current thinking on the gender dimensions of particular development and relief issues.

Other titles in the series are available from www.developmentbookshop.com and include:

Gender-Based Violence
HIV and AIDS
Climate Change and Gender Justice
Gender and the Economic Crisis
Gender, Faith and Development
Gender, Monitoring, Evaluation and Learning
Gender, Business and Enterprise
Gender, Development and Care

For further information on the journal please visit
www.genderanddevelopment.org

CHAPTER 1

Introduction: Gender and Inequalities

Naila Kabeer and Caroline Sweetman

Patterns of poverty and inequality are changing, and challenging the ways we understand development. In recent years, many countries that tell a story of economic growth at national level have also been showing worsening 'vertical' inequality (measured in terms of wealth or income). This increased polarisation between rich and poor in middle-income and high-income countries highlights the flaw in the (often implicit, but sometimes explicit) notion that economic growth heralds 'progress' and 'development' for humanity.

Gender and Inequalities presents a wide range of voices in international development research, policy and practice, and offers a gendered perspective on the question of inequalities. As Naila Kabeer states in her overview chapter, gender inequality is 'structured into the organisation of social relations in a society as fundamentally as class in capitalist societies, race in apartheid South Africa and caste in India. Women's location at the intersection between production and reproduction, between making a living and caring for the family, makes the organisation of gender relations central to the nexus between economic growth and human development, and hence central to the development agenda' (Kabeer, this book p. 18).

Human societies, in other words, are organised along gendered lines, giving gender inequality a special economic, social and political primacy. Gender relations, roles and unequal power imbue the lives of all women and girls in all societies; they intensify the disadvantages inherent in being born in a country in the global South, being part of a marginalised ethnic group, the experience of disability. The very pervasiveness of gender inequality demands that policymakers should focus on it as a central concern.

The goal of human development should be sustainable economies which support all the world's inhabitants, regardless of who they are or where they are located, to live decent, dignified lives characterised by fulfillment and wellbeing. The geographic distribution of poverty is altering, and our understanding of the drivers of poverty is becoming ever more sophisticated. With that comes new insight into the kinds of development policy and practice that might be effective in ensuring just and sustainable human development. Horizontal inequalities, including gender, race and caste, not only affect individual women's or men's chances of escaping or enduring poverty, but also shape the chances of households dependent on them.

http://dx.doi.org/10.3362/9781780447278.001

Diane Perrons' chapter considers the gendered nature of growing income inequality via an examination of the ways in which policymakers responded to economic crises, including structural adjustment (SAPs) in the 1980s and 1990s, and draws parallels with the more recent economic crisis in the supposedly 'advanced' economies of Europe and North America. The austerity policies of the past decade have marked parallels with earlier responses to SAPs. The world's economists and politicians continue to rely on the unpaid labour and unequal bargaining power of women in the market, to subsidise the costs of failed economic policies, and to justify unfair and unjust responses to the problems that these cause.

Daria Ukhova's chapter presents her research into gender relations in a range of countries which have shown significant economic growth in recent years, to ascertain the extent to which this has coincided with improvements in gender relations, measured across a range of indicators. There has been little attention thus far to this question. While gender equality indicators have improved in the main, these fail to capture the whole picture. Underlying gender inequality remains, and is morphing into new forms. To ensure economic progress and gender equality, these goals need to be worked on simultaneously and intersectionally, rather than in isolation, or sequentially. The aims of economic growth and prosperity, and anti-poverty, cannot be conflated with gender equality.

These insights should not only inform national and international development policymaking. They also hold for NGOs working at community level on anti-poverty and 'economic empowerment' aims. In their chapter Sheepa Hafiza, Mohammed Kamruzzaman and Hasne Ara Begum discuss work by BRAC, the world's largest NGO, to increase low-income Bangladeshi women's ability to earn income through directly challenging the gender-related barriers to them doing this. Insights from the Gender Quality Action Learning Programme (GQAL) confirm that economic empowerment projects cannot be the sole entry-point to wellbeing and security for women whose participation is constrained by gender inequalities operating within the household and the market. Instead, projects need to work with women and their communities to address gender inequality in parallel with economic poverty.

In their chapter Christine Hughes, Mara Bolis, Rebecca Fries and Stephanie Finigan also address the links between economic inequalities and gender inequality, from the point of view of development practitioners working to empower women through livelihood projects. They usefully survey the literature on the impact of women's economic empowerment programming on domestic violence. While gender and development researchers have focused on this connection, the evaluations and impact assessments undertaken by development organisations have not often focused on this area, despite its critical importance in informing current and future work with women who experience violence as the ultimate expression of extreme inequality, aggravated and perpetuated by poverty.

If poverty for women can mean violence and abuse within marriage and the family, heightened hunger due to norms of women eating last, and other gendered forms of suffering, why do the poverty measures used by policymakers fail to capture such dimensions? Two chapters here, by Sharon Bessell, and Gaëlle Ferrant and Keiko Nowacka, focus on the development of measures to understand poverty as an experience shaped by gender inequality. Development policymakers urgently need these measures to accurately trace and depict poverty as it is experienced by women and girls, and to relate the situation of poverty to the processes whereby individuals and households experience impoverishment (and enrichment). Development institutions and national governments need to understand how unequal and unjust gender roles and relations perpetuate poverty and drive inequality. The low-paid and unpaid labour of poor women and girls in poverty subsidises economic growth, and elites capture the gains, perpetuating current poverty, and ensuring it remains unchallenged into the future.

The current moment, when relationships which were previously assumed to be clear between economic growth and an end to poverty and inequality are being questioned afresh, is a moment to examine new research areas which reveal new and little-understood connections and disconnects. In their chapter Andrea Papan and Barbara Clow share insights from the Full Plate Project, which addressed women's experience of food insecurity, obesity, and chronic disease in Atlantic Canada. Learning more about low-income women's resourcefulness in evolving coping strategies to feed themselves and their dependents challenges old stereotypes about what poverty looks like and how people survive it. Such research is of critical importance to inform economic and social policy based on justice and an understanding of the centrality of women's rights to anti-poverty strategies.

In their chapter Jayshree P. Mangubhai and Chiara Capraro discuss ActionAid and its partner organisations' experience of work with single and Dalit women in India, in light of the Leave No-one Behind agenda of the Sustainable Development Goals (discussed in detail in Stuart and Woodroffe, 2016). This chapter shows both single women and Dalit women experiencing a range of gender-related barriers to the means to a livelihood, and facing gender-based violence which is intensified by the horizontal inequalities created by marital status and caste.

'Bridging inequalities through inclusion' by Abigail Hunt, Hannah Bond and Ruth Ojiambo Ochieng moves from the core focus of the issue to consider the need to work with women activists in the global South to get change for women. Women's rights organisations are key players challenging inequality within the development process, but national governments and international NGOs have often been slow to accept their critical role in bringing about any real progress on gender equality – and hence, on poverty. Women in poverty are excluded as a result of their unequal societal position, geographic location, and the predominance of 'top-down' and piecemeal policymaking processes carried out by donor governments. This chapter focuses on the agenda of Women, Peace and Security to argue that in-country women's rights organisations provide the 'missing link', bridging the disconnect between grassroots, marginalised women and donor decision-makers.

The message in every chapter in this book is that economic growth, if pursued without strategies to curb widening inequalities in society, is fundamentally fragile and precarious, depending as it does on the labour of a workforce whose wellbeing, security and long-term safety is threatened. The fabric of society is weakened when this happens. Aside from the economic cost to society of unsustainable wealth creation for the few based on exploitative wages and conditions for the many, there is high social cost. The arguments here range from the pragmatic – the cost to the wealthy as well as the impoverished in society of lack of trust, rising levels of crime and violence, alienation and guilt – to the ethical. Humanity should be profoundly disturbed by the injustice and indignity of witnessing extreme poverty and suffering which results from economic policies informed by a reductive understanding of the worth of fellow human beings.

A focus on inequalities should mean a renewal – or in some cases the adoption – of a gendered perspective on poverty. It also requires a new and wider focus on the relationship between social justice and economic wellbeing, to understand why some have so little, and others so much. Using the lens of political and social analysis as well as economics enables us to understand the complex relationship between intersecting power relations which shape the lives of all of us. Relative poverty or wealth at household level intersects with our personal identities (including our sex, age and position in the family, as well as other aspects, for example health status), to create very different interests and needs. Recasting the goal of development as one concerned with social justice and economic wellbeing would lead to a twin desire to generate sufficient resources for all the world's people, and to ensure that each of us has a fair share.

Reference

Stuart, Elizabeth, and Woodroffe, Jessica (2016), 'Leaving No-one Behind: can the Sustainable Development Goals succeed where the Millennium Development Goals lacked? *Gender & Development* pp.43-52 , https://doi.org/10.1080/13552074.2016.1142206

About the Authors

Naila Kabeer is co-editor of the Inequalities issue in the international journal *Gender & Development*. She is Professor of Gender and Development at the Gender Institute, London School of Economics. Email: N.Kabeer@lse.ac.uk.
Caroline Sweetman is Editor of the international journal *Gender & Development*. Email: csweetman@oxfam.org.uk

CHAPTER 2

Gender, poverty, and inequality: a brief history of feminist contributions in the field of international development

Naila Kabeer

Abstract

This chapter provides a brief history of feminist contributions to the analysis of gender, poverty, and inequality in the field of international development. It draws out the continuous threads running through these contributions over the years, as the focus has moved from micro-level analysis to a concern with macro-level forces. It concludes with a brief note on some of the confusions and conflations that continue to bedevil attempts to explore the relationship between gender, poverty, and inequality.

Keywords: poverty; inequality; gender; intersectionality; financial crisis; policy responses

Introduction: poverty and inequality

The *Gender and Development* series focuses on inequality, reflecting the current moment of focus on the rapid growth in income, and wealth inequality, in both poor and affluent countries in recent decades. This has helped to move distributional issues, and a concern with measuring what Frances Stewart calls 'vertical inequalities' (Stewart 2002), centre-stage. 'Vertical inequalities' rank individuals/households by their place in the income/wealth hierarchy, in contrast to 'horizontal inequalities', which refer to inequalities between socially defined groups that often cut across income groups. Vertical inequalities draw attention to class-based inequalities, while horizontal inequalities address discrimination based on marginalised social identities, such as gender, race, and caste. Development policy has touched on economic inequalities and social discrimination in an intermittent way but has remained largely focused on economic growth and the eradication of absolute poverty.[1]

In this overview chapter, I provide a brief history of feminist contributions to the analysis of poverty and inequality in the field of international development, drawing on my own experience. At this juncture, when development policymakers and planners are turning more systematic attention to inequalities of various kinds, feminists in development have much to bring to the table. We have decades of experience in analysing class inequalities through the lens of gender analysis to reveal the social and political aspects of phenomena that first appear to be purely economic in nature. Our work also reveals how horizontal inequalities of gender have served to differentiate the experience of class, particularly among those in the lower end of the income distribution. More recently, we have drawn attention to how *intersection* between vertical inequality with the multiple and overlapping horizontal inequalities of gender, caste, race, and ethnicity helps to explain the persistence of poverty, discrimination, and social exclusion, over lifetimes and generations.

Vertical inequality measures rank individuals/households by their position in the income/wealth hierarchy, and estimate what share of the total national income accrues to them. A recent study of global trends in income inequality between 1988 and 2008 found that while the top 1 per cent of the global income distribution reported a 60 per cent rise in their real incomes, there had also been significant gains all along the income distribution – with one striking exception. The bottom 5 per cent of the distribution had not shared in this progress: their real incomes had remained the same throughout this period (Milanovic 2012, 12).

This highlights the continuing need to retain a concern with those at the bottom end of the income distribution. While the definition of absolute poverty has moved from a very minimal concern with nutritional needs to a broader range of necessities, the fact that the poverty line is currently defined as $1.25 per person per day (adjusted for purchasing power parity) reminds us that the goal of poverty reduction sets the bar very low indeed. Even so, 48 per cent of the population in sub-Saharan Africa and 30 per cent of those in South Asia lived below this level in 2010 (UN 2013, 6).

Conceptualising poverty: state and process

Poverty used to be conceptualised in terms of the income needed to achieve a predetermined and physiologically-defined level of survival by members of the 'average' household. This poverty line served to distinguish the poor from the non-poor within a population. In early research on poverty, it was assumed that households were internally unified, and that their incomes were equitably distributed among their members. Consequently, all members of households were thought to be likely to be equally poor or equally well-off.

This assumption came under serious challenge from empirical evidence that income deficits impinged more severely and systematically on some members of the household than others, most often along lines of gender and age. The need to deconstruct households, and ask questions about the intra-household distribution of well-being, was thus the first step in the process of developing a gendered understanding of poverty. It revealed the relevance of identity-based inequalities, even among the poor.

My own entry into the field of poverty analysis began in 1987, when I was commissioned to develop an analytical framework for monitoring poverty from a gender perspective as part of a larger programme on poverty monitoring in Bangladesh. Because so little was known about the gender dimensions of poverty in Bangladesh at the time, I opted to combine available statistics on poverty and well-being with qualitative assessments of how poor women in different parts of Bangladesh described their own experiences (Kabeer 1989).

Central to the framework that came out of this research was the distinction between poverty as 'state' – expressed as a snapshot view of the basic needs deficits of the poor at a particular point in time; and poverty as 'process' – focusing on the 'causes and mechanisms of the generation and transmission of poverty' over time (Fergany 1981, 15). The two were, of course, closely interrelated, since deficits in needs at any particular point in time were both outcomes of ongoing processes of poverty, and contributory factors. Nevertheless, the distinction served to underline what emerged as the main finding of the study, that 'women and men experience the state of poverty differently and often unequally and become impoverished through processes that sometimes (though not always) diverge' (Kabeer 1989, 10).

I will retain the distinction between poverty as state and process in this chapter, and use it to explore some of the ways in which gender relations have differentiated the experience of poverty and inequality for men and women in different regions of the world, and the processes through which these differentiated experiences are reproduced over time.

The state of poverty

Let me take my own early study as a starting point, and use it to reflect on how the understanding of the gender dimensions of poverty has evolved since then.

A study of national statistics in Bangladesh at the time made it quickly clear that, as in many other regions of the world, household income was distributed in horizontally unequal ways, which systematically discriminated against women and girls in relation to basic survival and well-being, as measured by indicators of health, nutrition, and mortality. In addition, the Bangladesh data showed that while gender inequalities were not confined to the poor, they tended to be exacerbated by poverty.

I used qualitative interviews to explore the gender dimensions of poverty beyond these gender-disaggregated statistics. An important contribution to the literature at the time was the idea of a hierarchy of needs among the poor, in the sense that the basic survival needs of the present had to be satisfied before making plans for the future or concerning oneself with more intangible concerns with status, self-esteem, autonomy, and dignity (Chambers 1989). Much of the literature exploring this had focused on the generic category of 'the poor ', but my interviews suggested that this hierarchy played out in gendered ways. This was evident in one woman's explanation for doing agricultural waged labour in the fields in a country where norms of propriety required respectable women to remain secluded within the home:

> What need have the poor for self-respect or propriety? Everything is dic-
> tated by scarcity (abhab): scarcity of food, scarcity of clothes, scarcity of
> shelter, there is no end to scarcity ... there are mothers who cannot feed
> their children, can they afford propriety? (Kabeer 1989, 7)

This statement suggested that for those living on the margins of physical survival, the struggle to stay alive was indeed an overriding priority, as suggested
by Robert Chambers. But if the hierarchy of needs is imposed by one's objective position in society, rather than a reflection of subjectively-determined
preferences, the statement also conveyed the harsh nature of the trade-offs
that defined poverty. This woman could abide by her community's norms and
enjoy their approval, or she could feed her children.

Female-headed households and poverty

The fieldwork revealed some of the other ways in which gender inequalities
differentiated the experience of poverty. Female headship emerged as one
example of this. That female headship was empirically associated with poverty
in a country like Bangladesh, where women were largely dependent on male
earnings, was not surprising. However, it was also evident from the research
that it was *female-supported* households, those supported primarily or solely by
women's earnings, that were associated with poverty rather than households
deemed *female-headed* because they were being managed by women in the
temporary absence of men.

Mayra Buvinic and Nadia Yousseff (1978) had earlier drawn attention to
female household heads as a special category among the poor; indeed, as the
'poorest of the poor ' (1). Their typology of female heads, based on data from
Latin America and the Caribbean, distinguished between widows, divorced
women, women in consensual unions and single mothers. Data from the
region showed that these *de facto* (as opposed to *de jure*) female-headed households were indeed disproportionately represented among households below
the poverty line.

The use of the phrase 'the poorest of the poor' in relation to female headship, and the rise of female headship in a number of regions of the world,
served over time to establish it as a marker of the perceived process of the
'feminization of poverty' (Buvinic 1993, 1). Early efforts to distinguish between
different types of female heads were lost in the process, until the very presence
of households headed by women was taken as an indication of poverty.

Attempts to estimate the percentage of women and men living in poverty
have relied on this equation between female headship and poverty, which is
believed to have given rise to the ubiquitous statistic that 70 per cent of the
world's poor were women, advanced in the UN *Human Development Report
1995*. Alain Marcoux (1998) questioned this estimate. He pointed out that,

given the global estimate of people in poverty at the time was 1.3 billion, it suggested the improbable ratio of 900 million poor women and girls to 400 million poor men and boys. Such a claim could only be justified by making the improbable additional assumptions that male-headed households had a balanced sex composition, while female-headed ones were made up of an excess of female members.

However, female-supported households continue to be used widely as an indicator of poverty. A recent report by the UN Women (2012, 1) suggests that in all but three of 25 countries in sub-Saharan Africa, the ratio of women to men in the working age group in the poorest households varied from 110 to 130 to every 100 men. This estimate makes sense if we recognise that women are less likely to have paid work than men; that when they have paid work, they are likely to be paid less than men; and that, as a result, households that rely primarily on female rather than male earners are likely to be poorer on average.

Class, gender, and violence against women

The other gender dimension of poverty that emerged from the fieldwork related to violence. Participatory assessments of poverty in various contexts had highlighted the class-based nature of the violence experienced by poor people (Beck 1994), but had little to say about patriarchal forms of violence faced by women. My fieldwork offered additional insights. First of all, it suggested that gender mediated class-based violence when it came to women: many women I interviewed spoke of rape and sexual harassment by men from more affluent families. One young girl had been raped by the sons of the landlord she worked for and had turned to prostitution: 'Now she charges money for what they took by force' (Kabeer 1989, 22).

Secondly, class mediated certain forms of patriarchal violence through its link to scarcity. Conflicts revolving around food emerged as a frequent trigger for violence: women were beaten if there was not enough food, if it did not taste right or if they were found tasting it before their husbands had eaten. There also seemed to be a seasonal pattern to domestic violence in that it increased in the 'hungry' months. A similar observation was made in a study by Betsy Hartmann and James Boyce (1983) who had been told by a sharecropper's wife in the village they studied: 'When my husband's stomach is empty, he beats me, but when it is full, there is peace' (89). As the authors pointed out, wife-beating was frequently an outlet for men's powerlessness in the face of grinding poverty.

Multi-dimensional and intersectional understandings of poverty

Over time, qualitative assessments of poverty have helped to move the conceptualisation of 'poverty as state' beyond money-metric measures, to a more multi-dimensional conceptualisation which encompasses some of its less tangible dimensions. They have drawn attention, for instance, to gender differences in the priorities expressed by poor people, differences that reflect the roles and responsibilities assigned to men and women by households and communities. They have also drawn attention to women's greater workloads, giving rise to the concept of 'time poverty' (Hanmer *et al.* 1997).

At the same time, quantitative assessments have shown that it is the *intersection*, rather than the *addition*, of different kinds of inequality, vertical as well as horizontal, the fact that these inequalities overlap, reinforce, and exacerbate each other, that explains some of the most acute forms of disadvantage, what is referred to as 'extreme poverty'. Gender inequality cuts across both vertical inequalities and other horizontal inequalities including race and caste. Its intersection with these other forms of inequality means that it is women and girls from the poorest caste, ethnic, and racial groups who have poorer levels of health, nutrition, and education, and very often suffer higher levels of violence than other women, including women from similarly poor backgrounds (Kabeer 2010).

The processes of poverty: causal inequalities

The processes of poverty can be divided into those which explain why poor people remain poor over extended periods of time, the so-called 'poverty trap', and those which explain why people, both poor and non-poor, become poorer over time. A focus on processes necessarily draws attention to the unequal distribution of the means through which people in different contexts seek to meet their needs and pursue their goals. While the means themselves are clearly likely to vary across regions, the livelihoods literature has been useful in drawing out a number of generalisable insights. In particular, it has served to highlight the importance of human labour, skills, knowledge, and abilities (or what Amartya Sen [1992] called 'capabilities') to the livelihood strategies of poor people and to the extent to which largely unskilled family labour is the most abundant, sometimes the only, capability available to the very poorest.

In this analysis, the chances of poor households climbing out of poverty depend on the quantity of labour at their disposal, the productivity of this labour as determined by physical strength, education, skills and so on, and on their ability to mobilise other resources. These include material resources, including land and other natural resources, productive equipment, and credit, as well as social resources such as their claims on their kinship networks, the 'moral economy' of the community, and the state. It is of course the larger vertical inequalities in society that will determine what share of these resources accrue to the poor.

Analysis of the gendered causes of poverty requires attention to gender inequalities in access to, and control over the means of survival and security among households who are themselves disadvantaged in the distribution of these resources. Given the importance of physical labour as the predominant, and often the only, resource at the disposal of the poor, a critical insight into the gendered processes of poverty relates to asymmetries in the extent to which men and women are able to dispose of their own labour or enjoy command over the labour of others.

The first, and most widespread, form that this asymmetry takes relates to the fact that while everywhere in the world, households must allocate the labour at their disposal between earning a living and caring for the family, in much of the world, women bear a disproportionate share of the unpaid work of caring for the family. This 'reproductive tax' (Palmer 1995, 1981) on time, from which men are largely exempt, leaves women with less time for earning a living and hence dependent to a greater or lesser extent on male earnings.

Other asymmetries relate to the form taken by women's productive contributions. In areas of strict seclusion, women either work as unpaid family labour or in home-based forms of economic activity where they relinquish control over the production process and to the proceeds of their labour to male household members. Elsewhere, as in West Africa, women are obliged to provide labour on their husbands' farms before they can labour on their own, curtailing the returns they enjoy from their efforts.

Gender asymmetries are evident in the ability to translate labour effort into income in the market place. These reflect gender inequalities in endowments, such as education and productive assets. They also reflect the gendered organisation of economic opportunities. Labour markets across the world tend to be organised along hierarchical lines which reflect the intersection between income and group-based inequalities. As a result, women from poor and socially marginalised groups (lower castes or minority ethnic groups, for instance) tend to be concentrated in activities at the bottom of the hierarchy which are not only poorer-paid than the rest, but also the least desirable, because of the risks, stigma, and exploitative working conditions associated with them.

Gender asymmetries in livelihood opportunities are also reproduced through policy-related inequalities in access to credit, agricultural extension, and other services (Hanmer et al. 1997). As the Consultations with the Poor pointed out (Narayan et al. 2000), the problem is not merely one of neglect by public providers, but also of arrogance and disdain of those from better-educated and higher-status households towards those who occupy an inferior position by virtue of their gender, caste, class, and other marginalised identities.

The 'poverty trap' thus reflects how vertical inequalities of income and wealth are bound up with the multiple and overlapping horizontal inequalities associated with marginalised identities of various kinds to produce entrenched forms of disadvantage, referred to as 'chronic poverty'. The fact that gender inequality tends to exacerbate the disadvantages generated by the intersection between vertical inequalities and other forms of horizontal inequalities explains why poverty and inequalities continue to be reproduced over time in a gendered form.

Poverty as process: coping with idiosyncratic shocks and natural disasters

While the idea of the 'poverty trap' captures the way in which multiple, and reinforcing, inequalities keep people in poverty, research into the way in which households cope with various forms of crisis provides useful insights into the processes through which households, both poor and non-poor, slide into greater poverty. An early strand of this research focused on particular categories of 'shocks': idiosyncratic shocks, such as illness in the household; generalised but anticipated shocks, such as seasonal droughts; and unanticipated shocks, such as natural disasters (Agarwal 1990; Corbett 1988; Dreze 1988).

Detailed analysis of household strategies to deal with such shocks suggested that they could be classified along a loose continuum which gave a systematic pattern to the sequence of responses. Priority was given in the early stages of this sequence to responses which entailed less threat to the household productive base, and a greater degree of reversibility. These might include cutting back on number of meals consumed, purchasing less nutritious foods, foraging for wild food, borrowing from neighbours or money lenders, turning to wealthier patrons, letting illness go untreated, depletion of household stores, selling off smaller consumer durables, taking children out of school, and temporary migration in search of work. Much later in the sequence came the selling off of producer assets, which was likely to undermine the household's chances of recovery. The final stages could include permanent migration, and the breakdown of the family unit.

While the shocks in question were not confined to poor households, what distinguished poor from better-off households was their greater exposure to certain kinds of shocks (illness in the family; seasonal unemployment) as well as their lower likelihood of recovery. With fewer options available to them, poorer households arrived at the later, less reversible stages of the sequence outlined above with greater rapidity than other households and were more likely to permanently slide into greater poverty.

Horizontal inequalities among the poor frequently determined who bore the brunt of households' coping efforts. Thus, reduction of consumption was more often at the expense of female than male members. The mortality rates of girls peaked sharply relative to boys in times of drought in the Indian context (Rose 1999). John Hoddinott (2006) found that a drought in Zimbabwe in the early 1990s led to a decline in women's nutritional status, but not men's: this negative impact was strongest for women from poorer households.

Gender inequality was also evident in the sequence of household divestment strategies: women's goods were generally sold off earlier in a range of South Asian locations (Agarwal 1990). Janice Jiggins observed (1986) 'whatever women's personal earnings or assets, these (were) consumed *before* the point of family breakdown' (14). This meant that further down the spiral into greater poverty, when family inter-dependencies began to break down, women had fewer resources to fall back on than men.

The final stages of impoverishment were characterised by more drastic measures – the wholesale migration of family members, the sale of children, or abandonment of weaker members. Able-bodied male earners were very often the first to abandon the family unit, leaving women to look after the very young and the very old. At extreme levels of destitution, mothers might abandon their children to fend for themselves in the informal economy. Thus after the 1974 famine in Bangladesh, women who had been deserted by their husbands migrated to the cities and began to fill the vagrant homes, while in one district, special homes had to be set up for deserted children (Alamgir 1980).

Poverty as process: policy-induced shocks

The onset of structural adjustment policies in the 1980s in the wake of the debt crisis experienced by various countries in sub-Saharan Africa and Latin America signalled the beginning of a worldwide shift to market-led growth strategies, spearheaded by neo-liberal governments in powerful donor countries and promoted across the world through the lending policies of the international financial institutions. SAPs consisted of a number of key policy measures: downsizing of the state's role in the economy and cutback in public expenditure with a view to promoting private enterprise; the deregulation of labour and capital markets; and the liberalisation of trade and financial flows. The hypermobility of international capital and the exposure of countries to fluctuations in global markets meant that these policies inaugurated an era marked by a series of financial crises, of which the 1997–1998 East Asian crisis and the 2007–2008 financial crisis were only the most dramatic.

Structural adjustment policies introduced the concept of 'policy-induced shocks' into the development literature. Diane Elson (1991) summarised a number of such studies that dealt with responses to structural adjustment. She distinguished between two categories of responses. Income-generating responses referred to the increase in labour force participation by women and children and changes in household structure to increase ratio of earners to dependents. Consumption and expenditure responses included cutting down on meals, cheaper foods, borrowing in cash or kind, resort to borrowing, and reliance on the community.

Other studies have explored how households have coped with recent financial crises. Rasmus Heltberg *et al.* (2012) discuss some of the responses and consequences associated with the 2008–2011 financial, food, and fuel crises in developing and transitional economies. They divided coping mechanisms into three categories. 'Behaviour-based responses' referred to reducing quantity and quality of food and non-food expenditure, taking children out of school, intensifying work efforts, diversifying income sources, migration, and resort to illicit activities, such as sex work, drug dealing, and theft. 'Asset-based responses' included sale of assets, loans from moneylenders, microfinance organisations and families, and use of common property resources. Finally, 'assistance-based responses' included welfare assistance from governments,

NGOs, religious organisations, mutual solidarity groups, relatives, friends, and neighbours.

A number of general points can be made on the basis of this literature. First of all, there is a remarkable continuity in the crisis-coping responses reported in the later round of the literature, and those described in the earlier round. There are clearly a finite number of actions that households in poverty are able to take in order to protect themselves from the worst effects of crisis. At the same time, the fact that the study by Rasmus Heltberg *et al.* covered a wider range of countries than the earlier literature helps to make clear how certain options may vary between countries. For instance, formal government assistance was available to a greater extent in the former socialist countries than elsewhere. Moreover, while the sale of assets was reported as a crisis response across low- and middle-income countries, the reliance on common property resources for food and fuel was largely confined to low-income countries.

Secondly, these later studies make a distinction between the first- and second-order effects of shocks, crisis, and recession. The gendered impacts of the first-order effects varied considerably. For instance, in most countries, men lost their jobs in larger numbers than women as a result of the public sector entrenchments which accompanied structural adjustment since they made up the majority labour force – although women were often disproportionately represented among those who lost their jobs. The first round of impacts of financial crisis, on the other hand, varied from country to country because it depended on whether male- or female-intensive sectors were first hit (Aslanbeigui and Summerfield 2000).

However, regardless of the first-order effects, women's time emerged as 'a crucial variable of adjustment' in the second-order effects, given its allocation to a multiplicity of different responsibilities within the home, the market, and the community (Commonwealth Secretariat 1989, 71). One form this took was the entry of large numbers of women who had hitherto been economically inactive, leading to what is referred to as the 'added worker' effect. This led to the paradoxical result that in the midst of high levels of unemployment or under-employment, there were rising levels of female labour force participation. Women were often able to find jobs even when men were not, because they were willing to work for lower wages and to take up jobs wherever they could find them in order to ensure that household basic needs were met.

Micro-level studies carried out in the context of structural adjustment and economics recession also documented a 'scissors-effect' on women's time, as they sought to increase their unpaid labour to compensate for cutbacks in public services or to substitute for expensive items of food or clothing which were now beyond the financial means of the household while at the same time, increasing their time into paid work to compensate for rising male unemployment and the increases in the cost of living. As Caroline Moser (1989) pointed out in the context of her study in urban Ecuador, some women coped with these demands, others 'hung-on' but some simply 'burned-out', exhausted with the variety of conflicting responsibilities they had to juggle.

Later studies of the impact of the 1997 and 2008 financial crises reaffirmed the importance of women's time as a mechanism for adjustment to crisis. As men were laid off, women moved into various forms of paid work, putting in long hours of work for low pay, usually in the informal economy, often leaving small children in the care of older siblings. The more direct pressures they faced to feed their children led many to accept low status and physically demanding jobs like cleaning, laundry, and sex work.

Second-order effects of economic crises also affected children. For instance, in the context of the Indonesian crisis, entry into school was deferred for young children, while older ones, particularly girls, were withdrawn in order to contribute to household livelihoods:

> *Some wound up far away in cities where they could be easily exploited as domestic servants, factory labour, or street vendors. Those who became street children searching for food and money had little protection and became prey to pimps, policemen and gangs, who incorporated them in their criminal activities.* (Knowles *et al.* 1999, 44)

Second-order effects also affected social relations within the family and the community. In urban Ecuador, Caroline Moser noted that women who were dependent on their husbands to make ends meet were more likely to report a rise in domestic violence than those who had a reliable income of their own. In urban Zimbabwe as well, Nasneen Kanji (1994) reported higher levels of domestic conflict in households that were struggling to meet household needs with very little support from husbands.

The studies on the impact of the 2008 financial crisis note that in some sites, reduced incomes and rising unemployment had led to a rise in domestic violence, by men against women as well as by women against children. In others, domestic violence was exacerbated by the combination of high rates of unemployment and alcohol consumption by men (Heltberg *et al.* 2012). The study also reported a rise in female-headed households, as men migrated in search of jobs without necessarily sending remittances home or simply abandoning their families. Given that many resort to theft to cope with financial hardship, it is not surprising that in almost all the countries studied, concerns with crime had increased.

Thirdly, while later studies on response to adjustment, recession, and crisis do not refer explicitly to the sequencing considerations that had been identified in the earlier literature, they do note that some coping mechanisms had longer lasting – and less reversible – effects than others. As Rasmus Heltberg *et al.* point out, 'coping came at significant costs to poor individuals, families and communities and ... some of these costs may continue to be felt well after the crisis subsides' (8). As examples, they mention the impact of reduced food consumption in the context of chronic malnutrition, the sale of productive assets, the foregone education and health care, and the rise in anti-social behaviours which are likely to reverberate for a long time to come.

These studies also noted that some groups were more resilient in the face of crisis than others. In their study of the East Asian crisis, James C. Knowles *et al.* observed that while upper- and middle-income groups were able to cope with the crisis using strategies that avoided long-term damage, the same was not true of the poor. In relation to the impact of the more recent global crisis, it was noted that while groups tied to the formal economy were often hit first and most directly by lay-offs, they could also count on severance payments and live off savings without resorting to drastic measures that would hamper their chances of recovery as national economies started to grow. Most informal sector workers had been struggling to make ends meet before the crisis, and they saw the most damage to their livelihoods as a result of their coping responses. These groups were least likely to recover when their national economies started to grow again.

Fourth, it is clear that responses that are possible in the face of idiosyncratic or localised crises, for instance, drawing on common property resources or seeking help from family and neighbours, are likely to dry up in situations when large numbers of people were simultaneously resorting to these measures in the context of more generalised forms of crisis. At the same time, the fact that large numbers of people were engaging at the same time in the same strategies meant that they were driving changes at the macro-level.

For instance, the 'added worker' effect shows up at the national level. Sonia Bhalotra and Marcella Umana-Aponte (2010) used national survey data from 63 developing countries for the period 1986–2006 to study the impact of fluctuations in per capita GDP on women's employment status at the time of the survey. They found a strong counter-cyclical pattern in Asia and Latin America, with less-educated women dominating the 'added worker' effect, suggesting the effect was strongest among poorer households. Most of these women had not been working before and most went into self-employment, presumably in the informal economy. In sub-Saharan Africa, on the other hand, where many more women were already in paid work, women, particularly those from better off households and presumably in formal sector jobs, lost their jobs along with men in times of recession.

The spread of informal work can be seen as one of the longer-term changes at the macro-level, that has both accompanied and been a consequence of economic liberalisation policies. Workers laid off during an economic crisis or as part of public sector retrenchment generally turned to the informal economy for 'last-resort' survival activities. The fact that men and women fare very differently in the informal economy is evident from the fact that, in most developing country contexts, women are more likely than men to be in what the ILO terms 'vulnerable employment' (that is, own account work and unpaid family labour). Of men and women in vulnerable employment, women are more likely than men to be in unpaid family labour, and hence without an income of their own.

Gender, poverty, and inequality: disentangling the connections

I would like to conclude this brief account of feminist contributions to the field of gender, poverty, and inequality by highlighting a number of conflations and confusions that surface in the field from time to time. These frequently reflect how the relationship between vertical and horizontal inequalities is conceptualised.

One source of confusion is the widespread tendency in the development literature to conflate women's poverty with gender inequality. In her chapter on 'rescuing gender from the poverty trap', Cecile Jackson (1996) noted the tendency among a number of multilateral development agencies to engage with gender inequality only as this affects women in poverty, due to their focus on action to stimulate economic growth and/or to alleviate poverty. As she argued, 'the concept of poverty cannot serve as a proxy for the subordination of women ... and there is no substitute for a gender analysis which transcends class divisions and material definitions of deprivation' (489). Her point, therefore, was that gender inequality, and its impact on social relations, was not confined to the poor; rather, it cuts across socioeconomic classes.

The reverse problem was evident in the conceptualisation of Millennium Development Goal 3 on gender equality and women's empowerment, which failed to give attention to class and other differences among women. Thus, while the overall goal of the MDGs was the halving of extreme poverty in the world, MDG 3 was formulated in terms that might or might not be relevant to the needs and interests of poor and marginalised women across the world. For instance, tackling gender disparities in literacy and primary school enrolment rates is likely to be relevant to these groups, but less likely to be the case for secondary and tertiary education. Increasing the share of women in national parliaments, although important from a broader gender equality perspective, provides no guarantee that it would promote the needs and interests of women from poor and marginalised groups. Expanding the share of women in non-agricultural employment did little to address the poor pay and exploitative conditions that characterised the non-agricultural activities undertaken by poorer women from different social groups.

The third and final concern I want to raise is a tendency to lose sight of what distinguishes gender inequality from other relations of inequality. In recent consultations about the post-MDG agenda, it was widely agreed among those committed to social justice that a major limitation of the MDG agenda was its failure to acknowledge both vertical inequality and horizontal inequalities (beyond gender inequality) as major challenges facing the international community. One response to this has been advocacy for new ways to measure income-based 'vertical inequality', such as the Palma ratio.[2] These are better able to capture change than the traditionally used Gini coefficient,[3] but also ignore social discrimination.

The other has been to argue for greater attention to various forms of horizontal inequalities, such as age, disability, ethnicity, race, sexual orientation, and so on. In all of this, there has been a worrying tendency among some groups to treat gender as 'just one of many inequalities that generate poverty and exclusion … we don't lose points on gender if we admit that class, race and ethnicity also have a role – sometimes a primary role – in creating inequalities' (Melamed 2012, no page number). By way of conclusion, therefore, let me reiterate the arguments that I made over a decade ago in relation to the then newly-adopted MDGs as to why gender should not be treated as 'just another inequality' (Kabeer 2003).

First of all, gender inequality is more pervasive across societies than any other form of inequality, though it may take different forms in different societies. Consequently, understanding the causes and consequences of gender inequality is of concern to all societies in the world, rich as well as poor.

Secondly, gender inequality is also pervasive across different groups within societies, cutting across class, race, caste, ethnicity, and other forms of inequality. It is not simply one more horizontal inequality to be added to the others. Rather, it intersects with these other inequalities in ways that intensify the disadvantages associated with other forms of inequality.

Finally, gender inequality is structured into the organisation of social relations in society, as fundamentally as class is in capitalist societies, as race was in apartheid South Africa, and as caste is in India. Women's location at the intersection between production and reproduction, between making a living and caring for the family, makes the organisation of gender relations central to the nexus between economic growth and human development, and hence central to the development agenda.

Notes

1. By contrast, wealthier countries have been focused on 'relative poverty' despite the call by the 1995 Copenhagen Summit of Social Development for countries to develop measures of both absolute and relative poverty and the need for all nations to eradicate absolute poverty (Sarlo 2001).
2. The 'Palma ratio' measures the ratio of the income share of the top 10 per cent in the income distribution to the bottom 40 per cent, on the grounds that the income share of the middle 50 per cent has been relatively stable over time across countries.
3. The 'Gini co-efficient', which is the more commonly used measure of income inequality, compares how the actual distribution of income diverges from a perfectly equal distribution of income.

References

Agarwal, Bina (1990) 'Social security and the family in rural India coping with seasonality and calamity', *Journal of Peasant Studies* 17(3): 341–412

Alamgir, Mohiuddin (1980) *Famine in South Asia: The Political Economy of Mass Starvation*, Cambridge, MA: Oelgeschlager and Hain Publishers

Aslanbeigui, Nahid and Gale Summerfield (2000) 'The Asian crisis, gender, and the international financial architecture', *Feminist Economics* 6(3): 81–103

Beck, Tony (1994) *The Experience of Poverty: Fighting for Respect and Resources in Village India*, London: Intermediate Technology Publications

Bhalotra, Sonia and Marcela Umana-Aponte (2010) 'The dynamics of women's labor supply in developing countries', IZA Discussion Paper No. 4879, Bonn: Institute for the Study of Labour

Buvinic, Mayra (1993) 'The feminization of poverty? Research and policy needs', Presentation to Symposium on Poverty: New approaches to analysis and policy November 22–24, Geneva: International Institute for Labour Studies

Buvinic, Mayra and Nadia Yousseff (1978) *Woman-headed Households: The Ignored Factor in Development Planning. Report Submitted to the Office of Women in Development, USAID*, Washington, DC: ICRW

Chambers, Robert (1989) 'Editorial introduction: vulnerability, coping and policy', *IDS Bulletin* 20(2): 1–7

Commonwealth Secretariat (1989) *Engendering adjustment for the 1990s*, London: Common-wealth Secretariat

Corbett, Jane (1988) 'Famine and household coping strategies', *World Development* 16(9): 1099–112

Dreze, Jean (1988) *'Famine Prevention in India' Development Economics Paper No. 3, Suntory Toyota International Centre for Economics and Related Disciplines*, London: School of Economics and Political Science

Elson, Diane (1991) 'Household responses to stabilization and structural adjustment: male bias at the micro level', in D. Elson (ed.) *Male Bias in the Development Process*, 211–52 Manchester: Manchester University Press

Fergany, Nader (1981) 'Monitoring the condition of the poor in the third world: some aspects of measurement', ILO/WEP Research Working Paper WEP 10-6/WP52, Geneva: ILO

Hanmer, Lucia, Graham Pyatt, and Howard White (1997) *Poverty in Sub-Saharan Africa: What Can we Learn about the World Bank's Poverty Assessments?* The Hague: Institute of Social Studies Advisory Services

Hartmann, Betsy and James Boyce (1983) *A Quiet Violence. View from a Bangladesh Village*, London: Zed Books

Heltberg, Rasmus, Naomi Hossain, Anna Reva, and Carolyn Turk (2012) 'Anatomy of coping. Evidence from people living through the crises of 2008–2011', Policy Research Working Paper 5951, Washington: World Bank

Hoddinott, John (2006) 'Shocks and their consequences across and within households in rural Zimbabwe', *Journal of Development Studies* 42(2): 301–21

Jackson, Cecile (1996) 'Rescuing gender from the poverty trap', *World Development* 24 (3): 489–504

Jiggins, Janice (1986) 'Women and seasonality: coping with crisis and calamity', *IDS Bulletin* 17(3): 9–18

Kabeer, Naila (1989) 'Monitoring poverty as if gender mattered: a methodology for rural Bangladesh', IDS Discussion Paper 255. Brighton: IDS

Kabeer, Naila (2003) *Mainstreaming Gender and Poverty Eradication in the Millennium Development Goals*, London: Commonwealth Secretariat

Kabeer, Naila (2010) *Can the MDGs Provide a Pathway to Social Justice? The Challenge of Intersecting inequalities*, Brighton: IDS/UN MDG Achievement Fund

Kanji, Nazneen (1994) 'Structural adjustment in Zimbabwe. The way forward for low-income urban women', in Fatima Meer (ed.) *Poverty in the 1990s: The Responses of Urban women*, Paris: UNESCO, pp. 41–64

Knowles, J., E. Pernia and M. Racelis (1999) 'Social consequences of the financial crisis in Asia', Economic Staff Paper No. 60, Manila: Asian Development Bank

Marcoux, Alain (1998) 'The feminization of poverty: claims, facts and data needs', *Population and Development Review* 24(1): 131–39

Melamed, Claire (2012) 'Gender is just one of many inequalities that generate poverty and exclusion', http://www.guardian.co.uk/global-development/poverty-matters/2012/mar/09/gender-inequality-poverty-exclusion   (last checked by the author 7 July 2015)

Milanovic, Branko (2012) 'Global Income Inequality by the Numbers: In History and Now – An Overview', Policy Research Working Paper 6259, Washington, DC: World Bank

Moser, Caroline (1989) 'The impact of recession and adjustment policies at the micro-level: low income women and their households in Guayquil, Ecuador ', in UNICEF (ed.) *Poor Women and the Economic Crisis. The Invisible Adjustment*, Santiago: UNICEF, pp. 137–62

Narayan, Deepa, Chambers, Robert, Shah, Meera and Petesch, Patti (2000) *Voices of the Poor: Crying Out for Change*, Oxford: Oxford University Press

Palmer, I. (1995) 'Public finance from a gender perspective', *World Development* 23(11): 1981–6

Rose, Elaina (1999) 'Consumption smoothing and excess female mortality in Rural India', *Review of Economics and Statistics* 81(1): 41–9

Sarlo, Christopher (2001) *Measuring Poverty in Canada Critical Issues Bulletin*, Vancouver: Fraser Institute

Sen, Amartya (1992) *Inequality Re-examined*, Cambridge, MA: Harvard University Press

Stewart, Frances (2002) *Horizontal Inequalities: A Neglected Dimension of Development* (QEH Working Paper Series 81, 2002), Oxford: QEH, University of Oxford

UN Women (2012) 'The Millennium Development Goals Report: The Gender Chart', New York: UN Women

United Nations (2013) 'The Millennium Development Goals Report, 2013', New York: United Nations

About the Author

Naila Kabeer is co-editor of the Inequalities issue in the international journal *Gender & Development*. She is Professor of Gender and Development at the Gender Institute, London School of Economics. Email: N.Kabeer@lse.ac.uk

CHAPTER 3
Gendering the inequality debate

Diane Perrons

Abstract

In the past 30 years, economic inequality has increased to unprecedented levels, and is generating widespread public concern among orthodox, as well as leftist and feminist, thinkers. This chapter explores the gender dimensions of growing economic inequality, summarises key arguments from feminist economics which expose the inadequacy of current mainstream economic analysis on which 'development' is based, and argues for a 'gender and equality' approach to economic and social policy in both the global North and South.

Keywords: gender inequality; social norms; austerity; socially sustainable development

Introduction

Development has traditionally focused on economic inequality between countries, and different approaches to it have paid varying degrees of attention to the political roots of this inequality, and on the political and social impact of neo-liberal approaches to development. The new and growing public interest in increasing economic inequality within countries reflects widespread anxiety that contemporary levels of inequality within countries are unsustainable, undermining economic growth, social and political stability, as well as economic and social well-being. They also call into question the neo-liberal orthodoxies of global development policies.

These realisations have the potential to result in radical policies which change the course of global development. However, there is, as yet, little recognition on the part of global and national leaders of the importance of the moment. In particular, it is critical to devise policy that is founded on a recognition of how inequality is simultaneously gendered, racialised, and marked by other dimensions of social disadvantage if more equitable and economically and socially sustainable development is to be achieved. Yet the main policy recommendations from leading thinkers on the issues, similar to that of Piketty (2014), focus on attempting to effect some redistribution of wealth via taxation. Coincident with calls for redistribution and greater inclusion, the majority of countries worldwide (119 in 2013 and 132 in 2015)

http://dx.doi.org/10.3362/9781780447278.003

are pursuing and expected to intensify austerity policies (Ortiz and Cummins 2013, i) that for the most part have served only to aggravate inequality, especially gender inequality, and to date have not led to a reduction in sovereign debt, the stated rationale for their introduction.

This chapter argues for an 'equalities and gender' perspective on global development. This perspective highlights the need for redistributive economic policies to redress extreme inequalities to be accompanied by measures to *prevent* inequality. Feminist economists have long argued that international and national economic policies need to be rooted in a broad understanding of the economy. Macro-economic policies have *social content* (Elson and Cagatay 2000); that is, they have very different implications for differently positioned social groups. Nowhere is this more so than in the austerity policies developed in response to the economic crisis of 2007–8 which started in the financial sector of North America and Europe. These austerity policies are currently having very negative consequences for low-income people in general, and women and ethnic and racial minorities in particular, while the incomes of those responsible for the crisis have continued to increase. It is vital to challenge the view that what is considered good for the economy is good for everyone; or, in the case of austerity, anyone.

I argue here that economists need to question and change their fundamental ideas about the economy and to recognise the social implications embedded in orthodox macro-economic thinking and policymaking and the monetary values attributed to different forms of work. Gendered, class, and racialised social norms influence ideas of what constitutes the economy, and the worth attributed to different kinds of work. All work deserves to be remunerated fairly and equitably. A gender and equality approach would favour policies guaranteeing workers a basic income, and/or a living wage. This approach also calls into question the economic austerity policies adopted in the wake of the 2007–8 crisis in many countries, including the UK, since these are clearly unsustainable and inequitable. Instead, it challenges policymakers to evolve policies to reduce inequalities between countries as well as within them, in particular giving attention to the need to address the issue of sovereign debt and consider the different ways in which the debt issue can be resolved.

I begin by highlighting the gender dimensions of contemporary inequality in the next section. I particularly focus on wages and payments in the informal sector, showing how these are influenced by gendered social norms.

The gender dimensions of growing economic inequality

The burgeoning literature on growing economic inequality pays little or no attention to the enduring and universal question of gender inequality, and how economic inequality is simultaneously gendered, racialised, and marked by other dimensions of social disadvantage. While attention in North America and Europe is drawn to headline cases of maltreatment and injustice experienced by women, especially relating to violence and when it takes place in other countries, less attention is given to the everyday maltreatment and injustice experienced especially by women worldwide as a consequence of economic injustices within market economies.[1] With some exceptions, the economic dimensions of gender inequality have not aroused the same degree of public interest either among academics and policymakers, even though women continue to be disadvantaged in the labour market, under-represented in decision-making, and are more likely than men to experience domestic violence (ILO 2015). As Christine Lagarde (2014, 3) has put it, women are 'underutilised, underpaid, under-appreciated and over-exploited'.

What makes this situation in Europe and the United States surprising is that there have been five decades of equality policies[2] and the majority of countries worldwide have committed to a range of human rights including the Convention on the Elimination of All Discrimination Against Women (CEDAW) (ILO 2015) without acknowledging that their economic policies risk breaking their commitments to avoid retrogression and maximise the satisfaction of minimum essential levels of economic and social rights (Elson 2012). As the ILO (2015, 1) has pointed out, while progress has been made in terms of the scale of women's labour-force participation, the conditions identified in the Beijing World Conference on Women 20 years ago have not been addressed, and:

> ... in most parts of the world women are often concentrated in undervalued and low-paid jobs with poor working conditions. They suffer from lack of access to education, training, recruitment and equal remuneration, and have limited bargaining and decision-making power. Women have unequal access to productive resources, and are over-represented in informal work and non-standard forms of employment. They undertake a disproportionate level of unpaid care work, and many are at risk of violence at home and at work.

While gender inequality figures as a concern in many national and supranational policies, it is not considered intrinsic or central to the neo-liberal model of development, and is quickly sidelined in times of economic crisis. There is an implicit assumption that the economy and economic policies are wealth-creating or productive, and that social policies to address inequality concerns, including gender inequality, are costly, and concerned with redistributing rather than creating wealth; they should therefore be set aside in times of crisis, to enable policymakers to focus on the what is considered to be the more urgent task of dealing with the crisis, and restoring growth. An example is the EU Recovery Plan drawn up in the wake of the 2007–8 financial crisis, which mentioned neither gender nor economic equality (Bettio *et al.* 2012). The ideas that economic growth can be redistributive, or that social policy can be economically productive, are consequently overlooked (Perrons and Plomien 2013) – and yet austerity policies lead to low growth, and, as discussed below, have marked gender and class impact.

Furthermore, many of the solutions for greater equality, such as those proposed by Christine Lagarde (2014), the World Bank (2012), and the

European Commission (EC 2010) prescribe increasing women's integration within existing market economies as a resolution to gender inequality, without appreciating the significance of inequalities within the labour market, for both participation and levels of pay, and despite evidence of a worldwide gender pay gap in the formal sector and parts of the informal sector (Chant and Pedwell 2008). Outside of these policy circles, attention is given to the significance of wages as a primary source of increasing income inequality (OECD 2011; Piketty 2014), but these analyses still overlook gender issues. These macro- and micro-level issues relating to overall economic management and the value of labour are discussed below.

Inequality in returns to labour, and gendered social norms

Two key trends have influenced rising inequality in high- and medium-income countries. One is the growth in the proportion of service sector employment and a related polarisation in earnings between highly paid jobs – in professional, technical, and managerial occupations – and low-paid jobs in catering, cleaning, and security. Thus both ends of the service sector have expanded while the manufacturing sector, which provided relatively well-paid jobs for working people, has declined. Some economists have attributed these changes and corresponding polarisation in earnings to globalisation and increased trade as some manufacturing has been outsourced from the global North to lower-income countries, while other economists have focused on skill and argued that workers in highly paid jobs are paid a premium for their skill, while low-paid workers are assumed to be less skilled and therefore face increasing competition from workers in low-income countries and from inward migration (Krugman 2002). The OECD (2011) re-estimated the significance of these differing explanations, and found that weaker labour market regulation is also significant while David Rosnick and Dean Baker (2012) found the growth of the finance sector important.

The second and related trend influencing the polarisation in earnings which affects countries worldwide is the fall in the share of output or value added going to workers rather than to capital holders or owners and this is especially the case for low-paid workers (UNCTAD 2012). This decline in the workers' share has happened even though in many countries there have been increases in workers' productivity which is completely opposite to the predictions of conventional economic theory which links wages to the output produced. As a consequence this understanding of wages being connected to output has been challenged. Engelbert Stockhammer (2013, 4) in a study of 71 countries – '28 advanced and 43 developing and emerging economies' – between 1970 and 2007 found that globalisation processes had, overall, negatively affected the earning power of workforces in developing and emerging economies, as well as advanced economies. He also found that technological change had a negative effect on advanced economies, because skilled jobs had also shifted to developing and emerging economies, benefiting workers there.

However, he also found that the effect of these processes on workers' wages was much less significant than either the growing role played by the finance sector and (in the advanced countries), institutional change, in particular the retrenchment of the welfare state and the declining power of trade unions. As a consequence he argues that strengthening the welfare state and 'changing union legislation to foster collective bargaining could help increase the wage share with little if any costs in terms of economic efficiency' (viii). This finding is very important not only for discussions of inequality, but also with respect to austerity policies discussed in the final section.

Thomas Piketty (2014, 24) has shown that the rise of wage inequality in the United States since the 1970s (as well as other countries) is due mainly to the increasing earnings of an elite, which he terms 'supermanagers'. Their extremely high earnings cannot be explained (or justified) in terms of increased output, as there is no association between the pay of CEOs and company performance (Chemi and Giorgi 2014). Neither is there any association with education, skills or national growth levels. Instead, Thomas Piketty finds that these high earnings are a consequence of these super-managers' 'power(s) to set their own remuneration' (24), which, in turn, depends on their bargaining capacity and prevailing social norms, which vary between countries. This recognition matters, because it moves explanations for wage inequality away from purely individual characteristics and economic explanations, and invites a discussion of the social processes which influence wages and how these social norms are simultaneously gendered and racialised, though these issues are not developed by these writers.[3] It is important to note that Thomas Piketty rejects the conventional economic theory only for top earnings, maintaining that it offers 'plausible explanation of the long-run evolution of the wage distribution at least up until a certain level of pay and within a certain degree of precision' (2014, 333)

By contrast, feminist economists highlight the disjoint between the value of work performed, and the economic returns of the work, for all workers, not only the highest-paid. These insights are critical at this time of increased concern about extreme and growing inequality (Perrons 2014). Feminists recognise that there is a link between the value of the work that is done, and the social value attached to the individual who does it. This makes remuneration for work a subjective concern (Phillips and Taylor 1980) and something influenced by social norms or social expectations and traditions regarding the value of different forms of work, the value of different people and what their roles should be. Feminist economics therefore calls into question the idea of the economy as a concept free from 'the social'. This insight is useful when we look at the complexity of the tasks expected of economists in terms of measuring concepts such as 'individual output' for which a worker is supposedly rewarded in an objective and value-free way. In fact, it is very difficult to measure individual output in a wide range of occupations, especially in labour-intensive and highly feminised sectors such as caring, teaching, cleaning, or catering. Care provision, for example, is complex, consisting of guarding (preventing any harm), caring for identifiable bodily needs, and nurturing (Himmelweit 2007). It is relational, and so inherently encompasses an affective dimension that often is discernible only by the recipient, but has long-term social benefits for individuals and society. Despite the general view in society that care work is socially valuable, this is not reflected in economic value; care work is generally low paid. In the case of social care for the elderly and unwell, the average wage for a full-time worker in the UK in 2012 was £18,000 p.a. (ICF GHK 2013) which is £8,000 less than the average UK worker.

The low pay in the care sector is linked to the difficulty of raising productivity in this sector,[4] due to increasing privatisation and to the increasing presence of finance firms including private equity organisations which are motivated solely by profit. Private equity firms buy up existing companies with a view to making quick returns through modernisation and efficiency savings. However they raise the necessary funds by borrowing rather than by having shareholders, and interest on this borrowing has to be paid first, that is, before any profit can be taken. While the social care sector is growing and so attractive to private equity firms, its labour-intensive character makes it very difficult to increase profitability except by reducing employees' pay and conditions.[5] The growth of private firms in the care sector helps to explain why social care workers are increasingly those that experience labour market disadvantage, including women and migrants. In addition, their low wages are rooted in gendered social norms which admire and treasure women's 'natural' talents, rather than recognising and rewarding their skills and material competencies (Glenn 1992).

Overlooking how social norms are gendered reflects the customary gender-blindness in economic matters. Within orthodox economics, the economy is portrayed in a rather abstract way, as an entity with needs of its own, which have to be met in order to satisfy the needs of society as a whole. There is an assumption that everyone is affected equally by economic policies, and a disregard for the impact of gender, race, and class biases. Such a conflation between the interests of the economy and the interests of the people whose lives it shapes is dangerous, as it leads to the prioritisation of economic stability over economic and social well-being. This thinking is currently very evident in austerity policies discussed further below.

The macro-picture: austerity – economic necessity or class- and gender-biased policy?

Widening inequalities, a fall in wages for lower-paid workers and the corresponding lack of demand for goods and services were underlying causes of the 2007–8 crisis (Fukuda-Parr *et al.* 2013). As labour's share of value-added fell overall, and for low-paid people in particular, the effective demand for goods and services either declined, or was maintained only through credit expansion and rising consumer debt. It became difficult for investors to make a profit through traditional means of making and selling goods and services.

This led to the expansion of – and dramatic changes in – the finance sector. Rather than being a 'good servant' of the real economy, by providing funds for people to engage in material investments in small and medium enterprises and for social and physical infrastructure such as care services, hospitals, and transport and for mitigating risk, the finance sector has become a 'bad master', not only by failing to provide investment funds but also by aggravating risk (Griffith-Jones and Jolly 2013, 56).

In the US, the 2007–8 crisis was brought on by this dynamic, in combination with a fall in real wages which made it difficult for low-income workers to service their debt, leading to mortgage arrears and defaults. As the debt had been packaged and sold on to many financial institutions, when the income stream to service these products stopped (with the defaults) these institutions were unable to pay their savers.[6] To prevent the collapse of the banks and financial institutions, the public sector stepped in at a cost of trillions of dollars (in the US, $3 trillion) (Gill and Roberts 2011, 155), both domestically and worldwide, as these financial markets had become global. This collapse also led to a fall in bank lending to the real economy – which in turn led to low growth, unemployment, and sustained recession.

The first phase of austerity: Keynes revisited

In the first two years after the 2007–8 crisis, the G20 countries embarked on a response to it which reflected the economic approach of John Maynard Keynes, in a departure from the classic neo-liberal approaches which have dominated economic thinking over the past 30 years. Basic Keynesian economics suggests that the state should act in counter-cyclical ways (that is, to invest and spend in times of recession, and pay off the debt in times of growth) (Krugman 2013). Not only did decision-makers make public money available to bail out the banks, but the G20 engaged in a co-ordinated response to try and sustain the economy and employment more generally through increased state expenditure.

These policies were not gender-neutral in character, despite the conventional views that the economy is devoid of social content, due to the gendered nature of employment which generally sees women in lower-paid, 'feminised' parts of the labour market. Much of the state expenditure to stimulate the economy in the US and Europe went on physical infrastructure to boost male employment which had been badly hit by the decline in the construction industry and manufacturing, especially cars (Seguino 2010). Initially, female employment was more protected owing to the fact that in these countries women are disproportionately concentrated in the public sector (Fukuda-Parr *et al.* 2013). Perhaps of greater concern is the use of vast sums of public money to bail out the banks which is a highly regressive redistribution from tax payers to investors and creditors, who are disproportionately male and predominantly in the upper income groups. Had this not happened then the austerity policies which have had such negative effects on the well-being of ordinary people, and especially women, would not have been necessary.

The second phase: structural adjustment revisited

By 2010, there were a few small signs of recovery, and states became concerned about the high level of government spending, prompted in part by an economic theory that predicted a dramatic decline in growth if the public deficit exceeded 90 per cent of GDP (Reinhart and Rogoff 2010, 573) – a theory that was subsequently shown to be flawed (Krugman 2013). This led to a rapid reversal of strategy (Ortiz and Cummins 2013).

The features of the second-wave policies include efforts to reduce the scale of the public sector deficit and debt through cuts in public sector spending and with some countries, including Greece and Ireland, having to borrow from the IMF in order to remain solvent. Such policies, enforced in part by conditions attached to the borrowing, result in slower growth and reduced employment as well as cutbacks in public sector services and employment. The public sector cutbacks have particularly negative implications for women who, in many countries, are not only more likely than men to work in the public sector, but also more likely to be the users of government services and the ones who have to fill the gap when the services are withdrawn (WBG 2015).

The economic rationale for the second wave of austerity policies is highly questionable (Fukuda Parr *et al.* 2013); there is little evidence to suggest that they are working, and growing evidence, similar to their antecedents in the structural adjustment programmes of the 1980s and 1990s, that these policies are damaging the welfare of the vast majority of the population worldwide (Elson and Cagatay 2000; Ortiz and Cummins 2013). These policies contain three specific biases: deflationary-bias, male-bias, and a bias toward commodification (Elson 1991). Paul Krugman (2013) has suggested that the only possible explanation for their continuation is a political choice, reflecting the interests of the elites. Alternative positions, such as those adopted in the first round based on Keynes, are presented as being unsound and profligate (Elson and Cagatay 2000); yet, as Thomas Piketty (2014, 540) has shown with respect to Europe, the issue is clearly one of 'distribution rather than profligacy', as Europe currently has 'the highest level of private wealth per capita in the world and the greatest difficulty in resolving its public debt crisis – a strange paradox'.

Austerity policies and fiscal space

The three types of bias identified by Diane Elson are present in the second wave of austerity policies, have had a devastating impact, and are 'prevent[ing] the formulation of gender-equitable people-centred macroeconomic policies' (Elson and Cagatay 2000, 1348). In 2013, the International Monetary Fund (IMF) began to recognise that the new policies were having a much greater negative effect on economic growth than it had predicted (Blanchard and Leigh 2013).

These biases arise because economic stability is presumed to depend on the size and sustainability of the 'fiscal space' – that is, the public money available to spend which shapes a government's capacity for influencing economic and social development. Neo-classical economists consider that this fiscal space should be minimised, advocating a small state, low budgetary deficit, and minimum taxation, to allow maximum market flexibility. Peter Heller (2005, 1), writing in the IMF magazine, sees fiscal space as the 'room in a government's budget that allows it to provide resources for a desired purpose without jeopardizing *the sustainability of its financial position or the state of the economy'* (my emphasis).

In this definition, the needs of 'the state' or 'the economy' are prioritised over wider social well-being. This view presents what is in reality a political choice as a technical necessity, as the interests of the economy are assumed to be in the interest of all, and yet are much more to the advantage of wealth-holders protecting the value of their money. It makes the markets the arbiter of social decision-making, and restricts the size of government debt to the willingness of creditors to provide finance.

However, fiscal space can be seen in very different ways. The UNDP's definition fits within a wider view of the economy as serving human development and well-being:

> *financing that is available to government as a result of concrete policy actions for enhancing resource mobilization, and the reforms necessary to secure the enabling governance, institutional and economic environment for these policy actions to be effective, for a specified set of development objectives. (UNDP 2007, I)*

This definition could be modified further to recognise the existence of different interests within different groups in society, including gender and class interests. It could become

> *fiscal space is the available financing, designated by policy choices, to provide the necessary resources for a specific set of social, economic, and environmental objectives, taking into account the specific needs of marginalized groups using race, gender and class impact analysis. (Ida 2013)*

Such alternative definitions of fiscal space bring questions of social purpose and gender justice into decisions regarding fiscal policy, highlighting that these have a political rather than technical character. In effect, they understand the appropriate role of the economy as working for society, rather than vice versa. They show awareness of the impact of the economy on society, allowing for the possibility that particular policies will have an impact on poverty and inequality.

There are a number of ways in which fiscal space can, or could be, managed, in the wake of the 2007–8 crisis, and each of these has gender-differentiated outcomes. Figure 1 (modified from the UNDP [2007]) identifies the fiscal space or the capacity for government spending, which is determined by the elements identified on the four corners of the diamond. These are the amount received from official development assistance, the amount of domestic revenue raised

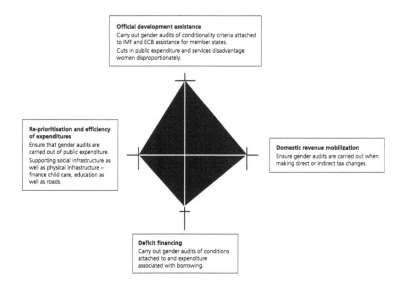

Figure 1 A gender perspective on public finances
Source: Modified from UNDP (2007).
Note: There are few technical constraints on the size and shape of the fiscal space but rather the space could be pulled in different directions depending on political decisions that ideally would be in the social interest, which includes gender equality. For example, with respect to domestic revenue mobilisation a gender audit is likely to show that women, as lower earners, are more likely to benefit from reducing indirect taxes while men are more likely to benefit from lowering the tax thresholds.

through taxation, the extent of government expenditure, and the deficit or the gap between the amount of government expenditure and the amount of revenue raised either through taxation or borrowing (UNDP 2007; Figure 1).

The relative size of all these elements can vary; as John Loxley – one of the leaders of the Canadian Alternative Federal Budget – has pointed out, 'there is always an alternative macroeconomic strategy that is economically feasible; but different strategies imply different distributions of the costs and benefits' (cited by Diane Elson [2006, 120]). Clearly, countries cannot create more fiscal space by running up government deficits and debt indefinitely, not least because large amounts of public money would have to be spent on interest repayments to creditors. But there is no clear idea as to what a maximum should be, and this would depend in part on what the additional money borrowed was being used for – whether it was generating returns in the future or whether it was being dissipated in unproductive ways.

To maintain returns on their investments, creditors prefer low inflation and low government expenditure – so leading to what Diane Elson (1991), mentioned earlier, terms a 'deflationary bias'. This bias has particularly negative effects for women, as they are more likely to be employed by the public sector and so face unemployment; to have greater reliance on state entitlements, which are often cut; and have fewer safety nets to draw on, owing to their lower level of labour market attachment (Elson and Cagatay 2000). Diane

Elson's 'male bias' (1991) refers to the way that state entitlements are based largely on assumptions of a pattern of full-time working over the lifetime, something that women (given the uneven division of labour with respect to domestic work and caring) are less likely to do. Finally, the 'commodification bias' (Elson 1991) refers to the privatisation of public services such as education, health, or care, discussed above, which have to be paid for at the point of use, rather than being entitlements paid for indirectly, via taxation.

Conclusion and alternatives to austerity

To reduce inequality, not only does there need to be an increase in the taxes on high incomes and wealth-holders in society, but there also needs to be a radical reassessment of the social worth of different kinds of work, and an assertion of labour and social rights through living wages and a basic income (Davala *et al*. 2015). As the OECD (2008, 116) has pointed out with respect to formal employment in medium- to high- income countries, 'relying on taxing more and spending more as a response to inequality can only be a temporary measure. The only sustainable way to reduce inequality is to stop the underlying widening of wages'. A gender and equalities approach reminds us of the politics which exists beneath the ostensibly technical and value-free concept of the economy, and alerts us to the insights of feminist and other alternative economists which challenge the idea that the economy either is or should be separate from society and where market forces should be allowed to operate in a 'free 'way. Instead they recognise that the economy is part of society and this relationship should be acknowledged in order to shift understandings of the relationships of the economy to society.

So far, the response to the economic crisis in the global North which started in 2007–8, and the issue of rising public debt has predominantly been one of austerity, and not one of taxation. As Piketty (2014, 541) argues, this prolonged austerity is 'the worst solution in terms of both justice and efficiency'; a problem magnified when also taking into account, as I have here, the issue of gender inequality.

In terms of justice, both the structural adjustment programmes of the 1980s and 1990s and contemporary austerity policies embed gender and class bias to the disadvantage of women, given the prevailing gender division of labour, with women being over-represented among those working in the public sector, using state services, and being more likely to be entitled to various forms of income support, where available. Since care work which is largely unpaid or paid at very low rates, yet invaluable to society, is also largely performed by women, a focus on this is critical.

However, these biases, which profoundly shape both the economy and the lives and well-being of women, their households, and communities, are not recognised in orthodox economic thinking which divorces the economy from society and presumes that issues of low levels of inflation and government deficit are purely technical necessities in the sense that they are politics-free by ultimately benefiting everyone equally, rather than political priorities that favour wealth holders and increase inequality. As Paul Krugman (2013) among many others has argued, the consequences of second-wave austerity policies have been devastating for ordinary people, especially women and the socially marginalised – whether the impact is measured at household level, or for individuals. However, austerity continues reflecting the long standing wishes of elite groups to reduce the role of the state.

Many alternative and transformative proposals have been put forward which link social and economic objectives and challenge the desirability of austerity policies. These include the Casablanca group and their vision for a better world (UNDP 2010) and proposals linked with gender budgeting including the Feminist F plan (WBG 2015). To date, few if any of these proposals have been implemented. However, Syriza, a leftist party, was elected in Greece in January 2015, on a platform based on challenging austerity. Rania Antonopolous, a feminist economist, has been appointed Deputy Minister of Labour and Social Solidarity. In her academic work with Kijong Kim (Antonopoulos and King 2011) she demonstrated the social and economic benefits of increasing state employment in times of low growth. She also showed that expenditure on social infrastructure, such as social care, has a higher multiplier effect or positive impact on overall growth and creates more jobs, especially for low-income women than equivalent levels of expenditure on physical infrastructure, such as road building. So far the Greek government has introduced policies to expand employment but it is not clear yet whether these will be in the care sector. Hopefully, policies related to this analysis will be implemented in Greece and elsewhere. More generally what is undoubtedly clear is that austerity policies have had a profoundly negative impact on the vast majority of the populations in the global North and South and while there are some signs of economic 'recovery' this has yet to affect the wellbeing of those who were least responsible for the crisis and who have suffered most through the attempts to restore the economy via austerity.

Notes

1. For example, the gang rape in Delhi which led to days of protest in India, but was also reported widely in the UK press and TV (Kabeer 2013).
2. By 'equality policies' I am referring to the continual presence of strategies for economic and social cohesion in the European Union as well as for gender equality since the original Treaty of Rome in 1958, though in practice commitment has varied.
3. Financialisation refers to 'the increase in quantity, velocity and complexity of financial transactions in the global economy; the expansion of financial motives in the operation of the economy and the expanded power of financial interests' (Fukuda-Parr *et al.* 2013, 8). This expansion has led to increasing instability in the global economy and increasing pressure for quick returns on investments which leads to a deterioration in working conditions.

4. See Diane Perrons (2014) for a fuller explanation.
5. The low pay can to some extent be attributed to the difficulties of increasing the productivity of caring for dependents, and corresponding tendency for costs to rise (Baumol 1967). Productivity is difficult to increase owing to the relational qualities of the work: that is, affective labour itself cannot be reduced without changing the actual character, content, and end result of the work. To illustrate this problem, William Baumol (1967) gave the example of trying to increase the productivity of a string quintet, that is a piece of music played by five players with stringed instruments. Just as speeding up the tune would change the quality of the music, likewise, expecting childminders to look after six, rather than four, children, undermines the attention and care each child can receive.
6. This change to finance has happened as finance increasingly takes on an immaterial form, such as financial derivatives and 'collatorised debt obligations' (CDOs) and the connection with any real assets declines. A collatorised debt obligation (CDO) is an asset-backed security that arises from the pooling of debt linked to bonds or mortgages, and the investors will be paid from the income arising from debt repayments. CDOs arise from the pooling of debt (for example from mortgages) and are used 'as a platform for ever more speculative financial constructions that can be so complex they challenge empirical analysis, let alone moral evaluation' (Sassen 2014, 117).

References

Antonopoulos, Rania and Kijong Kim (2011) 'Public job-creation programs: the economic benefits of investing in social care? Case studies in South Africa and the United States', Working Paper, Levy Economics Institute, No. 671

Baumol, William (1967) 'Macroeconomics of unbalanced growth: the anatomy of the Urban Crisis', *American Economic Review* 57(3): 415–26

Bettio, Francesca, Marcella Corsi, Carlo D'Ippoliti, Antigone Lyberaki, Manuela Lodoviciand, and Alina Verashchagina (2012) *The Impact of the Economic Crisis on the Situation of Women and Men and on Gender Equality Policies.* Luxembourg: European Commission

Blanchard, Oliver and Daniel Leigh (2013) 'Growth forecast errors and fiscal multipliers', IMF Working Paper, 13/1, https://www.imf.org/external/pubs/ft/wp/2013/wp1301.pdf (last checked by the author 10 April 2015)

Chant, Sylvia and Caroline Pedwell (2008) *Women, Gender and the Informal Economy: An Assessment of ILO Research and Suggested Ways Forward'*, Geneva: ILO

Chemi, Eric and Ariana Giorgi (2014) 'The pay-for-performance myth, Bloomberg Businessweek; Data: Equilar' http://www.businessweek.com/articles/2014-07-22/for-ceos-correlation-between-pay-and-stock-performance-is-pretty-random (last checked by the author 10 April 2015)

Davala, Sarath, Renana Jhabvala, Soumya Kapoor Mehta, and Guy Standing (2015) *Basic Income*, London: Bloomsbury

European Commission (2010) *Strategy for Equality between Women and Men 2010–2015*, Luxemburg: European Commission

Elson, Diane (1991) *Male Bias in the Development Process*, Manchester: Manchester University Press

Elson, Diane (2006) *Budgeting for Human Rights*, New York: UNIFEM

Elson, Diane (2012) 'The reduction of the UK budget deficit: a human rights perspective', *International Review of Applied Economics* 26(2): 177–90

Elson, Diane and Nilufer Cagatay (2000) 'The social content of macroeconomic policies', *World Development* 28(7): 1347–64

Fukuda-Parr, Sakiko, James Heintz, and Stephanie Seguino (2013) 'Critical perspectives on financial and economic crises: heterodox macroeconomics meets feminist economics', *Feminist Economics* 19(3): 4–31

Gill, Stephen and Adrianne Roberts (2011) 'Macroeconomic governance, gendered inequality, and global crises', in Barbara Young, Isabella Bakker, and Diane Elson (eds.) *Questioning Financial Governance from a Feminist Perspective*, London: Routledge, pp. 155–172

Glenn, Evelyn Nwanko (1992) 'From servitude to service work: historical continuities in the racial division of paid reproductive labour', *Signs* 18(1): 1–43

Griffith-Jones, Stephany and Richard Jolly (2013) 'Be outraged by austerity', *Challenge* January/February 55(4): 40–60

Heller, Peter (2005) 'Back to basics – fiscal space: what it is and how to get it', *Finance and Development A Quarterly Magazine of the IMF* 42(2): 1, http://www.imf.org/external/pubs/ft/fandd/2005/06/basics.htm (last by the author checked 10 April 2015)

Himmelweit, Susan (2007) 'The prospects for caring: economic theory and policy analysis', *Cambridge Journal of Economics* 31(4): 581–99

ICF GHK (2013) *The Economic Value of the Adult Social Care Sector in England, London: Skills for Care*, http://cdn.basw.co.uk/upload/basw_114055-9.pdf (last checked by the author 10 April 2015)

Ida, Katy (2013) *LSE Feminists Economics Graduate Option Week 4 Discussion Blog*, Internal University Blog

International Labour Organisation (2015) *Women and the Future of Work: Beijing + 20 and Beyond*, Geneva: International Labour Office, http://www.ilo.org/gender/Informationre-sources/Publications/WCMS_348087/lang–en/index.htm (last checked by the author 10 April 2015)

Kabeer, Naila (2013) 'Grief and rage in India: making violence against women history?', https://www.opendemocracy.net/5050/naila-kabeer/grief-and-rage-in-india-making-violence-against-women-history (last checked by the author 10 April 2015)

Krugman, Paul (2002) 'For richer ', *New York Times*, 20 October http://www.pkarchive.org/economy/ForRicher.html (last checked by the author 10 April 2015)

Krugman, Paul (2013) 'How the case for austerity has crumbled', *New York Times* June 6th, http://www.nybooks.com/articles/archives/2013/jun/06/how-case-austerity-has-crumbled/ (last checked by the author 10 April 2015)

Lagarde, Christine (2014) 'Empowerment – the Amartya Sen Lecture 2014', Transcript http://www.lse.ac.uk/assets/richmedia/channels/publicLecturesAndEvents/transcripts/20140606_1830_theAmartyaSenLecture2014_tr.pdf (last checked by the author 10 April 2015)

OECD (2008) *Growing Unequal. Income Distribution and Poverty in OECD Countries*, Paris: OECD

OECD (2011) *Divided We Stand: Why Inequality Keeps Rising*, Paris: OECD

Ortiz, Isabel and Matthew Cummins (2013) 'The Age of Austerity: A Review of Public Expenditures and Adjustment Measures in 181 Countries', Initiative for Policy Dialogue and the South Centre Working Paper http://policydialogue.org/files/publications/Age_of_Austerity_Ortiz_and_Cummins.pdf (last checked by the author 10 April 2015)

Phillips, Anne and Barbara Taylor (1980) 'Sex and skill: notes towards a feminist economics', *Feminist Review* 6(1): 79–88

Piketty, Thomas (2014) *Capital in the Twenty-First Century*, Harvard: Belknap Press

Perrons, Diane (2014) 'Gendering inequality: a note on Piketty's Capital in the Twenty-First Century', *British Journal of Sociology* 65(4): 667–677

Perrons, Diane and Ania Plomien (2013) 'Gender, inequality and the crisis: towards more equitable development', in Maria Karamessini and Jill Rubery (eds.) *Women and Austerity The Economic Crisis and the Future for Gender Equality*, 295–313, London: Routledge

Reinhart, Carment and Kenneth Rogoff (2010) 'Growth in a time of debt', *American Economic Review* 100 (May): 573–78

Rosnick, David and Dean Baker (2012) *Missing the Story. The OECD's Analysis of Inequality*, Washington, DC: Centre for Economic Policy Research

Sassen, Saskia (2014) *Expulsions. Brutality and Complexity in the Global Economy*, Harvard: Belknap Press

Seguino, Stephanie (2010) 'The global economic crisis: its gender and ethnic implications and policy responses', *Gender and Development* 18(2): 179–199

Stockhammer, Engelbert (2013) *Why Have Wage Shares Fallen? A Panel Analysis of the Determinants of Functional Income Distribution, Conditions of Work and Employment Series No. 35*, Geneva: ILO

UNCTAD (2012) *Policies for Inclusive and Balanced Growth, Trade and Development Report, 2012*, http://unctad.org/en/publicationslibrary/tdr2012_en.pdf (last checked by the author 10 April 2015)

UNDP (2007) *Primer: Fiscal Space for MDGs*, http://www.sarpn.org/documents/d0002584/ Fiscal_Space_UNDP_Jun2007.pdf (last checked by the author 10 April 2015)

UNDP (2010) *Vision for a Better World: From Economic Crisis to Recovery*, http://www.inclusivecities.org/wpcontent/uploads/2012/07/Jain_Elson_UNDP_Crisis_to_equality.pdf (last checked by the author 10 April 2015)

WBG (2015) *PLAN F: A Feminist Economic Strategy for a Caring and Sustainable Economy*. http://wbg.org.uk/ (last checked by the author 10 April 2015)

World Bank (2012) *Gender and Development, World Development Report 2012*, Washington: World Bank

About the Author

Diane Perrons is Professor Emerita in Feminist Political Economy, Department of Gender Studies, London School of Economics and Political Science. Email: d.perrons@lse.ac.uk

CHAPTER 4

The Individual Deprivation Measure: measuring poverty as if gender and inequality matter

Sharon Bessell

Abstract

As inequality deepens globally and within countries it is vital that we know how poverty shapes, constrains, and often destroys the lives of women and men. We know from decades of research that poverty is experienced differently by women and men, yet existing mainstream measures of poverty have been blind to gender. This chapter focuses on the Individual Deprivation Measure (IDM), a multi-dimensional measure of poverty and inequality designed to illuminate rather than obscure gender differences. Developed over the past five years by an inter-disciplinary research team based at the Australian National University, the IDM is grounded in research with women and men across 18 sites in six countries. Unlike most mainstream measures of poverty, the IDM takes the individual, rather than the household, as the unit of analysis. As a result, the IDM is able to capture gendered differences in the ways poverty is experienced, and also differences according to other markers of identity or social status, such as age, ethnicity, or geographic location.

Keywords: poverty measurement; gender sensitive; multi-dimensional poverty; Individual Deprivation Measure

Introduction

How we measure poverty matters. As inequality deepens globally and within countries, the need to know how poverty is shaping, constraining, and in many cases, destroying the lives of women and men becomes more acute. There is an urgent need to reconceptualise definitions and measures of poverty in ways that take gender seriously. Measures of poverty need to illuminate when and how gender inequality results in particular forms of deprivation for women *and* men across the life course. Yet existing measures are inadequate to provide the insights needed to respond to poverty as different social groups experience it. In particular, the gender-blindness of most mainstream measures of poverty undermines their utility and value.

http://dx.doi.org/10.3362/9781780447278.004

This chapter focuses on the Individual Deprivation Measure (IDM): a multi-dimensional measure of poverty developed between 2010 and 2014 through an inter-disciplinary, cross-national research project, involving 1,800 participants across 18 sites in six countries. The starting point for the research that resulted in the Individual Deprivation Measure was the dissatisfaction of the team which developed the IDM with the gender insensitivity of most existing measures of poverty (Bessell 2010; Pogge and Minar 2009). From its inception, the IDM was envisaged as a just, and justifiable, measure of poverty. Just in the sense that it would reveal how poverty impacts differently on different individuals, particularly those individuals who are marginalised or disadvantaged not only in society broadly, but within their own households. A just poverty measure must be capable of assessing each individual's overall level of disadvantage. Only when the individual – rather than the household – is the unit of analysis can we reveal inequality between women and men, between social and identity groups, and across geographic locations.

We aspired that the IDM be *justifiable*, in the sense of our approach being transparent, and grounded in research with people with lived experience of poverty. While the many decades of knowledge accumulated by experts must influence any new approach to poverty measurement, it is our contention that a measure of poverty cannot be fully justifiable, if it is driven solely by expert knowledge. Certainly, participatory approaches to poverty research have been influential at the policy level. Arguably, both the shift to an understanding of poverty as multi-dimensional and the emphasis on promoting empowerment within development discourse is largely attributable to participatory research. Yet, while there is a wealth of literature using participatory methods to explore the causes, experiences, and impacts of poverty, our review of the literature revealed no comprehensive studies of how the poor think poverty should be *measured*. Our review demonstrated the need for a measure of poverty capable of illuminating individual deprivation and inequality at multiple levels and across multiple dimensions, which is grounded in participatory research.

This chapter describes the development of the IDM and its innovations in more detail. It begins with a brief summary of the shortcomings of existing poverty measures, before relating the features of the IDM and the process through which it was created. Our methodological approach was underpinned by two principles. First, we were committed to the idea that development theories, policies, and practices must be grounded in an understanding of poverty and inequality as complex, individual- and context-specific. Poverty needs to be measured in a way which captures the lived experiences of women and men whose perceptions and understandings remain marginal to the decisions of elites which shape their lives. Second, we recognised that any measure of poverty must be practicable and comparable.

The team working on the IDM was based at the Australian National University and was composed of academics from a range of disciplines, including philosophy, political science, public policy, development studies, and economics, as well as practitioners with considerable experience in working on issues of poverty and gender in the global South.

Why a new measure of (gendered) poverty?

That experiences of poverty are gendered has long been recognised. Since the early 1990s, this recognition has been taken up – albeit somewhat unevenly – by policy-makers. However, in some cases the result has been sloganeering, rather than well-crafted policies. Claims that 'poverty has a woman's face' and of the 'feminisation of poverty' are commonplace, but do not illuminate the extent, depth, or nature of this perceived 'feminisation', and what it means for our understandings of poverty and its links to inequality. Jane Millar and Caroline Glendinning (1989, 369) challenged such simplistic representations of a complex and layered social problem, arguing that 'understanding the gender dimensions of poverty means more than making the simple empirical observation that women are at greater risk of poverty than men'. Instead, they argued, we need to fundamentally reconceptualise poverty from a gender perspective.

In highlighting the ways in which 'gender equality is part and parcel of the processes of poverty and discrimination', Naila Kabeer (2003, 3) has argued cogently that gender inequality must also 'figure just as integrally in the set of measures to eradicate these conditions'. Equally, the fact of gender inequality must be taken seriously within efforts to measure the extent and intensity of poverty, which in turn form the basis for policy and action to overcome poverty.

Debates about how poverty should be measured are by no means new. A long-standing issue of contestation is the relative merits of income-based and multi-dimensional approaches to conceptualising and measuring poverty. Another central concern, particularly for feminist scholars, is the continued focus on the household as the appropriate unit of analysis.

Income-based poverty measures

The International Poverty Line, established by The World Bank, provides an example of income-based measures of poverty. Here poverty is calculated according to the daily amount required by a person to meet his or her food requirements (typically 2,100 calories per person per day) and essential non-food needs. The amount of money required per person per day is then calculated according to costs in a particular country (known as purchasing power parity), and converted into a common currency (US dollars) for the purposes of comparison across countries (Ravallion *et al.* 2008). Many countries have national income-based poverty lines. In some cases, such as India, poverty lines are different for rural and urban areas. Households are generally the unit of analysis, with a household determined as poor or not according to the amount of income divided across the number of members.

Income-based measures of poverty calculated in this way are particularly problematic from a gender perspective. They pay no heed to details of what happens to income once it enters households – that is, to access to and control over money and how it is spent, which means these measures fail to track different outcomes for individuals within the household (Chant 2005). Households are institutions distinguished not by relationships of harmony presided over by a benign household head, but by relations of conflict and co-operation rooted in gender and other dimensions of difference (Sen 1990). In households, there are 'multiple actors, with varying (and often conflicting) preferences and interests, and differential abilities to pursue and realize those interests' (Agarwal 1997, 3). Gender, age, and position in the family are among the many dimensions of difference which shape reality and power for an individual. Differences in the bargaining power of household members, and gender norms, necessarily have implications for the intra-household distribution of resources. For example, hardship resulting from seasonal shortages or economic crisis falls disproportionately on women within poor households, as they reduce consumption, deplete their assets as a coping strategy, and take on heavier work burdens (Agarwal 1990, 392).

Moreover, income-based measures of poverty are entirely unable to capture the full range of value of household labour. They ignore the economic worth of unpaid work: subsistence agriculture, family labour of women and children in production, and unpaid care work undertaken within the households and communities. This is critical to a gendered understanding of poverty, since unpaid work is overwhelmingly performed by women and children.

In addition to needing to reveal difference and inequality with the household, it is also important that any measure of poverty should reveal and provide insight into differences between households in different contexts. Sonalde Desai (1992, 711) correctly reminds us that 'the conditions that affect cooperation and conflict in the relationship between family members ... vary across cultures and across socioeconomic contexts'. Poverty measures therefore need to focus on individuals, not households, in order to gain a nuanced understanding of what poverty actually means to individual women and men, boys and girls. They also need to move beyond income alone.

Multi-dimensional poverty measures

Multi-dimensional approaches to the conceptualisation and measurement of poverty have their theoretical origins in the capability approach pioneered by Amartya Sen (1984), and offer greater potential than income-based measures to be gender-sensitive. Martha Nussbaum (2001) has sought to illuminate the intersections between a capabilities approach and feminism. In practice, however, multi-dimensional approaches have yet to fulfil their promise of sensitivity to gender difference and inequality.

The Multi-dimensional Poverty Index (MPI), developed via the Oxford Poverty and Human Development Initiative at the University of Oxford, is described by its creators as 'an index of acute multidimensional poverty ... [reflecting] ... deprivations in very rudimentary services and core human functionings' (Alkire and Santos 2011, 7). Reflecting the increasing influence of multi-dimensional approaches to poverty measurement, the MPI was adopted by UNDP in 2010 and is used in several countries, often alongside income-based measures. The MPI determines poverty not by income, but by deprivation in health, education, and standard of living, measured at household level using ten indicators. The MPI is described as revealing 'the combination of deprivations that batter a household at the same time' (Alkire and Santos 2011, 7). Such revelation is important, but the MPI has a critical weakness in that it does not delve beneath household level to reveal the different experiences of individuals according to gender, age, and other important aspects of identity. While households collectively suffer from poverty, deprivation, and unequal access to services, not all members of a household suffer in the same way or to the same extent.

Conversely, several well-known measures of gender equality/inequality have little light to shed on the gendered experience of poverty and economic inequality. For reasons of space these will not be discussed here, but examples are the Gender-related Development Index (GDI) and the Gender Empowerment Measure (GEM), launched by UNDP in 1995.[1]

Addressing the challenges: the Individual Deprivation Measure (IDM)[2]

The Individual Deprivation Measure seeks to overcome the gender insensitivity of existing measures of poverty, and in doing so reveals both gendered and other forms of inequality. The IDM captures an individual's status using two axes. Financial deprivation is plotted on the y axis, and 15 dimensions of poverty are plotted on the x axis. These are intended to capture the individual's experience of individual, multi-dimensional deprivation (see Wisor *et al*. 2014 for more detail). Financial deprivation is featured on a different axis rather than including it among the dimensions since it is clearly central to measuring poverty (indeed, during our research participants over-whelmingly identified income and ownership of assets as central to measuring poverty, deprivation, and inequality). Yet, including income or wealth in the dimensions may have a distorting effect on participants' response to questions relating to other dimensions. By plotting financial deprivation on one axis and multi-dimensional poverty on another, policymakers and practitioners are able to identify and track the relationship between the two forms of deprivation. This is an approach that is accepted and used in other multi-dimensional poverty measures.

Each dimension has one or more indicators, developed from research with participants with experience of living in poverty in different contexts, a review of the relevant literature and existing measures, and consultation with expert stakeholders. The indicators are a distillation of those raised in different contexts into a universal list to ensure the measure can be used in different contexts in the global South and potentially in the North. The IDM includes dimensions such as food/nutrition, water, shelter, and health care, which are shared by some existing measures of poverty or inequality. In some of these dimensions, however, the indicators are somewhat different from those used in existing poverty measures. For example, in relation to health, the IDM's indicators measure both health status, and access to health care. An additional question is asked of women who are pregnant or have been pregnant in the past three years, in order to measure access to maternal health care. The IDM also includes various dimensions that are rarely included in measures of poverty, inequality, or deprivation, but were identified by participants as very important. Three examples, freedom from violence, time use, and voice, are discussed in more detail later in this chapter.

The 15 dimensions and associated indicators that make up the IDM are provided in Table 1.

Table 1 The Individual Deprivation Measure

Dimension	Indicators
Food/Nutrition	Hunger in the last four weeks
Water	Water source, water quality
Shelter	Durable housing; Homelessness
Health care/Health	Health status, health care access; For women who are pregnant or have been pregnant in the past three years, access to pre-natal care, trained health care worker in attendance at birth
Education	Years of schooling completed; Basic literacy and numeracy
Energy/Cooking fuel	Source of cooking fuel; Health impacts; Access to electricity
Sanitation	Primary toilet, secondary toilet
Family relations	Control of decision-making in household; Supportive relationships
Clothing/ Personal care	Protection from elements; Ability to present oneself in a way that is socially acceptable
Violence	Violence (including sexual and physical violence) experienced in the last 12 months; Perceived risk of violence in the next six months
Family planning	Access to reliable, safe contraception; Control over use of contraception
Environment	Exposure to environmental harms that can affect health, well-being and livelihood prospects
Voice	Ability to participate in public decision-making in the community; Ability to influence change at community level
Time use	Labour burden; Leisure time
Work	Status of and respect in paid and unpaid work; Safety and risk in relation to paid and unpaid work

Using the Individual Deprivation Measure

The IDM is administered via a survey, which was explicitly designed to be practicable in a range of contexts, both in terms of cost and the technical ability of survey-takers. The survey requires approximately one hour per individual, and should be administered to every adult member of the household. In trialling the survey through a nationally representative sample in the Philippines, we found return visits to house-holds are often necessary in order to survey all members. This requires more time than approaches that survey only (usually male) household heads, but is essential in overcoming the problem of gender-bias from which most surveys suffer.

The IDM uses a simple asset index as an approximate measure of financial status, capturing the assets that are shared across household members and able to be compared across contexts.

Multi-dimensional status is calculated from survey questions for each of the 15 dimensions and associated indicators. An individual is scored on a scale from one to five for each dimension; where dimensions have multiple indicators, the scores for each indicator are averaged. A score of one indicates extreme deprivation in a particular dimension, while a score of five indicates that an individual is not deprived in that dimension. Scores are then aggregated for each individual across all dimensions to provide an overall score. While there is debate around the appropriateness of aggregating information to form a score for individuals (Ravallion 2011), we argue that without a combined total score for each individual it is not possible for identify who is multi-dimensionally poor. The great value of the approach taken by the IDM is that because scores are aggregated *for each individual* it is possible to *disaggregate* in order to identify which groups are deprived in specific dimensions (for example, according to sex, age, ethnicity, location). It is also possible to gain insight into which individuals within a household are deprived and in which dimensions. Thus, the gendered nature of inequality – both within and beyond the household – is not hidden as in many measures of poverty but illuminated.

What makes the IDM different?

The IDM is distinct from other measures in three important ways. First, it is grounded in participatory research with people in poor communities in 18 sites across six countries. Unlike most mainstream measures of poverty or inequality, the IDM explicitly incorporates the priority issues identified by those living in poverty. Second, the IDM departs from the dominant measures of poverty in taking the individual, rather than the household, as the unit of analysis. This enables it to reveal the details of experiences of inequality within households. We can analyse how individuals in the same household experience the impact of financial deprivation differently, as well as the role of non-monetary deprivation in the ways individual household members experience poverty. Crucially, this enables comparison of how a particular social category – for example, adolescent girls – experience poverty in a particular community. Third, the IDM is not constrained by existing (and limited) data sources, which are often insensitive to gender-based inequality and do not reveal the dimensions of poverty that are important to poor people.

I go into each of these three points in more detail in the sections that follow.

Taking the priorities of the poor seriously

As David Hulme (2010) observes, definitions of poverty are often polarised as objective or subjective. 'Objective' definitions of poverty – and the measurement tools that flow from those definitions – are specified by experts who determine not only definitions but the ways in which data are collected and analysed. Objective approaches are grounded in positivist assumptions about the possibility of defining a social problem, and measuring it in a way that is value-free. While justifiable in terms of rigour and comparability, objective definitions and measures of poverty are never actually that, since they are never really free from the normative assumptions that, often implicitly, drive them. 'Subjective' definitions produce very different approaches, whereby poor women and men make assessments of their own situation and status. Subjective approaches provide depth and nuance that objective approaches rarely achieve, but are generally undertaken on a small, local scale, and produce detailed and often very context-specific data that cannot be easily compared across contexts or over time.Subjective approaches are necessarily coloured by individuals' experiences, knowledge, priorities, and interests.

In developing the IDM, we drew on feminist and participatory research principles that challenge the idea that poverty can be defined and understood free of the social structures that produce it (Kabeer 1991). We dismissed an 'objective' approach to the task of reconceptualising poverty measurement as replicating existing problems. However, we were conscious of the shortcomings of localised participatory approaches that generate data which cannot be used in comparisons across contexts or among groups. We therefore rejected the objective/subjective dichotomy, and developed a participatory research methodology to build a measure of poverty, deprivation, and inequality from the ground up, while taking heed of the vast expert literature around defining and measuring poverty.

The IDM is grounded in research carried out by local research teams in six countries: Angola, Fiji, Indonesia, Malawi, Mozambique, and the Philippines. In each country, we worked in three sites: one urban, one rural, and one marginalised. The marginalised site was selected not because of its geographic location, but because the community was known to suffer not only from poverty but from deep stigma, exclusion, and marginalisation. In each site, we worked separately with women and men, in order to understand deeply the ways in which participants thought poverty and deprivation impacts differently according to gender. We asked both women and men how poverty and deprivation should be conceptualised and measured for people of their own sex, and also for people of the opposite sex. Here, we gained insight into the complex ways in which participants considered the intersection between gender and poverty. As will be discussed later, gender roles and responsibilities were fundamental in shaping experiences of poverty.

In addition to exploring the gendered dimensions of poverty measurement, the first phase of the research sought also to illuminate the generational dimensions. In each site, we worked with participants across the life course: young women and men from their mid-teens to early twenties; women and men in middle life; and elderly women and men.[3] While we used chronological age as a rough guide to identifying generational cohorts, we relied more heavily on social age and forms of responsibility. Indeed, chronological age made little sense as a determinant of stage within the life course, since life expectancy ranged from 70 in Fiji and Indonesia, to just 49 in Mozambique.

The focus on both generation and gender proved to be important, particularly in understanding both how inequality plays out and which dimensions of poverty are most acute across the life course. While most existing measures of poverty are insensitive to gender, they are also insensitive to generation – yet one's position within the life course is fundamentally important to experiences of poverty, inequality, and deprivation.

The first, qualitative, phase of the project was carried out by local research teams in each country, each of which had deep knowledge of the country context, necessary language skills, and experience in conducting participatory research. While the length of time research teams spent at each site varies, teams were at each site for at least a week during phase one, returning for several days in phase two. In phase one, we used participatory research principles and methods to explore what constitutes poverty, how gender and age determine the constitution of poverty, and whether there are different levels of poverty. This phase of the research focused on which dimensions of poverty participants considered important for policymakers to recognise and understand in order to effectively combat it. Based on the analysis of the qualitative research and an extensive review of the relevant literature and existing measures, we identified 25 dimensions of poverty, each of which was a candidate for a gender-sensitive measure. Research teams then returned to all sites to ask participants to respond to and rank the dimensions, and also to identify important dimensions that were not on the list of 25. As in phase one, the phase two research was structured around sex and age, with the number of participants increasing to 1,800 across the 18 sites (approximately 100 participants per site; 300 participants per country).

From phase two, we developed a measure of deprivation comprising 15 dimensions. The final 15 dimensions were those most commonly identified by participants across sites and countries and those identified from the literature review or by participants as particularly important in uncovering gendered poverty. Pre-testing for this phase found that while participants tended to have strong views about the dimensions they considered to be a high priority in the measurement of poverty, they did not have strong views on the relative priority of the dimensions at the bottom of the list. For example, in phase one, both freedom from the disruptive behaviour of other people and spending on discretionary items were identified as important, but were not prioritised in phase two. By contrast, food or adequate nutrition, water, and shelter consistently received a high ranking by the majority of participants across sites in phase two.

The resulting IDM therefore not only relies on expert knowledge developed over decades of research and debate about poverty measurement, but is grounded in the views and experiences of those who have lived and experienced poverty. The participatory nature of the development of the IDM is a remarkable strength shared by few existing mainstream measures of poverty. In the past, participatory methodologies have been used very effectively to understand the extent and nature of poverty at the local level (see for example Chambers 1994). Such participatory appraisals are important in revealing the extent and nature of poverty in a specific area, and often highlight and reflect local perceptions of poverty. However, the findings are often difficult to generalise. Poverty measurement on a large scale has tended to rely on high level data on income, health, or education gathered through censuses and household or labour force surveys. Such approaches produce statistically significant results and provide important insights into broad trends. However, they are often unable to reveal nuance and context. The IDM offers an alternative to either small-scale, local, and highly contextualised assessments of poverty, or measures based on large scale data sets that have no participatory element.

The individual as the unit of analysis

The second important and distinctive feature of the IDM is the identification of the individual, not the household, as the unit of analysis. As discussed earlier, the remarkably enduring assumption that household poverty can adequately reveal the status of individual members is flawed, and is at the heart of our critique of most existing measures of poverty.

Couched in feminist principles, this research began with recognition of the ways in which measures of household poverty mask inequalities in intra-household. The IDM is designed to aggregate the 15 dimensions for each individual, thus providing a holistic of individual deprivation. From here, it is possible to identify if, and how, inequalities play out *within* a household. Data collected at the individual level can then be aggregated to illuminate the nature and extent of deprivation, and to identify changes over time, for particular groups; for example, women, older women, older women living with a disability. The IDM can also be used to measure deprivation not only according to gender, but according to geographic location, ethnicity, religion, language, and so on. Consequently, and importantly, the IDM offers a means of establishing baseline data and tracking changes for each individual and for specific groups. This level of insight is essential if inequality is to be seriously addressed.

It is important to emphasise that in moving to the individual as the unit of analysis, we do not imply that the household is unimportant. We heard from participants about the survival strategies of households. In several communities during the first phase of the research, we heard from participants that if a household is poor, everyone is poor. In one group discussion of middle-aged women in Indonesia, one participant said that there is little difference about the effect of poverty within the household:

> All are the same, poor men and poor women are the same, they are all suffering.

Yet we also heard that poverty plays out differently according to one's place in the household. Participants spoke of the very different burdens that fall to different individuals, often as a result of gender and/or generation. As the discussion about poor men and women both suffering unfolded, the different impacts of poverty on women and men began to emerge. Another woman participating in the discussion provided an additional perspective:

> Poor men and poor women are the same, but women may have more burdens than anyone else in the family because women have responsibility to take care of household affairs. If a woman or a wife wants to cook but she does not have money, she will feel sad, if the children ask for pocket money but she cannot give them any, she will feel terrible, if she wants to buy on credit from a warung (food stall), the owner of the food stall won't believe she will pay it back.

This comment reveals the ways in which women's ascribed gender roles and responsibilities create obligations within and beyond the family, leading to a deep sense of inadequacy and shame when those obligations cannot be met.

In Indonesia, we found few overt examples of food or clothing being distributed on the basis of sex. We did find that gender roles and responsibilities act to shape deprivation in often quite subtle ways, as individuals – and particularly women – make choices about their own use of resources. A typical comment in Indonesia, where social expectations dictate that mothers should sacrifice for their families, was made by a woman in middle-age: 'For me the first thing is fulfilling my children's needs, if I may say; I don't care if I suffer, children should eat properly'. That women's role in caring for family members, particularly children, comes at the cost of their own welfare in situations of poverty was a common theme across sites.

Significantly, participants noted that gendered expectations also shape the context within which men experience poverty. One elderly woman observed, 'We feel so sorry if we see a man does not have a job because they have responsibility to their family, usually they easily get angry'. Here we see both the pressure on men to fulfil socially expected roles, and gain a glimpse of the consequences of them being unable to fulfil those roles.

Our aim is not to dismiss the significance of the household, but to illuminate the poverty of *individuals* within the household as the basis for effective interventions. As we move from the household to the individual as the unit of analysis, the centrality of gender in shaping experiences and burdens of poverty is clearly apparent. It is also clear that while gender differences are universally important to the way poverty is experienced, gender plays out differently across contexts – including across different households and household-types.

Considering new sources of data

The third feature of the IDM is that it is a survey-based multi-dimensional poverty measure that does not solely rely on existing data. In reviewing the literature and existing measures of poverty and inequality, and based on the experience of several team members, we were acutely aware from the outset of the research of the ways in which current measures of poverty rely on existing – and often inadequate – data sources. That measures of poverty rely on existing data is understandable. Clearly, having data that are reasonably reliable and comparable is important if any measure is to be robust. Yet, we were also cognisant of the problems of reliability and of patchy data that exist in some of the countries in which we worked, and in many countries of the global South. Moreover, and more importantly, much existing data are not adequate to measure the dimensions of poverty that matter most to people, and particularly to women. So long as we remain limited by existing data sources, we are destined to remain limited in our understanding of poverty and limited in our responses. Very importantly, while we are limited by existing data sources, we are ill-equipped to identify and respond to the gendered dimensions of poverty.

In its conceptualisation and development, the IDM was not bound by existing data. Had we been, the first participatory phase of the research would have provided little value. The IDM is able to take people's views seriously – on the importance, for example, of measuring the strength of family relationships or on exposure to violence – despite the current absence of reliable or comparable data. Nevertheless, despite moving beyond existing data sources, in designing the survey we were conscious that it must be practically feasible and easy to administer. We were also conscious of the need for a survey that can be used at various levels, from local to national or global, or with specific population groups. A trial of the IDM in the Philippines, using a nationally representative sample of 750 households whereby most adult household members were interviewed, demonstrated that it is easy to administer and relatively low-cost. Each individual survey takes under one hour to administer. While the IDM does not resolve the problems of limited data, it does aim to expand thinking about the kinds of data that are collected, including through nationally representative censuses and surveys, and used in poverty measurement.

Tracing the inter-connections between poverty and (gender) inequality

Earlier, I noted that the IDM includes dimensions, such as freedom from violence, time use and voice, which were considered very important by participants across sites, but rarely feature in mainstream measures of poverty or deprivation. In the following sections, I briefly discuss why these three dimensions were important to participants. In doing so, the complex inter-connections between gender, poverty, and inequality emerge, as does the importance of holistic, individualised measures of poverty to efforts to understand and overcome inequality.

Freedom from violence

Participants across all sites spoke of violence as a pervasive reality confronting people living in poverty. Violence was described as plaguing the lives of the poor in multiple ways. Public violence was experienced as inter-personal violence, perpetrated by other individuals or groups, and as structural violence, perpetrated or tacitly endorsed by the state. Inter-personal violence had a strong gendered dimension. In Malawi, for example, both male and female participants from the urban site spoke of the violence to which women are subjected. Domestic violence, often related to husband's alcohol use or to financial pressures, was a common theme. Other forms of family violence were also identified, including 'property-grabbing', whereby a widow is confronted by her husband's relatives, who claim 'his' land as belonging to them, not his wife. Participants pointed out that women are often unable to repel such claims, and are left destitute as a consequence.

Both women and men described the vulnerability of the poor to violence in public spaces. Violence was often associated with stigma and discrimination against particular groups, and people living in the marginalised sites described themselves as being most vulnerable. Young men in the marginalised site in the Philippines, where fishing was one of the few sources of livelihood, described being subjected to physical violence and having their boats or catch stolen. In the urban site in Malawi, women of all ages faced the possibility of violent attack and rape when they went to collect water. Participants noted that the problem was worse in the rainy season, when foliage around the river was thicker and assailants could wait unseen. In all of these cases, a common experience was the impunity with which perpetrators could act. Participants told us that the poor are not only vulnerable to violence, but also that they have no recourse.

While inter-personal violence, or perceived risk of violence, was identified as a dimension of poverty by participants across sites, structural violence was also a feature of the lives of the poor, particularly in marginalised sites. Arguably, poverty itself is a form of structural violence; and many participants, for example in the marginalised site in Indonesia, described being excluded from health, education, and other services. Poverty, stigma, and discrimination combined to create an environment of violence, particularly in the marginalised sites, which manifest most obviously in vulnerability to state efforts to define their living arrangements as illegal and to use security forces to clear communities. The resulting insecurity and stigma of people living under the threat of violent eviction both deepens and broadens the ways in which poverty is experienced.

Time use and labour burdens

In both the first and second phases of our research, the way in which poverty intersects with time use and labour burdens was highlighted by participants. Feminist scholars have critiqued the ways in which measures of gender equality have ignored the care economy, often opting to focus exclusively on paid employment at the expense of unpaid care (Folbre 2006). Similarly, measures of poverty have paid little attention to the care economy and time burdens. Yet, as Sylvia Chant (2007) points out, it is inputs of time and energy rather than incomes that are crucial in analysing women's experiences of poverty. In Indonesia, for example, time burdens were identified as central to poverty by women in the 19–40 age-group. Women explained that meeting their family's daily needs, food preparation, house cleaning, and childcare left them with no free time. As a result, women said they rarely engaged in activities other than those associated with their gender-specific caring roles. Moreover, they said a lack of time had a deleterious effect on their ability to take care of themselves. A particularly significant finding in Indonesia is that the caring and household maintenance burdens on poor women result in them having limited time in which to engage in paid labour, and when they do so, it is likely to be irregular and insecure. Consequently, poor women are more likely to be financially dependent on working age males, at least for part of the time. They are also particularly vulnerable to insecure and exploitative forms of paid work.

Voice

Lack of voice was identified across all sites as a dimension of poverty, but played out in different ways. Very often, being poor and marginalised equated to having little power to influence decision-makers, policy, or public debate at any level. In Malawi, participants said they felt they had no voice because parliamentarians did not represent them or their interests. Lack of voice also disempowered people at the local level, sometimes in unanticipated ways. For example, in one site in Mozambique men migrated to South Africa in search of work, leaving their wives and children behind and often without support. Participants explained the women and children were particularly vulnerable to poverty when men migrated, but in a patriarchal society women had no access to community forums or deliberation processes. In the absence of a male head of household, women were effectively without a voice in the community.

Clearly, violence, time burdens, and lack of voice are not *only* related to poverty. People who are well-off on other measures may also be deprived in one or more of these dimensions. Our research indicates, however, that each has a strong inter-relationship to poverty, and the poor experience deprivations in each of these dimensions in particular ways – *as a result of their poverty*. Moreover, experiencing deprivations in these dimensions may exacerbate poverty. Our research is not able to – and does not seek to – suggest causation. It does however reveal the complex webs of connection between poverty, deprivation, *and* inequality across the dimensions that make up the IDM. Unless we are able to understand and measure these webs of connection, we have an insufficient basis for interventions that are able to respond to the most insidious dimensions of poverty and inequality for any given group or in any given context.

The potential of the IDM

The IDM is by no means the perfect tool. It does, however, demonstrate how we can do better in measuring poverty in ways that are sensitive to inequalities on the basis of gender, generation, and other individual characteristics. The IDM provides far deeper insights and nuance than income-based measures of poverty and moves well beyond the comparatively limited dimensions included in other multi-dimensional measures.

The IDM provides a way of taking gender seriously as an analytic category in the measurement of poverty, and revealing the depth and nature of poverty among women and men. By focusing on the individual, it is sensitive not only to gender, but also to other individual characteristics that may intensify poverty. It moves beyond income, and towards the dimensions of poverty that those with lived experience of poverty consider important. As such, the IDM provides a potentially powerful tool in understanding the complexities of poverty and in contributing to policy responses. The research project that produced the IDM began with the aim of producing a measure of poverty that is sensitive to gender and capable of illuminating disparities between men and women. By taking the individual as the unit of analysis, it is also capable of revealing inequalities based on a range of other characteristics. Revealing the nature, depth, and trends of inequality, and revealing who is deprived and in which dimensions, is essential if the widening gap between the wealthy few and the poor majority is to be both understood and countered.

Acknowledgement

This research project was funded by an Australian Research Council Linkage Grant LP0989385, *Assessing Development: Designing Better Indices of Poverty and Gender Equity*. The research was led by the Australian National University in Canberra, and supported by additional funding and in-kind support from the International Women's Development Agency (IWDA), Oxfam Great Britain

(Southern Africa), Oxfam America, Philippine Health and Social Science Association and the University of Colorado at Boulder. Invaluable additional support was provided by the Centre for the Study of Mind in Nature, Oslo University.

I am grateful to all those involved, especially Thomas Pogge, Scott Wisor, Jo Crawford, Janet Hunt, and Kieran Donaghue, who have been central to the development of the ideas in this paper. Any errors are, of course, my own. My particular thanks go to the research teams in each country, and to the hundreds of participants who were prepared to share their time, knowledge and insights.

Notes

1. See Bessell (2010) and Pogge (2010) for more on these.
2. Full details of the project, including the full report, and of the researchers involved are available at http://www.iwda.org.au/research/assessing-development/ (last checked by the author 16 April 2015).
3. We did not include children younger than mid-teens in this research due to resource and ethical issues. We are, however, currently planning a research project, using a similar methodology, that will focus on children and childhood deprivation.

References

Agarwal, Bina (1990) 'Social security and the family: coping with seasonality and calamity in rural India', *The Journal of Peasant Studies* 17(3): 341–412

Agarwal, Bina (1997) '"Bargaining" and gender relations: within and beyond the house-hold', *Feminist Economics* 3(1): 1–51

Alkire, Sabina, and Santos, María Emma (2011) 'Acute multidimensional poverty: a new index for developing countries', Proceedings of the German Development Economics Conference, no. 3. Berlin

Bessell, Sharon (2010) 'Methodologies for gender-sensitive and pro-poor poverty measures', in Sylvia Chant (ed.) *The International Handbook of Gender and Poverty: Concepts, Research and Policy*, 59–64, Cheltenham: Edward Elgar

Chambers, Robert (1994) 'Participatory rural appraisal (PRA): challenges, potentials and paradigm', *World Development* 22(10): 1437–54

Chant, Sylvia (2005) 'Re-thinking the "Feminization of Poverty" in relation to aggregate gender indices', *Journal of Human Development* 7(2): 201–20

Chant, Sylvia (2007) *Gender, Generation and Poverty: Exploring the 'Feminisation of Poverty' in Africa, Asia and Latin America*, Cheltenham: Edward Elgar

Desai, Sonalde (1992) 'Children at risk: the role of family structure in Latin America and West Africa', *Population and Development Review* 18(4): 689–717

Folbre, Nancy (2006) 'Measuring care: gender, empowerment, and the care economy', *Journal of Human Development* 7(2): 183–99

Hulme, David (2010) *Global Poverty: How Global Governance is Failing the Poor*, New York: Routledge

Kabeer, Naila (1991) 'Gender dimensions of rural poverty: analysis from Bangladesh', *The Journal of Peasant Studies* 18(2): 241–62

Kabeer, Naila (2003) 'Gender equality, poverty eradication and the millennium development goals: promoting women's capabilities and participation', *Gender & Development Paper Series No 13,* Economic and Social Commission for Asia and the Pacific

Millar, Jane, and Caroline Glendinning (1989) 'Gender and poverty', *Journal of Social Policy* 18(3): 363–81

Nussbaum, Martha C. (2001) *Women and Human Development: The Capabilities Approach,* Cambridge: Cambridge University Press

Pogge, Thomas (2009) 'Developing morally plausible indices of poverty and gender equity a research program', *Philosophical Topics* 37(2): 199–221

Pogge, Thomas (2010) *Politics as Usual: What lies Behind Pro-poor Rhetoric,* Cambridge: Polity Press

Ravallion, Martin (2011) 'On multidimensional indices of poverty', *Journal of Economic Inequality* 9(2): 235–48

Ravallion, Martin, Shaohua Chen, and Prem Sangraula (2008) 'Dollar a day revisited', Policy Research Working Paper 4620, Washington: The World Bank. http://www-wds.worldbank.org/external/default/WDSContentServer/IW3P/IB/2008/09/02/000158349_20080902095754/Rendered/PDF/wps4620.pdf (last checked by the author 19 June 2015)

Sen, Amartya (1984) 'Rights and capabilities', in Amartya Sen (ed.) *Resources, Values and Development,* Cambridge, MA: Harvard University Press

Sen, Amartya (1990) 'Gender and cooperative conflicts', in Irene Tinker (ed.) *Persistent Inequalities: Women and World Development,* New York: Oxford University Press, pp. 123–148

Wisor, Scott, Sharon Bessell, Fatima Castillo, Joanne Crawford, Kieran Donaghue, Janet Hunt, Alison Jaggar, Amy Liu, and Thomas Pogge (2014) *The Individaul Deprivation Measure: A Gender-sensitive Approach to Poverty Measurement,* Project Report https://www.iwda.org.au/assets/files/IDM-Report-16.02.15_FINAL.pdf (last checked by the author 19 June 2015)

About the Author

Sharon Bessell is Professor of Public Policy and Director of the Individual Deprivation Measure Program at the Crawford School of Public Policy, The Australian National University. Email: sharon.bessell@anu.edu.au

CHAPTER 5

Gender inequality and inter-household economic inequality in emerging economies: exploring the relationship

Daria Ukhova

Abstract

While most emerging economies have been characterised by persistence/growth of inter-household economic inequality in recent decades, and simultaneous poor performance on gender equality, the intersecting relationship between these two trends so far has not received much attention. This chapter is an initial attempt look at this relationship, showing how gender inequality has both contributed to, and been affected by, growing economic inequality. It focuses on eight emerging economies – Brazil, Russia, India, China, South Africa, Mexico, Indonesia, and Turkey (dubbed the BRICSAMIT countries). The chapter analyses Gini coefficient trends and Global Gender Gap Index trends, and draws in addition on insights gained from seven exploratory interviews with Oxfam colleagues and partners working on women's rights in the considered countries. It concludes with a reflection on the possible future policy agenda that would allow one to simultaneously address the issues of gender inequality and economic inequality in the analysed countries.

Keywords: economic inequality; gender inequality; BRICS; emerging economies

Introduction

Since the beginning of the 2000s – and, especially, following the 2007–2008 financial crisis leading to global recession – the eyes of the international expert community have been drawn towards emerging economies[1] (including BRICS,[2] a number of other major economies in Latin America, Asia, and Africa, and some of the new European Member States). This increased attention has been, on the one hand, caused by their unprecedented economic performance, and mostly fast and successful recovery post-2008. These countries are of interest due to their increasing importance in the international arena, as can be seen from the institutionalisation of the BRICS process and establishment of the BRICS bank.

http://dx.doi.org/10.3362/9781780447278.005

On the other hand, many emerging economies are also creating concern about the inclusiveness of their growth, which is viewed as one of the key threats to sustainability of their economic development and, consequently, economic development of the world in general (GovInn 2013; Gower *et al.* 2011; OECD 2011). Indeed, many of the countries belonging to this group have the highest economic inequality in the world. In some of them, for example China and Russia, it has grown with unprecedented speed over the last decades (Ortiz and Cummins 2011). There is a growing concern that the socioeconomic model being advanced by these countries is nothing more than a slightly different mode of neoliberalism, rather than a real developmental alternative (Prashad 2013).

It is not only vertical economic inequality – that is, inter-household inequality – that poses obstacles to inclusive development of these countries. In addition, most of them also rank comparatively low – and very low, as, for example, in the case of India – on gender equality in global rankings of gender inequality, including UNDP's Gender Inequality Index and WEF's Global Gender Gap Index. So far, the discussion about the relationship between trends of economic and gender inequality seen in these countries has been quite limited (exceptions are Heintz 2013; Wakefield 2014). This discussion is, however, particularly important. Feminist scholars and activists have drawn attention to the cost to women of the socioeconomic models embraced by emerging economies (for example, Campbell 2014; Torabian 2014); these critiques have been responded to by voices questioning this analysis and suggesting it is a misconception (for example, Hewlett and Rashid 2011; Khalaf 2014). How are the issues of gender inequality and vertical economic inequality in emerging economies related? As economic inequality worsens or improves, what happens to gender inequality? These are the questions this chapter sets out to explore. Studying the relationship between trends of gender and economic inequality is crucially important, in view of the need to develop policies that can ensure more inclusive and gender-sensitive economic growth, in emerging economies and beyond.

To shed light on these concerns about the relationship between economic inequality and gender inequality in emerging economies, I focus here on the group of emerging economies that Oxfam has been working in over recent years, and which we dub the BRICSAMIT countries: Brazil, Russia, India, China, South Africa, Mexico, Indonesia, and Turkey. In seven of these countries (the exception is Turkey), Oxfam is also currently implementing a project on empowering local civil society to advocate on issues of inequality at relevant global fora.[3]

The chapter is arranged as follows. The first section provides an overview of economic inequality trends in emerging economies, as well as highlighting key statistics and the current state of the debate on the progress of emerging economies on gender inequality. The second section presents an original analysis of intersection of gender inequality and economic inequality trends in BRICSAMIT, undertaken by the author, based on the World Economic Forum's Global Gender Gap data, and the results of seven exploratory interviews with gender equality experts from across the BRICSAMIT. The chapter concludes with a discussion of the potential future policy agenda for inclusive and gender-sensitive growth in emerging economies.

Economic inequality and gender inequality in emerging economies: what we already know

Economic inequality: negative trends, but not everywhere

As already mentioned above, the problem of economic inequality is most acute in the emerging economies, where rapid economic growth over the past decades has in many cases not been inclusive (Gower *et al.* 2011; OECD 2011; Ortiz and Cummins 2011).

Due to data limitations, it is difficult to trace inequality trends in the countries under consideration over a short period of time. Therefore, for the purposes of this analysis, I rely on information about long-term trends since the end of the 1990s. Table 1 outlines the major trend of economic inequality for each country based on the data from All the Ginis Dataset created by Branko Milanovic, which is a unique source providing comparable data on trends of economic inequality across countries (Milanovic 2014).

The overall levels of inequality in BRICSAMIT countries remain substantially higher than in the OECD countries. However, over the past 20 years, the emerging economies which are the focus of this chapter have had diverging economic inequality trends. While most of them have witnessed long-term growth in economic inequality, two countries – namely, Brazil and Mexico – have made clear notable progress to reduce economic inequality (see Figure 1). This is a particularly notable achievement in times when even most developed countries have also seen economic inequality increase (Cingano 2014).

Table 1 Level of economic inequality in BRICSAMIT and OECD, Gini index* of disposable income

	Brazil	Russia	India	China	South Africa	Mexico	Indonesia	Turkey	OECD average
Gini index	52.7	42.2	33.9	47.8	66.5	47.5	32.3	42.2	31.54

Sources: All the Gini Dataset; OECD Statistical Database.
Note: Latest available data used for each country.
*The Gini co-efficient measures the extent to which the distribution of income or consumption expenditure among individuals or households within an economy deviates from a perfectly equal distribution, a value of 0 expressing total equality and 1 absolute inequality where one person owns all the income or performs all the consumption. The Gini index is the Gini coefficient expressed as a percentage, and is equal to the Gini coefficient multiplied by 100.

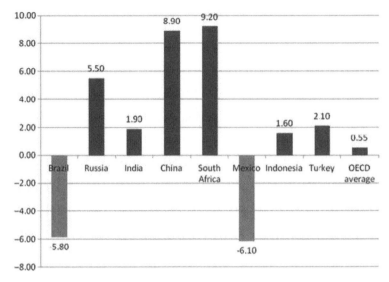

Figure 1 Absolute changes in levels of economic inequality from 1999/2000 to late 2000s, Gini index percentage points

Gender inequality in emerging economies: neoliberal neopatriarchy or global future gender champions?

The issue of gender inequality in emerging economies has so far received less attention than the issue of economic inequality. In addition, while there is general broad agreement that economic inequality in emerging economies is a concern, gender inequality is a more contested issue.

On the one hand, there are those that view gender inequality in emerging economies as a very big challenge. In 2013, Oxford University organised its first symposium on Gender Inequality in Emerging Markets, at which 50 leaders from emerging economies gathered to discuss the issue under Chatham House rules.[4] The key message that emerged from that meeting was that *gender discrimination and gender inequality are particularly prevalent in emerging economies, the growth in many of which has not been equally inclusive for men and women.* Similarly, recently Elham Torabian (2014, 29) argued that 'the scale and speed at which their [auth. – BRIC's] societies have entered global markets have not been equally translated into transformation of gendered roles and norms'. Emerging economies, indeed, mostly rank comparatively low in global indexes of gender inequality (Table 2).

On the other hand, since 2013, the mainstream media have seen a new kind of headline appearing, challenging the gloomy view of gender inequality in emerging economies. Here, I offer a few examples. Article headings included: 'How women will dominate the workplace BRIC by BRIC' (a 2014 article by Saadia Zahidi, a Senior Director and Head of the Women Leaders and

Table 2 BRICSAMIT performance in key global rankings of gender inequality

Country	Ranking	
	World Economic Forum Global Gender Gap Index 2014	UNDP Gender Inequality Index (GII) 2013
Brazil	71	85
Russia	75	52
India	114	127
China	87	37
South Africa	18	94
Mexico	80	73
Indonesia	97	103
Turkey	125	69

Gender Parity Programme at the World Economic Forum); 'Want more gender equality at work? Go to an emerging market' (NPR 2013); and 'Growth helps narrow gender gap in fast-growing economies' (Khalaf 2014).

The key argument of the group having an optimistic view of gender equality trends in emerging markets could be summarised as follows:

> the rapid economic growth of emerging markets in recent years has greatly increased opportunities for women in business, giving them a boost over their counterparts in developed countries. (Khalaf 2014, 1)

These experts even see emerging economies as potential gender equality champions in the future:

> Will we see a world where these countries [auth.: emerging economies] become world leaders on gender equality in the economy? The economic, political and social trends we are witnessing suggest this may be the case. (Zahidi 2014, 1)

Gender inequality and economic inequality trends in emerging economies: an overlooked link

What the experts working on the issues of gender inequality in emerging economies, however, have only tangentially explored so far has been the relationship between trends of economic and gender inequality. Notably, this has been considered only by those adhering to the 'pessimistic' view of gender equality trends in those countries.

From the data that is available, we could assume that the relationship between levels of gender (in)equality and inter-household economic (in)equality is cyclical, with gender (in)equality both contributing to, and being affected by, economic (in)equality between households. On the one hand, a range of studies in some of the BRICSAMIT countries showed that gender inequality, especially, in wages and employment rates contribute to higher levels of economic inequality between households (Costa *et al.* 2009; Ding *et al.* 2009; Kaya and Senesen 2010). On the other hand, in another stream of debate, economic inequality in emerging economies is viewed as having negative implications for gender equality. At the Oxford University Symposium on Gender Inequality in Emerging Markets mentioned above, it was suggested that:

> ... *gender inequality may be a larger issue in emerging markets than anywhere else in the modern world (...) because public policy has failed to mitigate the distributive consequences of rapid growth in emerging markets that, in the last thirty years has outstripped growth in the rest of the world.* (Symposium on Gender Inequality in Emerging Markets 2013, 2)

In a similar vein, in her recent book *The End of Equality* (2014), Beatrix Campbell presents powerful arguments about what she perceives as the dangerous mix of neoliberalism and neopatriarchy in these countries, pushing women to the bottom.

However, what these arguments clearly lack is an analysis of longitudinal and cross-country trends in gender inequality, and their intersection with economic inequality. In what follows below, based on an analysis of the World Economic Forum Global Gender Gap data and exploratory interviews with civil society leaders from BRICSAMIT countries, I propose a closer look at this intersection.

Economic inequality and gender inequality in emerging economies: taking a closer look at the data

Gender inequality trends in BRICSAMIT countries: looking beyond the rankings

To understand what has actually been happening in terms of gender inequality, we need to turn from rankings (which compare countries against each other in ways which actually say very little about the actual state of affairs relating to gender inequality, bearing in mind that the number of sample countries used in such rankings changes from year to year – and quite significantly so – meaning that the changes in the ranks often do not reflect actual advancement or deterioration of the country's position). Instead, we can more helpfully look at the absolute value of composite indices, and see how those values have been changing. The analysis below is founded on my own calculations, based on a dataset I compiled from data in World Economic Forum 2006–2014 reports and UNDP Human Development reports.

Both indices suggest that, as a group, the analysed emerging economies have been closing the gender gap equally fast or even faster than the countries of the world on average. (It should be noted that there are some variations in estimations of the extent to which this is happening.) According to the World Economic Forum data, between 2006 and 2014, BRICSAMIT countries' progress in reduction of the gender gap[5] was 5.1 per cent , while the average for all the countries for which data have been consistently collected since 2006 also stood at 5.1 per cent.[6]

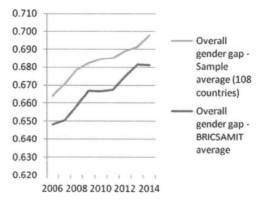

Figure 2 Trends of gender gap in BRICSAMIT countries and globally, according to WEF Gender Gap Index, 2006–2014

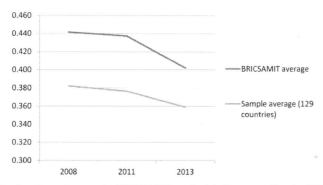

Figure 3 Trends of gender gap in BRICSAMIT and globally, according to UNDP Gender Inequality Index, 2008–2013

If we compare BRICSAMIT with countries divided by income groups (the World Economic Forum compared countries by income groups in its latest report), we see that between 2006 and 2014, low-income countries made gains of nearly 5 per cent (WEF 2014, 32). Lower-middle income countries made the second-largest gains, at 3.4 per cent (WEF 2014, 32). Next were high-income countries, at 3.3 per cent (WEF 2014, 32). Finally, upper-middle income countries – the category that most of the BRICSAMIT countries belong to – came in at 2.2 per cent (WEF 2014, 32; see Figures 2 and 3).

UNDP's Gender Inequality Index, which covers the 2008–2013 period, indicates even more favourable trends in BRICSAMIT countries. In that period, their progress was 8.9 per cent, while the average for all the countries that UNDP consistently collected data for stood at 6.0 per cent.[7]

To conclude, overall trends of gender inequality across BRICSAMIT countries thus seem to provide some confirmation of the optimistic view of emerging economies as potential 'gender champions'.

However, to understand gender inequality trends, we certainly could not rely on aggregated data alone.[8] In what follows, I look at the individual countries, using the WEF Gender Gap Index to shed further light on the issues. Among existing international indices, WEF GGI is considered by the advocacy and campaigning organisation Gender Action to be the most comprehensive one in terms of the number of dimensions included in it (Gender Action 2013), and it also covers a longer period of time (see Table 3).

This more detailed analysis suggests that clearly not all the analysed countries have been progressing with the same speed, which clearly could be one of the explanations for the diverging views on the issue of gender inequality in emerging economies. Crucially, none of the BRICSAMIT countries has seen regression on gender inequality, but important differences among them can be found regarding the relative speed with which they have been reducing the gender gap. China, Indonesia, Russia, and Turkey have been closing their gender gaps at below the global average speed. Brazil, India, South Africa, and Mexico have been progressing faster than the global average. Moreover, it can also be seen that countries differ in terms of the number of sub-areas across which they have been faster or slower in closing the gender gap.

Further attention to progress across sub-areas also suggests that there are quite clear cross-BRICSAMIT trends. The gender gap in economic participation and opportunity is an area where most of the BRICSAMIT countries have seen the slowest progress over the last decade (compared to global averages). This contradicts the view that economic growth has empowered women

Table 3 Gender gap reduction, relative percentage change in the 'remaining gap' between 2006 and 2014

	Overall score	Economic	Educational	Health	Political
Brazil	11.5	11.3	100	0.2	9.2
Russia	4.8	9.7	77.1	−0.2	3.4
India	11.1	2.1	17.4	−68.6	20.5
China	7.8	9.2	65.9	7.6	4.5
South Africa	14	20.6	−84.9	16.4	10.5
Mexico	12.4	13.8	−14.9	0.2	12.1
Indonesia	5.3	0.1	78.5	24.1	2.8
Turkey	8	3.3	58.9	34	3.8
Global average (108 countries)	10.1	15	23.8	0.4	6.8
BRICSAMIT average	9.3	8.4	43.5	0.5	8

Shaded boxes denote percentage changes are higher or equal to the average global speed of gender gap reduction
Source: Author's calculations based on Global Gender Gap Index data.

living in emerging economies to participate in business – a view which is common among those that express optimism about gender equality progress in those countries (Khalaf 2014; Zahidi 2014). As BRICSAMIT profiles in the Global Gender Gap Report of 2014 show (WEF 2014), they still have low scores on women's labour force participation (with the exception of Russia and China, with their histories of socialism – under the socialist model, all women were mobilised as workers, which continues to affect the structure of the post-socialist labour markets in those countries). BRICSAMIT countries also perform poorly on gender wage gap for similar work and gender gap in estimated earned income (the latter clearly caused by the former, as well as by low labour force participation and large gender gaps in part-time work).

This persistent gap in economic participation and opportunity stands in contrast with achievements in the educational sphere, in which many of the BRICSAMIT have been performing comparatively well. The data show that some of them, like Brazil, are global champions in terms of success in closing of the educational inequality gap. Reductions to the economic participation gender gap and the educational gender gap across BRICSAMIT have clearly not gone in tandem, highlighting the fact that improvements in women's educational achievements do not necessarily translate into similar-scale improvements in the economic sphere.

Notably, alongside the achievements in education, the gender gap in political empowerment has also been closing in many BRICSAMIT countries faster than average. However, a clear divide between BRICSAMIT countries is visible in terms of women's political empowerment, which appears to be linked to the degree of the overall development of democratic institutions in those countries, with China, Indonesia, Russia, and Turkey clearly lagging behind.

BRICSAMIT's performance on the health and survival index is something that really requires unpacking, but not in terms of the speed with which the countries have been closing this gap. This index consists of two components – the gender gap in healthy life expectancy, and the sex ratio at birth. And it is performance against the latter that is particularly telling about the situation in some of the BRICSAMIT countries. China and India are among the lowest ranking countries in the world on sex ratio at birth – in the 2014 WEF GGI, they ranked 140 and 141 out of 142 respectively on Health and Survival Index. The problem of sex-selective abortion to rid families of unwanted daughters before birth in those two countries has been quite widely discussed in the literature already (Hesketh *et al.* 2011) – but this issue needs to receive attention in light of their status as emerging economies, and the growth of economic inequality within them. A number of studies clearly suggest the links between economic inequality and this phenomenon (Das Gupta *et al.* 2003; Gaudin 2011):

> *In the present state of development and income inequality in India, there are many parents who have some extent capitalistic attitude. That actually generates two things – son preference and gender bias against female for human capital accumulation.* (Ghose 2011, 119)

As Table 3 suggests, over the last eight years, however, these countries have had diverging trajectories in this area.

Taking into account all the above, we could conclude that BRICSAMIT as a group have, indeed, been progressing equally fast as the global average, and in some areas have actually been global leaders of gender inequality reduction. But, importantly, they have not progressed at this pace in the areas of women's economic participation and opportunity, as has been quite recently argued. However, looking at specific country cases, it also shows clearly that faster-than-average progress has not been a universal trend among them.

Vertical economic inequality and gender inequality trends in BRICSAMIT countries: exploring the relationship

It is possible to see the relationship between gender equality and long-term trends in economic inequality in BRICSAMIT countries, using a form of 'truth table', as Table 4, shows.[9]

The BRICSAMIT countries that have seen slower-than-global-average reduction in gender inequality are those that have also experienced long-term economic inequality increases, and those that have experienced the most significant and dramatic increases, for example Russia and China. Slower gender inequality reduction is thus clearly associated with long-term growth of economic inequality.

However, two countries, India and South Africa, appear to have been able to reduce the overall gender gap faster than the global average, even though they are experiencing an upward trend in economic inequality. However, if we look closely at them, we see that, in the case of India, the overall progress in reduction of gender inequality has been mainly due to the closing of the gap in women's political participation, but this needs to be set against a worrying setback in the sphere of health, very slow progress in education, and lack of any progress in the economic area. In the case of South Africa, the gender gap in economic participation and opportunity has not been successfully closed;

Table 4 Long-term economic inequality trends and gender inequality trends in BRICSAM

		Long-term economic inequality trend, 1999/2000–late 2000s	
		Increase	*Decrease*
Gender inequality trends, 2006–2014	Faster than global average reduction	India	Brazil
		South Africa	Mexico
	Slower than global average reduction	China	
		Indonesia	
		Russia	
		Turkey	

Source: Author's calculations based on all the Gini datasets and Global Gender Gap Index Data.

since 2011, there has actually been continuous deterioration of this indicator (WEF 2014).

Finally, those BRICSAMIT countries that have seen a long-term reduction in economic inequality – that is, Brazil and Mexico – have also been faster than the global average in closing the overall gender gap, and, in addition, have been closing the gender gap faster across a wider number of areas. Put against the fact that no single BRICSAMIT country with a slower-than-average rate of gender inequality reduction has managed to reduce economic inequality, this suggests the hypothesis that a reduction of economic inequality needs to be accompanied by faster-than-average – and more comprehensive – reduction of gender inequality.

To conclude, an examination of how BRICSAMIT countries are progressing against these particular indicators of gender equality clearly suggests that the dynamics of gender inequality – represented in these ways, at least – are less dependent on the dynamics of economic inequality than the other way round. The gender gap has been closing across all BRICSAMIT countries, independently of the dynamics of economic inequality within them; however, in the countries with long-term trends of worsening economic inequality, progress on gender inequality reduction has been slower, and less comprehensive across the range of different indicators. At the same time, faster-than-average, and more comprehensive, progress in reduction of gender inequality appears to be a necessary precondition of economic inequality reduction.

It is beyond the scope of this paper, due to data limitations, to analyse quantitatively the relation between different dimensions of gender inequality and economic inequality. But as Table 3 suggests, one of the key dimensions of gender inequality that needs detailed attention is the gender gap in economic participation and opportunity. Even in countries that have been relatively successful in reduction of inter-household – that is, vertical – economic inequality, like Brazil and Mexico, the gender gap in the economic domain has been reducing slower than globally.

As individual countries, all BRICSAMIT countries have seen – though rather unevenly – progress on gender equality over the last decade. What the statistical data cannot fully tell is the story about the ways in which gender inequality morphs in response to economic change. As Diane Elson (2009, 42) argues, 'economic growth is a gendered process in which old forms of gender inequality are weakened but new forms of gender inequality emerge'. Economic growth accompanied by growing/persistently high economic inequalities could, arguably, produce even more acute new forms of gender inequality.

To shed further light on this emerging area for research, I carried out a small number of interviews with expert informants, during November 2014–January 2015. These informants were colleagues and partners working in the BRICSAMIT countries.[10] Their insights highlight the need to closely look at the likelihood that women – especially, poorer and migrant women – in emerging economies are undertaking an increasing burden of unpaid care (caused by a mix of demographic and socioeconomic transformations, including ageing populations), and at possible changes in the extent and nature of gender-based violence (including, but not limited to, sex selective abortion; sexual violence; sexual harassment at work; sex trafficking) under the changing economic conditions.

To see if this is the case in BRICSAMIT countries, we need more data – both quantitative and qualitative. We also need to note the *increasing importance of an intersectional approach to inform analysis of the problem of gender inequality* in the considered countries. Part of an intersectional analysis is to analyse how relative wealth or poverty affects individual women's experience of gender inequality, and vice versa. Gender inequality has different expressions in different 'economic layers' of society. Some women have benefitted from the type of economic growth that has been seen in BRICSAMIT countries, while others have been left behind. This sheds light on the apparent disagreement between 'gender inequality pessimists' and 'gender equality optimists' writing about emerging economies, as discussed earlier in the chapter.

Conclusion: future policy agendas to support gender equitable and inclusive growth

As the empirical evidence presented in this chapter suggests, the near-complete omission of the relation between gender inequality and economic inequality from the current debates on inclusive growth in emerging economies is unjustified and alarming, for two key reasons. First, it leads to overlooking of gender discrimination as a mechanism through which economic inequalities get reproduced – and consequently – could be countered in the emerging economies. Second, this results in the virtual absence of discussion about impacts of growing/persistently high economic inequality witnessed by most emerging economies on gender relations and policies needed to offset those impacts.

Analysis of the relationship between economic inequality trends and Global Gender Gap Index trends in BRICSAMIT countries clearly confirms that a more intensive and comprehensive gender inequality reduction represents a necessary precondition for inter-household economic inequality reduction. These findings provide further evidence for arguments developed by James Heintz (2013) and Shawna Wakefield (2014), that addressing gender inequality thus represents an important entry point through which growth of economic inequality could be countered in the context of emerging economies. However, as the example of such BRICSAMIT countries as India and South Africa show, addressing gender inequality is a necessary, but insufficient measure for reduction of economic inequality, as economic inequality is a complex phenomenon.

Analysis of the dynamics of economic, educational, health, and political dimensions of gender inequality across BRICSAMIT countries also indicates that contrary to optimistic views expressed in some recent publications discussed above (Khalaf 2014; NPR 2013; Zahidi 2014), emerging economies appear to fail women precisely in the economic area. Most BRICSAMIT countries have some of the largest employment and wage gaps in the world. In addition, even though they have been progressing equally fast or even faster than the world on average in closing the overall gender gap, most have made below-average progress in closing the gender gap in economic participation and opportunity. Targeting the economic dimension of gender inequality through women's economic empowerment programming and policy work thus remains crucially important in emerging economies.

In considering the intersection between vertical economic inequality and gender inequality trends, even in countries that have been relatively successful in reduction of inter-household inequality, like Mexico and Brazil, the gender gap in economic participation and opportunity has been persistent. To re-phrase Naila Kabeer 's (1996, 14) argument that the 'forces that create inequalities of wealth and opulence in a society embody quite different social norms and material practices to those which create inequalities of gender ', current analyses suggest that we also cannot assume that forces/ policies that lead to reduction of inter-household economic inequality would by default reduce gendered economic inequality. Along with redistributive fiscal policies targeting vertical economic inequality, specific policies addressing gendered economic inequality need to be put in place across emerging economies.[11]

Economic growth accompanied by growing/persistently high inter-household economic inequality is likely to cause gender inequality and gender discrimination across BRICSAMIT countries to morph and reconstitute. Further research, with a particular attention to the issues of carework and gender-based violence, is needed to explore this dynamic further.

Finally, I have argued that we need to understand that inequalities of different kinds intersect (Kabeer 2010). In particular, analysing the ways economic status/class and gender inequality intersect now in emerging economies is essential for design of effective policies targeted at reduction of both gender and economic inequality. Over the past decade, overall gender inequality reduction has, indeed, been comparatively fast across most of the analysed emerging economies. But the benefits of this reduction have clearly not been equally distributed among women living in those countries. Neither do the new/re-emerging forms of gender inequality triggered by the increased economic inequality look the same across different economic classes.

To conclude, any progress on gender inequality and economic inequality reduction in emerging economies will depend of the ability of both policymakers and civil society to recognise the need to address both of these phenomena in parallel, rather than either viewing them as independent or prioritising one of them as primary.

Notes

1. No commonly-agreed definition of an emerging economy has been coined to date, although the term is being increasingly used both in economics and sociology. The commonly-agreed characteristics of emerging

economies include intermediate income (emerging economies are most often classified as middle-income countries by the WB), catching-up growth over a relatively long-term period of time, which allowed these countries to narrow the economic gap with the developed countries, and finally institutional transformations and economic opening (Vercueil 2012). Social impact of the above processes on the societal change in those countries is being increasingly scrutinised both by international development professionals and scholars, and this chapter aims to contribute to this emerging scholarship.

2. The acronym BRIC was coined in 2001 by Goldman Sachs' economist Jim O'Neill to refer to Brazil, Russia, India, and China as the new global economic powers. The group institutionalised itself by holding its first summit in 2009, and in 2010 was joined by South Africa, which tuned the group's name into BRICS. BRICS countries are developing their economic, political, and cultural co-operation. And in 2014, BRICS founded their own development bank (most recently referred to as the New Development bank) that is expected to boost greater financial and development co-operation between BRICS countries, as well as between BRICS and other developing countries.

3. For details about the project, see the following web page: http://csnbricsam.org/about-ecsn-bricsam/ (last checked by the author 21 May 2015).

4. The Chatham House Rule refers to the principle that participants at a meeting are free to use the information received, but neither the identity nor the affiliation of the speaker(s), nor that of any other participant, may be revealed.

5. The 'gender gap' as measured by the World Economic Forum's Global Gender Gap Index is the relative gap between women and men across four key areas: health, education, economy, and politics. For more on the Global Gender Gap Index, see the World Economic Forum's annual reports, http://reports.weforum.com/global-gender-gap-report-2014 (last checked by the author 21 May 2015).

6. A note on methodology used in this section and further in the chapter for calculation of the percentage change in the gender gap should be made. The WEF forum calculates the percentage change in the gender gap in relation to the gap *already* closed by the countries. This implies that the 5 per cent change in the gender gap cited in this section means that the progress of the countries in the period 2006–2014 equalled 5 per cent of the value of the 'closed gap' that they had achieved by 2006. However, for individual country comparisons presented later in the section, to ensure better comparability, I focus on the percentage change in the 'remaining gap'. The reasoning is that this method for calculating individual countries' progress is more valid, because it allows one to better grasp the relative progress of countries that initially had relatively small remaining 'gaps' in attainment in some areas – for example, as in the case of education for Russia.

7. The challenge with UNDP data is that on their website they have only the latest year, i.e. 2013 (http://hdr.undp.org/content/table-4-gender-inequality-index, last checked by the author 21 May 2015). Since I needed to look at the trends, I found an xls file, which contained the data on

the trends (http://capacity4dev.ec.europa.eu/public-gender/blog/gender-inequality-index, last checked by the author 21 May 2015); I then added the 2013 data into that file and used it. I took out the 1995 data, since it was retrospectively calculated. The index itself was published in UNDP's 2010 Human Development Report, and the first reference year is 2008.

8. Although this chapter refrains from the detailed discussion of pros and cons of using aggregate gender indices, I do endorse a position earlier expressed by a number of authors (see, for example, Chant 2006; Permanyer 2010). Use of aggregate gender indices has clear advantages and disadvantages. On the 'minus' side, as Sylvia Chant rightly argues, aggregated scores can't do much more than permit rather top line comparative assessments of national achievements in gender equality or to track broad movements in individual countries over time. On the 'plus' side, to echo a point made by Inaki Permanyer (2010, 196) in his critical assessment of various gender indices, 'the proper measurement of gender inequality is an extremely important issue that must be addressed in order to monitor the degree to which gender related policies are achieving their goals. Moreover, the publication of gender inequality indices can stimulate many countries to pay more attention to these issues and to introduce the corresponding policies'.

9. A truth table is essentially a logic table introduced as a method of comparative research into social science by Charles Ragin (see Ragin and Amoroso 2011). The method allows one to explore the presence/absence of a simple dichotomous causal relationship.

10. The interviews were carried out as part of an ongoing research project of mine on gender inequality and economic inequality in emerging economies, part of which this chapter represents. Overall, seven semi-structured phone interviews were carried out with Oxfam staff and partners working on issues of gender inequality across BRICAMIT countries. The interviewees included Lai Shan Chung (China Programme Officer on Gender, Oxfam Hong Kong); Elena Fedyashina (Executive Director at Committee of the 20, Russia); Carolina Maldonado Pacheco (Campaign Coordinator, Oxfam Mexico); Taufiqul Mujib (Knowledge and Capacity Building Coordinator Oxfam in Indonesia); Graciela Rodriguez (Brazilian Network for Peoples' Integration representative); Parvinder Singh (National Manager Campaigns at Oxfam India); and Lanying Zhang (GCAP China).

11. These policies, among others, may include gender-responsive budgeting (that some of the BRICSAMIT, i.e. Brazil, India, Mexico, and South Africa, have started implementing with the support of UN Women) and gender-sensitive tax systems (organisations such as Christian Aid and Oxfam (Capraro 2014; Oxfam 2014) have recently started developing programming and policy work in this area).

References

Campbell, Beatrix (2014) *End of Equality: The Only Way is Women's Liberation*, London: Seagull Books

Capraro, Chiara (2014) *Taxing Men and Women: Why Gender is Crucial for a Fair Tax System*, London: Christian Aid

Centre for the Study of Governance (GovInn) (2013) *On the BRICS of Collapse? Why Emerging Economies Need a Different Development Model*, New York: DEMOS/Rockefeller Foundation

Chant, Sylvia (2006) 'Re-thinking the "feminization of poverty" in relation to aggregate gender indices', *Journal of Human Development* 7(2): 201–2020

Cingano, Federico (2014) Trends of Income Inequality and Its Impact on Economic Growth, OECD Social, Employment and Migration Working Paper no. 163, OECD: Paris

Costa, Joana, Elydia Silva, and Fabio Vaz (2009) *The Role of Gender Inequalities in Explaining Income Growth, Poverty and Inequality: Evidences from Latin American Countries*, Brasilia: UNDP-International Policy Centre for Inclusive Growth

Das Gupta, Monica, Jiang Zhenghua, Li Bohua, Xie Zhenming, Woojin Chung, and Bae Hwa-Ok (2003) *Why Is Son Preference So Persistent in East and South Asia? A Cross-country Study of China, India and the Republic of Korea*, Washington, DC: World Bank

Ding, Sai, Xiao-yuan Dong, and Shi Li (2009) 'Women's employment and family income inequality during China's economic transition', *Feminist Economics* 15(3): 163–90

Elson, Diane (2009) 'Gender equality and economic growth in the World Bank World Development Report 2006', *Feminist Economics* 15(3): 35–59

Gaudin, Sylvestre (2011) 'Son preference in Indian families: absolute versus relative wealth effects', *Demography* 48(1): 343–70

Gender Action (2013) *Gender Toolkit for International Finance Watchers*, Washington, DC: Gender Action & Oxfam Novib

Ghose, Manas (2011) 'Gender bias in education in India', *Journal of Economic and Social Development* 7(2): 118–28

Gower, Richard, Caroline Pearce, and Kate Raworth (2011) *Left behind by the G20? How inequality and environmental degradation threaten to exclude poor people from the benefits of economic growth*, Oxfam Briefing Paper, Oxford: Oxfam International

Heintz, James (2013) *Missing Women: The G20, Gender Equality and Global Economic Governance*, Washington, DC: Heinrich Böll Stiftung

Hesketh, Therese, Li Lu, and Zhu Wei Xing (2011) 'The consequences of son prefenrence and sex selective abortion in China and other Asian countries', *Canadian Medical Association Journal* 183(12): 1374–7

Hewlett, Sylvia Anna and Ripa Rashid (2011) *Winning the War for Talent in Emerging Markets: Why Women Are the Solution*, Boston, MA: Harvard Business Review Press

Kabeer, Naila (1996) 'Agency, well-being and discrimination: reflections on the gender dimensions of poverty', *IDS Bulletin* 27(1): 11–21

Kabeer, Naila (2010) *Can the MDGs Provide a Pathway to Social Justice? The Challenge of Intersecting Inequalities?* New York: UNDP

Kaya, Ezgi and Umit Senesen (2010) 'Gini decomposition by gender: Turkish case', *Brussels Economic Review* 53(1): 59–83

Khalaf, Roula (2014) 'Growth helps narrow gender gap in fast-growing economies', *Financial Times*, 7 March 2014, http://www.ft.com/cms/s/2/99d7d6c2-8f21-11e3-be85-00144feab7de.html#axzz3LyrQ2Up2 (last checked by the author 31 December 2014)

Milanovic, Branko (2014) *All the Ginis Dataset*, October 2014, http://econ. worldbank.org/WBSITE/EXTERNAL/EXTDEC/EXTRESEARCH/0,,content MDK:22301380~pagePK:64214825~piPK:64214943~theSitePK:469382,00. html (last checked by the author 26 June 2015)

National Public Radio (2013) 'Want more gender inequality at work? Go to an emerging market', 22 April 2013, http://www.wbur.org/npr/177511506/ want-more-gender-equality-at-work-go-to-an-emerging-market   (last checked by the author 31 December 2014)

OECD (2011) *Divided We Stand: Why Inequality Keeps Rising*, Paris: OECD

Ortiz, Isabel and Michael Cummins (2011) *Global Inequality: Beyond the Bottom Billion – A Rapid Review of Income Distribution in 141 Countries*, Working Paper, New York: UNICEF

Oxfam (2014) *Ajustar la Lente. Fiscalidad desde un enfoque de genero: Metodologia de analisis*, Oxford: Oxfam International

Permanyer, Inaki (2010) 'The measurement of multidimensional gender inequality: continuing the debate', *Social Indices Research* 95(2): 181–198

Prashad, Vijay (2013) *Neoliberalism with Southern Characteristics: The Rise of the BRICS*, New York: Rosa Luxembourg Foundation

Ragin, Cahrles C. and Lisa M. Amoroso (2011) *Constructing Social Research: The Unity and Diversity of Method* (2nd ed.), Thousand Oaks, CA: Sage

Symposium on Gender Inequality in Emerging Markets (2013) *Findings and Recommendations*, Oxford: University of Oxford

Torabian, Elham (2014) 'BRIC by BRIC: realities and challenges for women', *The Paris Globalist* 2014: 25–29

Vercueil, Julien (2012) *Les Pays Emergents. Brésil – Russie – Inde – Chine… Mutations Economiques et Nouveaux Défis* (Emerging Countries. Brazil – Russia – India – China. Economic change and new challenges, in French) (3rd ed.), Paris: Bréal

Wakefield, Shawna (2014) *The G20 and Gender Equality: How the G20 Could Advance Women's Right in Employment, Social Protection and Fiscal Policies*, Oxfam Briefing Paper 183, Oxford: Oxfam International & Heinrich Böll Stiftung

World Economic Forum (2014) *The Global Gender Gap Report 2014*, Geneva: World Economic Forum

Zahidi, Saadia (2014) 'How women will dominate the workplace BRIC by BRIC', *CNN*, 22 January 2014, http://edition.cnn.com/2014/01/22/opinion/how-women-will-dominate-the-workplace-bric/ (last checked by the author 31 December 2014)

About the Author

Daria Ukhova is Ph.D. fellow in sociology at the Bremen International Graduate School of Social Sciences (BIGSSS), Germany. Email: daria.ukhova@ gmail.com

CHAPTER 6

'Leave no one behind' and the challenge of intersectionality: Christian Aid's experience of working with single and Dalit women in India

Jayshree P. Mangubhai and Chiara Capraro

Abstract

The principle of 'leaving no one behind' is strongly emerging as a defining aspect of the new development framework under negotiation in 2015. This stems from an acknowledgement of the failure of the Millennium Development Goals in securing benefits for the most marginalised groups, those suffering from economic deprivation and discrimination as a result of intersecting inequalities. As the new development framework takes shape, national-level experiences of tackling intersecting inequalities can provide lessons on the shifts required in policy and practice to address the specific needs of women experiencing deprivation, violence, and discrimination because of their gender and other identities. This case study illustrates lessons learnt from Christian Aid's programmatic experience in several states of India in support of Dalit women and single women as they individually and collectively struggle to gain dignity and realise their rights.

Keywords: gender; inequality; caste; empowerment; India; intersectionality

'Leave no one behind': from theory to practice?

The limitations of the Millennium Development Goals (MDGs) in benefitting the poorest of the poor have increasingly been realised. With achievements based on averages, MDGs could virtually be met even when the most marginalised missed out. Very early in the discussions around the new post-2015 Sustainable Development Goals (SDGs) development framework, a new principle started emerging – to 'leave no one behind'. This ambition – that no human development goal or target should be met unless met for all social and income groups – is a principle worth fighting for, and provides an opportunity to reframe and reprioritise action at both the global and national level (High Level Panel Report 2013). It will require governments to identify those

http://dx.doi.org/10.3362/9781780447278.006

people and communities who are failed by the *status quo*, falling through the gaps of policy-formulation and implementation. We will need to look beyond quintiles,[1] and beyond the ways single categories of difference create relations of inequality between individuals and groups (for example gender, ethnicity, caste, or [dis]ability). Meeting the post-2015 ambition will necessitate understanding the interests and needs of those who experience multiple disadvantages and exclusion, as a result of intersecting inequalities.

Already, international human rights law – including the Convention on the Elimination of All forms of Discrimination Against Women (adopted by the UN General Assembly in 1979) and the International Covenant on Economic, Social and Cultural Rights (adopted by the UN General Assembly in 1966) – acknowledges the existence of intersecting inequalities, and the way in which different inequalities compound each other to create unique and complex disadvantage for the individuals facing them.[2] The obligation placed on states is to eliminate intersectional discrimination by preventing, diminishing, and eliminating the conditions and attitudes which cause or perpetuate it, and to enact specific measures to attenuate or suppress conditions that reproduce this discrimination (CEDAW 2010; ICESCR 2009). To respond to their international legal obligations and the SDG agenda will require states to go beyond merely seeking GDP growth boosting strategies to also concentrate on redistribution by closing the gap between the wealthy and the poor, and prevent further marginalisation and deprivation, by redistributing resources and power in ways which benefit those experiencing complex inequalities.

This chapter seeks to explore and underscore the importance of these issues, via a discussion of Christian Aid's programme work to support women who have Dalit caste identity, and women with single marital status. Christian Aid has been working on this agenda under both its general India national programme, and its Poorest Areas Civil Society (PACS) programme, a DFID-funded programme managed by Christian Aid.[3] The programmes are based on awareness that the root causes of poverty in India cannot be explained without a reference to caste and gender. Both these characteristics cause marginalisation and exclusion. Further, in a context of gender inequality, marital and family status shapes women's gendered experience of poverty, creating particular challenges for single women. Development initiatives and social policy programmes need to support single women and Dalit women to claim their entitlements through collective action and advocacy.

Current public policies, including social protection and anti-poverty policies, fail to respond to the intersectional nature of inequalities faced by single Dalit women. This results in these women falling into the gaps of social provisions, and continuing to experience discrimination, violence, and destitution arising from deeply-engrained, complex, and shifting social norms. The programmes focused on in this chapter aim to support women who experience discrimination based on both these aspects of identity, promoting opportunities for them to organise, and building their leadership to claim their rights and entitlements vis-à-vis the state, dominant castes, and their own menfolk and families.

We write this chapter as colleagues who work on issues of gender justice policy and advocacy, respectively at the South Asia level and at the global level, both with knowledge and expertise on the gender and inequality issues in the Indian context. The chapter draws on information from several sources: the personal experiences of staff members managing the programmes, captured via informal interviews; impact assessments and learning studies written up as grey literature to use in reporting and organisational learning; the annual reports of partner organisations; and finally, interviews conducted by one of the authors with some of the organisation heads.

The first section sets the context for single women and Dalit women in India. The second section looks at programmatic approaches in support of single women in the northern state of Jharkhand, while the third section looks at approaches to build the collective action of Dalit women, including those engaged in manual scavenging, to claim their rights and fight against discrimination and violence. The fourth section then examines the challenges and lessons learnt from programmatic experience, and ends with some implications for development programming and policy.

The status of Dalit and single women in India

India currently ranks 135 out of 187 countries on the UNDP's gender development and equality index (UNDP 2014, 172–9). Despite a slew of gender-responsive laws, policies, programmes, and budgets,[4] the majority of women still endure inequality in all major areas of life. The situation of the country's roughly 587 million women, however, is not uniform. Women from certain marginalised groups consistently appear at the bottom of poverty indicators. Two such groups of women are Dalit or scheduled caste[5] women, and single women. The former face exclusion and discrimination foremost on the basis of their caste and gender, the latter on the basis of their gender and marital status. These inequalities intersect with economic disadvantage, and are mutually reinforcing.

Overcoming challenges in the struggle for the rights of women experiencing intersecting inequalities requires a deep understanding of the lived experiences of these women and the power dynamics that reinforce their marginalised position not only in society at large, but also within their own communities. The experiences of single women and Dalit women in India are masked by a national discourse on diversity which seeks to acknowledge different (read, discrete) identities to be promoted within the notion of an overarching nationalistic identity. The discourse of diversity, which is familiar in the popular media and underpins state policies, results in lack of space to identify and problematise the unequal power relations which exist between different social groups (Pandey 2010).

Dalit women in India

The approximately 98 million Dalit women in India (Data Table A10, Census of India 2011) live spatially segregated on the outskirts of villages or in over-crowded urban slums. They are denied equal access to and command over resources and services, as well as public and cultural spaces. Caste and gender inequalities intersect where, for example, Dalit women face 'untouchability'[6] practices and discrimination related to the collection of water, an activity ascribed to women under the sexual division of labour. Dalit women are less likely to own land than women of other castes, which pushes them into low paid and often exploitative labour. They are primarily agricultural labourers, but also take on non-farm labour, including traditionally ascribed 'polluted' tasks such as manual scavenging (the manual removal of human excreta from dry latrines) and sweeping.

Violence is perpetrated against Dalit women with impunity by other castes, taking advantage of their relatively powerless position. If they assert their right to resources and spaces, this is seen as a transgression of social norms on their part and punished with violence (Irudayam *et al.* 2011). Much of this violence is sexualised in nature. According to the National Crimes Record Bureau data (2014, 424), five Dalit women report rape in India every day. These figures mask a far higher estimated number. The author was involved in one study of 500 cases of violence across four states, which showed that 67.1 per cent of cases of rapes of Dalit women went unreported due to the women not report-ing for reasons including fear of the perpetrators or fear of bringing dishonour to the families, or else family/community/dominant castes intervening to prevent registration of the cases (Irudayam *et al.* 2011).

Significantly, studies show that caste-based social exclusion is more acutely felt by Dalit women than by Dalit men because the women experience greater 'untouchability', and ill-treatment, from dominant caste women and men (Shah *et al.* 2006). Political exclusion then denies these women a voice and an equal say in decision-making on the issues that affect their lives. This situa-tion is compounded by gender discrimination and violence within the family, influenced by the wider dynamics of caste and class oppression.

Single women in India

'Single' women (defined as women who are widowed, divorced, separated, or women older than 30 who have never married) face significant chal-lenges, starting with the basic challenge of survival. The number of widowed, divorced, or separated women alone is 48 million (Data Table C2, Census of India 2011). A study of 386 single women in six states (National Forum for Single Women's Rights 2011) highlighted a number of significant trends. Over half of the women were below the age of 45, under half were literate (24), and a disproportionately higher percentage (43.5 per cent) came from his-torically excluded scheduled caste (Dalit) and scheduled tribe (Indigenous) communities (27). Most of the women were employed in daily wage labour, subsisting on below minimum wages, and lived in small houses that lacked basic amenities. While at least 60 per cent of widowed women were able to retain control of their marital homes (51), most separated and divorced women were dispossessed when the marriage broke up. Despite this, only 12.7 per cent had benefitted from government housing schemes (49) and only 24.8 per cent (57) received a pension or some kind of social security entitlement. Moreover, few single women enjoyed participation in local political processes outside of exercising their vote (ibid).

Behind the poverty and marginalisation of single women lies their perceived 'failure' to conform to social norms that demand good women be faithful wives and mothers within male-headed households. These norms prescribe male control over female sexuality, which then deems women who are living in female-headed house-holds without the 'protection' of men to be morally suspect. Hence, negative stereotypes about these women enhance their vulnerability to harassment, evictions, sexual exploitation, and abuse from family members and others. Even widows, who have not left their marriages but who are involuntarily single, attract social sanctions in the form of strong superstitious beliefs, such as accusations of being witches, and social rejection. Widows have the right in civil law to inherit property from their husbands in their own right, but traditional practices in patrilineal societies pass property down the male line, leaving widows to be supported as dependents by sons or other male relatives (Agarwal 1998), and vulnerable to psychological and physical abuse.

Policy shortcomings for Dalit women and single women

Public policies intended to benefit Dalits as a caste group, and women as a sex, do not fully respond to the specific interests and needs of Dalit women or single women, let alone addressing the intersecting issues faced by women who have both these identities. While it is true that there are targeted development programmes and affirmative action (reservation) provisions for scheduled castes and women in local governance, education, and government employment, social norms cause *de facto* exclusion of Dalit women. Further, the tendency among policymakers to focus on a single aspect of identity-based discrimination rather than understanding intersecting inequalities leads to individuals who belong to two marginalised categories falling into the gaps. For example, in work and higher education Dalit women often become excluded because of the existence of two separate quotas they could be eligible for; that is, they are told to apply for the women's quota when they try to access the scheduled caste quota, and they are directed towards the scheduled caste quota when they apply for the women's quota (Singh 2000, quoted in Grey 2005). As a result, the majority of the beneficiaries of reservation are Dalit men or dominant caste women respectively (National Human Rights Commission 2004). Additionally, quotas operate as a form of rationing: because of the existence of quotas, Dalit women are deemed ineligible for unreserved categories (Das 2006).

Similarly, in the case of 'single' women, a number of lacunae exist. The existing social security net in the form of pensions and other entitlements for the poor do not extend to separated and divorced women, or unmarried older women, or widows younger than 40. The underlying assumption is that young, able-bodied single women can fend for themselves (Dhar 2011). Many single women lack legal papers to establish marital status, especially in cases of permanent separation, leaving them with few rights and the burden of providing for themselves and their children. Similarly, the complicated and lengthy bureaucratic procedures to access social security and other entitlements, including the need for multiple documents to prove one's single status (for example, death certificates of husbands in the case of widows' pensions), coupled with the frequent need to pay bribes or a percentage of one's entitlement to officials, serve to increase the burden on these women (National Forum for Single Women's Rights 2011).

Single but not alone: realising rights for single women

Ekal Nari Sashakti Sangathan (Association of Empowered Women Alone, or ENSS) was established in the north Indian state of Jharkhand in 2005. The association today comprises around 34,000 members spread across 21 districts of the state (internal report). ENSS is led by low-income single women, most of whom enjoy little or no family support. The women are facilitated to organise themselves into associations at the village *panchayat* level,[7] which are federated at the block, district, and state levels. ENSS focuses on developing and enhancing the capacities and leadership of single women, so that they are able to tackle their multiple vulnerabilities, demand access to resources and entitlements, as well as solve the socioeconomic problems of their communities. It also seeks to empower the women to engage in lobbying and advocacy to reform laws and policies in order to ensure the rights of single women.

Christian Aid's involvement with ENSS is via local implementing partners.[8] It has focused on strengthening the collective, democratic functioning of the association at all levels, through the facilitation of regular meetings, training sessions, and the building of linkages to other like-minded networks. We have also encouraged ENSS to widen its focus to address issues including discrimination against single women, campaigning and advocating for equal land rights for single women, and awareness-raising and campaigning against violence against single women, for example witch-hunting (internal programme document). Taking into account large-scale poor literacy levels and lack of access to information, a key component of the programme has focused on supporting women to make a decent, independent livelihood. The programmes aim to generate and build women's knowledge about how to go about this, not only on practical issues of how to access entitlements, but also to build common perspectives on core issues of discrimination, gender equality, exclusion, rights, and entitlements. Women need access to land, health, and livelihood-related entitlements and associated skills, and this can be achieved in part by building their awareness of their independent rights to resources and services. They can then raise their voices and claim entitlements. For example, supporting women's access to the government's Mahatma Gandhi National Rural Employment Guarantee Scheme[9] is emerging as a priority.

A formal evaluation of the programme was carried out in 2011. This, together with subsequent research in 2013–2014, suggests it has helped to generate rising levels of confidence and motivation among single women association members to organise and take action to claim entitlements. A number of women have filed complaints regarding domestic violence, trafficking, the denial of maintenance, official corruption in the distribution of entitlements, and other issues. An indicator that women find this approach helpful is the increasing membership, and regular participation, which we have seen at all levels of the ENSS organisational structure, as well as greater participation of single women in local village-level committees. Increasing participation in different decision-making bodies at the local level is significant; women are claiming spaces to speak up and take part in decision-making on issues of development, health, water, sanitation, and forest protection on behalf of their communities.

By widening and deepening organisation-building, ENSS aims to reach from village to state to ensure greater public awareness that single women's issues are specific and need to be acted upon (ENSS Objectives Statement). In the words of Prameela Devi, an ENSS member and separated woman who successfully petitioned to receive a share of the marital property in her name, empowerment stems from a feeling that 'I am single but not alone'. Beyond this, several thousand single women have accessed formal avenues of credit in order to move into self-employment in allied agriculture, animal husbandry, or small businesses in the villages (internal programme documents 2013–2014).

Increasing the agency of women is only one side of the coin. For women to be able to claim equal rights to services and resources, institutional gender biases need to be removed, which requires attitudinal change. Research into the ENSS experience suggests such changes are taking place. ENSS undertook sustained engagement, through discussions and evidence-based representations, which led to the Jharkhand state government providing for the inclusion of single women in several key entitlement schemes such as pensions for young widows, labour cards in the name of single women, and 10 per cent quota for the daughters of single women in government Kasturba schools.[10]

Advocacy at the national level is also a key component of ENSS' work, through the National Forum for Single Women's Rights, a network in which ENSS participates with seven other single women associations across north and central India. The Forum has operated since 2008. Its success can be gauged from representatives being included in the consultative process for writing the 12th Five Year Plan of the Government of India.[11] The Minister of Finance subsequently noted single women as a group requiring special action and allocated, for the first time in the 2013–2014 financial year, a separate budget for the development of single women (Union Budget Speech 2013–2014 and Union Budget 2013–2014), while also considering a separate quota for single women under two of its key housing entitlement schemes (Dhar 2012).

Shifting mind-sets together: working towards dignity for Dalit women

In the southern state of Andhra Pradesh, Dalit Stree Shakti (DSS) has been working since 2005 to organise Dalit women to struggle for their rights. The organisation emerged out of the perceived failures of both the Dalit and women's movements in the state to address the specific issues of Dalit women, particularly gender-based caste violence and caste-class-gender based exclusions from access to quality education, entitlements under government schemes and from political representation (interview with DSS director, Hyderabad, 20 August 2014).

DSS work concentrates on these issues by supporting Dalit women to form collectives at the village level, federated to the state level, where they receive training to build their capacity to engage in independent decision-making. At present, over 1,000 collectives involving around 6,000 women have been initiated in seven districts (DSS annual report 2014–2015).

Almost all the members and co-ordinators have moved from a process of surviving discrimination and other rights violations to becoming human rights defenders and most are Dalits themselves. DSS aims to support the building of 'collective agency' – that is, organised action – through different issue-based campaigns, meetings, training sessions, and engagement with the media and government officials. A central understanding is that the women have been traditionally excluded from access to knowledge, and that knowledge means respect and power, especially the power to act. In addition to knowledge on rights, entitlements, and the institutional structures of government, sessions support women to analyse their situation and the current political context. The organisation also works with women to devise strategies for change, boosting self-confidence and self-esteem as Dalit women.

One core aspect of the work involves supporting the women's collectives to take up cases of caste-based gender violence, as well as domestic violence, in order to ensure access to justice. The collectives work with the DSS district co-ordinator, conduct fact-findings for incidents, ensure immediate relief for the survivor and assist her to file a complaint with the police. Where domestic violence is involved, the collectives begin with a series of counselling sessions for both parties in order to halt the violence and resolve the conflict. If this fails, then the woman is supported to take recourse to legal interventions. The collectives monitor the ongoing cases, especially to support the survivors to pursue justice and not to be pressured into compromises with the perpetrator. The collectives are encouraged to work in a collaborative manner with the government, in order to gain credibility and influence among officials. At the same time, where police negligence is found, the collectives have strongly protested to the higher authorities. The result is that DSS increasingly has become a point of contact for officials seeking collaboration in cases of atrocities, and around 75 per cent of cases where the women's collectives and DSS have accompanied the victims/survivors to court have led to convictions over a period of five years (interview with DSS Director, Hyderabad, 15 September 2013).

The work on the ground by the women's collectives is complemented by evidence-based engagements between Dalit women collective members, DSS, police, and government officials, in order to promote more Dalit women inclusive policies and schemes and strengthen the implementation of protective laws. As a result of DSS advocacy, for example, the Women and Child Welfare Department now ensures that compensation is paid immediately to rape victims, and a number of government orders have been promulgated to establish stringent procedures for the distribution of compensation following such violence.

In a similar manner, a PACS programme partner organisation, Jan Sahas Social Development Society, which is based in the central Indian state of Madhya Pradesh, has been engaged since 2000 with one specific section of Dalit women, those who do the work of manual scavenging. This practice continues to blight the lives of an estimated 1.2 million Indians, around 90 per cent of whom are women and belong to specific 'low caste' Dalit communities (Human Rights Watch 2014). Over 20 years after its legal prohibition and despite a new law enacted in 2013, this indecent and inhuman work continues under both government and individual employers (Human Rights Watch 2014).

Jan Sahas identifies and liberates those engaged in manual scavenging into decent livelihoods. For many of these women, this is the only work they have known and, given their precarious economic situation, that income is vital for running their homes. At the same time, all are aware of the undignified nature of the work, and the consequent discrimination that especially their children face. Jan Sahas supports women to access government rehabilitation and livelihood schemes, and skills development opportunities, to gain alternative, decent work. Women also form community-based organisations of liberated manual scavengers, in order to support and motivate others. A focus on dignity enables members to articulate the problem and develop leadership skills to take forward the struggle to eradicate this practice. These community-based organisations are then brought together in a national movement for dignity, which currently runs across around 110 of the 676 districts in the country (http://www.jansahasindia.org/, last checked by the authors 15 May 2015). The movement has been responsible for organising rallies and foot marches to spread awareness about the need to end manual scavenging and restore dignity to these women. At the same time, the organisation aims to fill a key supportive role to foster movement-building around the issues on which it works, in order to build alliances that can pressurise the government to eradicate manual scavenging. It also operates a resource centre providing legal support to women, taking up cases of rights violations.

A large focus of Jan Sahas' work has been on advocacy. The organisation has been part of a three-year campaign which has seen women marching across the country to demand stronger legal measures. All this led to the enactment of the Prohibition of Employment as Manual Scavengers and their Rehabilitation Act 2013, and to continuing efforts now to enforce the law to end this practice. Moreover, whereas the benefits of the government's rehabilitation schemes primarily went into the hands of Dalit men, regular advocacy has led to greater government focus on Dalit women as the key beneficiaries of such schemes.

Challenges and lessons learnt

Balancing immediate practical needs with longer-term strategic needs

Economic disadvantage and gender inequality intersect to create poor educational levels among women, which in turn constrain their ability to transcend poverty and inequality. As a result, the securing of employment opportunities for socially isolated low-income single women or Dalit women is a basic and immense challenge, which leads to a focus on maintaining survival-level livelihoods rather than supporting women to aspire to greater prosperity. This means, in effect, a focus on meeting immediate practical needs and does not help to challenge the lower status of single women and Dalit women in society. In the absence of more targeted programmes for these women to promote their entry into higher-value areas of the labour market, there are too few opportunities for them to shift into better employment.

Hence, interventions have to be flexible and operate on a long-term trajectory in order to increase their opportunities to break the cycle of poverty. This takes place by accommodating the women's multiple roles and responsibilities, while motivating and facilitating them to shift from a focus on individual benefits attained through the women's associations to working together towards long-lasting change in the lives of all single or Dalit women.

Engaging men, leaders, and the wider community

If programmes only focus on supporting women's individual agency, this may place them at risk of increased violence and abuse. Overcoming intra-family and community resistance has to be consciously built into interventions. An example comes from DSS. The success of the Dalit women's collectives depends in part on engaging with Dalit men, especially the Dalit male leaders in the local communities. Men have to be convinced of the need for women to engage in empowering economic and political activities. The challenge here is to shift attitudes which consider it appropriate for women to take part in economic empowerment processes focusing on a self-help group model, which traditionally engages with savings schemes, but inappropriate for women to engage in a more political model of organising to secure rights and entitlements for the community (and themselves!).

In the experience of DSS (interview with DSS director, Hyderabad, 20 August 2014), the key is to emphasise the good of the whole community of women taking part in political action, and the need for gender equality if a community is to be harmonious and prosperous. The underlying message is that the collectives are not about women dominating over men; rather, they are to promote spaces for women to equally contribute to bettering the lives of their community. This includes not only taking up issues of livelihood entitlements such as land and work, but also addressing cases of domestic violence. This is complemented by interventions with youth, understood as a critical stakeholder in widening spaces for Dalit women's rights, in terms of personality and leadership development as well as debates on key political issues such as affirmative action.

In a similar manner, the challenge for Jan Sahas is to focus on rights, in order to support women and their families to give up manual scavenging and move into other work. This is challenging as it flies in the face of economic realities for these very poor individuals, families, and communities: average manual scavenging work in central India earns around Rs.10 to Rs.20 (USD 0.16–0.32) per private household per month (Jan Sahas 2014, 18). Where women are key breadwinners for their families and where they have been socialised into believing that it is their duty to continue this work, any attempt to increase the economic vulnerability of the family is met with resistance. It is for this reason that the liberation of those engaged in manual scavenging to be able to regain their dignity has to be tied to messages of mobilisation, liberation, and rehabilitation into dignified livelihoods. This requires that women be provided with new skills to engage in productive employment, but also elements of social and political consciousness-raising in order to be able to demand the right to live with dignity. Engrained beliefs about caste and gender have to be challenged.

Jan Sahas premises its work on an understanding that manual scavenging cannot be eradicated through technical solutions alone, for example shifting women into new occupations and replacing dry latrine with flush water-based toilets. Such strategies fail to grapple with caste and gender inequalities that keep women in this degrading occupation. This includes recognising that Dalit men may discriminate against these women while pressuring them to continue this occupation. In other words, challenging the mind-set that reinforces the boundaries keeping certain castes of women in this illegal occupation remains crucial.

Creating and maintaining new power dynamics for positive change

India has yet to see clear, time-bound plans of action to ensure caste and gender equality, and to eradicate manual scavenging. Government's challenges to caste-based discrimination and violence against women do not fully address the interests and needs of Dalit women. Certain state governments continue to deny the very existence of manual scavenging, despite all evidence to the contrary. Dominant caste employers of cleaners support the continuation of manual scavenging. Informal caste institutions and actors are often still clearly exerting influence over formal state actors, a link that remains to be severed. Collectives and organisations fighting for Dalit women's rights need long-term encouragement and support to sustain their actions.

One way to gain more support for the collectives and their agenda is to eventually admit non-Dalit female members, in order to provide space for Dalit and non-Dalit women to interact and break down social barriers. This, however, requires first that the Dalit women members feel empowered enough to engage on equal terms with other women, in order for their leadership potential to remain.

Another challenge comes from the shifts in power relations that occur as the women organise and become more independent and assertive of their rights. The resulting backlash and threats to ENSS members from middle men and money lenders, who traditionally have had a great sway over poor single women's lives, are an example. Only when members are able to form good relations with the officials in their localities have they been able to counter the negative reactions from family and community. Overall progress has also been slow in terms of shifts in property rights in favour of single women, including land, which would signal a strong challenge to gender- and marital-status induced inequalities.

Engagements with government stakeholders are also marked by the need to recognise that progress will be slow in building understanding and political will to create equitable measures and to ensure that government mechanisms are functioning to check violence against Dalit and single women. Strongly-ingrained institutional biases based on caste, class, and gender need to be broken. Moreover, the adequate representation of these women in governance structures, and subsequently their free and informed political participation, remains to be realised given the continuing hostile socio-political environment in which these women live. Hence, while significant advocacy gains have been made over the years, the stronger political participation in, for example, the village *panchayats* by single or Dalit women would only further support their agenda to be pushed.

A further challenge lies in the relationship with the wider women's movement in pushing for the recognition of difference, of intersecting inequalities, and how they increase the vulnerabilities of certain categories of women. While there has been some agreement on the recognition of Dalit women's issues, this is yet to translate into more concrete forms of engagement and alliance building between the women's movement and Dalit women's organisations such as DSS. Similarly, the issue of manual scavenging has always been perceived as a 'Dalit' issue, not as a women's issue, thereby narrowing civil society response to it.

Working for individual and collective resilience

Another significant challenge concerns the fact that gains in terms of economic rights – that is, improvements in the extent to which single Dalit women can engage in productive activities and make a livelihood – does not necessarily lead to challenges to the norms producing stigma, isolation, and abuse of these women. In other words, a focus on economic development alone is insufficient to shift these women from the margins. For instance, liberated Dalit women who shift from manual scavenging into alternative small businesses in their villages often continue to face stigma and discrimination on the basis of their caste and former occupation.

In response to this challenge, Jan Sahas continues to use public marches and demolitions of dry latrines in order to help people to understand the problem and challenge the mind-sets that stigmatise the women. It also has recognised the need to engage with the private employers of manual scavengers in order to support their access to government entitlements to water-flush toilets as part of its interventions.

Conclusion

What do these experiences tell us about meeting the immediate and longer-term needs of women experiencing intersecting inequalities? First, the dynamics of intersecting inequalities as they affect individuals need to be recognised and addressed in policies and programmes. As we have seen, governments and NGOs which choose to intervene on the basis of one identity are problematic: the different identities are experienced together and simultaneously, and this approach risks many interests and needs falling into the gaps, unaddressed.

Secondly, interventions need to be built supporting the organisation of individual women into a structure to advance group-based demands for rights and justice through collective agency. Obviously collective action is a challenge for women whose identities are shared to some extent but not on every point; the more sophisticated an analysis of intersecting inequalities becomes, the greater the challenges for organisation. In addition, rehabilitation and consciousness-raising is particularly important for women whose oppression feels common-place and goes unquestioned, even by them. This requires providing safe spaces for women to come together and recognise their personal struggle as part of a collective, wider movement that builds a sense of dignity and strength to bring about change. This needs to be complemented with an approach that seeks to involve the wider community, starting with male leaders of the community to advocate for a shift in the way in which political and social spaces are created and occupied in order to advance community demands. There is a need to make conscious efforts to build institutions and spaces for Dalit women in particular in order to bridge voice, representation, and leadership gaps.

Thirdly, looking at the wider single identity-based movements such as the women's or Dalit movements, there is a continuous need to build new perspectives to challenge the idea that taking up single or Dalit women's rights – or single Dalit women's rights! – can dilute attention to the issues of gender discrimination or caste discrimination. Instead, acknowledging difference, and how this is converted into different oppressions and disadvantages, strengthens solidarity and widens the range of interventions to transform gender and interlinking inequalities.

Finally, work towards an enabling legal and policy environment that addresses intersecting inequalities cannot be divorced from interventions to change mind-sets, and the social norms that underlie them. While able to achieve success at the individual level, the case studies highlight how damaging social norms constitute the most significant resistance to widespread change. Integrating these findings into a new and transformative post-2015 agenda will be challenging – they point to a need for intelligent and integrated planning, which draws energy and political impetus from the headlines (for example, Gender Equality and Women's Empowerment, and Addressing Inequality – both current proposals for stand-alone goals),[12] but which avoids siloes. It will require a long-term approach which includes indicators which track changes in social norms over time, and invests in the required data. And it will require a strong consensus on the achievement of human rights for all, including the political leadership to name the inequalities which continue to exclude at a national and local level, and which can intersect to reproduce the most extreme forms of poverty and marginalisation. If these points are recognised, then the new agenda may succeed in leaving no one behind and in the words of the UN Secretary General, putting us on 'the road to dignity by 2030' (UN Secretary General 2014).

Acknowledgement

We would like to gratefully acknowledge the contribution of Helen Dennis, Senior Adviser on Poverty and Inequality with Christian Aid, to the thinking and analysis in this chapter.

Notes

1. Evidence suggests that those most likely to be excluded by progress in development are those groups of people whose economic deprivation intersects with 'culturally devalued identities, locational disadvantage and lack of political representation' (Paz Arauco *et al.* 2015, viii).
2. In recent years, the committees that monitor the international laws CEDAW and ICESCR have provided detailed comments that explain what constitutes the obligations of states when it comes to respecting, protecting, and fulfilling human rights in terms of addressing the multiple discrimination that certain groups face due to the intersection of two or more identities. For more information, please see CEDAW and CESCR references provided below.
3. More information can be found at the Christian Aid website: http://www.christianaid.org.uk and PACS website: http://www.pacsindia.org (last checked by the authors 22 June 2015).
4. For example, India has a constitutional right to non-discrimination on the basis of gender and affirmative action provisions for women (Article 15), laws on anti-trafficking, anti-dowry, sexual harassment of women and domestic violence laws, a National Policy on the empowerment of women, and has undertaken gender-responsive budgeting. For more information

please go to Ministry of Women and Child Development website: http://wcd.nic.in/ (last checked by the authors 22 June 2015).

5. Scheduled caste is an official term used for those communities listed by the Government of India as castes characterised by extreme social, educational, and economic backwardness arising out of the traditional practice of untouchability. Notably, Dalit Christians and Muslims are left out of the scheduled caste list. In this chapter, all those who face untouchability are considered to be Dalits irrespective of their religion. For more information please go to http://idsn.org/countries/india/ (last checked by the authors 22 June 2015).

6. 'Untouchability' refers to the imposition of social disabilities by reason of a person's birth into certain 'polluted', 'low' castes to which historically prescribed, degrading occupations linked to death, dirt, and menial labour are attached. For more information please go to http://idsn.org/countries/india/ (last checked by the authors 22 June 2015).

7. Lowest unit of local governance, comprising several villages.

8. These organisations are Samuel Hahnemann Associates & Research Centre and Shramjivi Mahila Samiti.

9. The Mahatma Gandhi National Rural Employment Guarantee Scheme specifies the right of every rural household to 100 paid work days for one household member. Women and men are both eligible to apply and receive equal pay.

10. Kasturba Gandhi Balika Vidyalayas, or government residential schools for girls of families living below the poverty line in 'educationally backward blocks'.

11. For more information on the Government of India's planning process and the 12th Five Year Plan, please go to http://planningcommission.gov.in/index_oldpc.php & http://12thplan.gov.in/ (last checked by the authors 22 June 2015).

12. The proposed goals, at the time of writing, are respectively Goal 5 'Achieve gender equality and empower all women and girls' and Goal 10 'Reduce inequality within and among countries'. The final goals will be agreed at the UN General Assembly in September 2015.

References

Agarwal, Bina (1998) 'Widows versus daughters or widows as daughters? Property, land, and economic security in Rural India', *Modern Asian Studies* 32(1): 1–48

Census of India (2011) New Delhi: Ministry of Home Affairs, Government of India

Committee on the Elimination of Discrimination against Women (CEDAW) (2010) 'General Recommendation No.28: Core Obligations of States Parties under Article 2 of the Convention on the Elimination of All Forms of Discrimination against Women. UN Doc. CEDAW/C/2010/47/GC.2', Geneva: United Nations

Committee on Economic, Social and Cultural Rights (CESCR) (2009) 'General Comment No. 20: Non Discrimination in Economic, Social and Cultural Rights. UN Doc. E/C.12/ GC/20', Geneva: United Nations

Das, Maitreyi Bordia (2006). 'Do Traditional Axes of Exclusion Affect Labor Market Outcomes in India? Social Development Papers, South Asian Series 97', Washington DC: The World Bank

Dhar, Aarti (2012) Special Housing Quota for Single Women Proposed, *The Hindu Newspaper*, (17 December 2012)

Dhar, Aarti (2011) Low Income Single Women Demand Public Funds to Live with Dignity, *The Hindu Newspaper*, (11 October 2011)

Grey, Mary (2005) 'Dalit women and the struggle for justice in a world of global capitalism', *Feminist Theology* 14(1): 127–49

Human Rights Watch (2014) *Cleaning Human Waste "Manual Scavenging," Caste, and Discrimination in India*, New York: Human Rights Watch

Irudayam, Aloysius, Jayshree Priyadarshani Mangubhai, and Joel Guyton Lee (2011) *Dalit Women Speak Out: Caste, Class and Gender Violence in India*, New Delhi: Zubaan

Jan Sahas Social Development Society (Jan Sahas) (2014) 'Socio Economic Status of Women Manual Scavengers: Baseline Report 2014', New Delhi: UN Women, Fund for Gender Equality

National Crimes Records Bureau (2014) *Crimes in India 2013*, New Delhi: National Crimes Records Bureau

National Forum for Single Women's Rights (2011) *Are We Forgotten Women? A Study of the Status of Low-income Single Women in India*, Udaipur: National Forum for Single Women's Rights

National Human Rights Commission (NHRC) (2004) 'Report on Prevention of Atrocities against Scheduled Castes: Policy and Performance, Suggested Interventions and Initiatives for NHRC', New Delhi: National Human Rights Commission

Pandey, Gyanendra (2010) 'Politics of difference: reflections on dalit and African American struggles', *Economic and Political Weekly* 45(19): 62–84

Paz Arauco, Veronica, Haris Gazdar, Paula Hevia-Pacheco, Naila Kabeer, Amanda Lenhardt, Syeda Quratulain Masood, Haider Naqvi, Nandini Nayak, Andrew Norton, Nidhi Sadana Sabharwal, Elisa Scalise, Andrew Shepherd, Deepak Thapa, Sukhadeo Thorat and D. Hien Tran (2015) *Strengthening social justice to address inequalities post-2015*. London: Overseas Development Institute

Secretary General (UN) (2014) 'The Road to Dignity by 2030: Ending Poverty, Transforming All Lives and Protecting the Planet', Synthesis Report of the Secretary-General on the Post 2015 Agenda, http://www.un.org/disabilities/documents/reports/SG_Synthesis_Report_Road_to_Dignity_by_2030.pdf (last checked by the authors 24 April 2015)

Shah, Ghanshyam, Harsh Mander, Sukhadeo Thorat, Satish Deshpande, and Amita Baviskar (2006) *Untouchability in Rural India*, New Delhi: Sage Publications

The Report of the High-Level Panel of Eminent Persons on the Post-2015 Development Agenda(UN) (2013) 'A New Global Partnership: Eradicate Poverty and Transform Economies through Sustainable Development', http://www.un.org/sg/management/pdf/HLP_P2015_Report.pdf (last checked by the authors 24 April 2014)

United National Development Programme (UNDP) (2014) 'Human Development Report 2014', New York: UNDP

About the Authors

Jayshree P. Mangubhai is the South Asia Senior Programme Officer for Policy and Advocacy with Christian Aid, based in New Delhi. Email: jmangubhai@christian-aid.org.
Chiara Capraro is the Gender Policy Adviser with Christian Aid, based in London. Email: ccapraro@christian-aid.org.

CHAPTER 7

Women's economic inequality and domestic violence: exploring the links and empowering women

Christine Hughes, Mara Bolis, Rebecca Fries and Stephanie Finigan

Abstract

Economic empowerment of poor households is a key entry point for development organisations concerned with economic inequality. Over the decades, gender inequality has emerged as a key concern, and the result has been women's economic empowerment (WEE) programming. This chapter is a study of the impact of WEE programming on domestic violence (DV) against women. While this link has received some attention in gender and development literature, evaluations and impact assessments in development organisations have not consistently focused on the possibility of increased or decreased DV as a result of the challenge WEE represents to gender power relations. Drawing on the experience of Oxfam and other development organisations, we offer recommendations for practitioners aimed at better programme integration and more holistic empowerment. Aiming to challenge economic inequality between households involves better understanding of the impact of WEE programming on intra-household gender inequality, including rates of DV. This requires planning to anticipate these possible impacts and ensure women are able to gain from programming without placing themselves at risk.

Keywords: women's economic empowerment; violence against women; domestic violence; microfinance; women's economic leadership; holistic empowerment

Introduction

Economic poverty and gender inequality are interlinked. Globally, women are more likely to live in poverty and economic insecurity than men (UN 2014; World Bank/ International Bank for Reconstruction and Development 2011). Meanwhile, and with implications for women's economic participation, one in three women has experienced sexual or physical violence in her lifetime (WHO 2013). Rights-based approaches to development support women's struggles for and access to their rights to economic participation and security,

http://dx.doi.org/10.3362/9781780447278.007

and to live free from violence. Yet these areas of work are often treated in separate programmes, to promote women's economic empowerment (WEE), and to combat violence against women (VAW). These two siloed development domains need to be seen as connected in order to provide effective responses to gendered poverty and inequality. This is not least because research into the impact of women's economic empowerment (WEE) programming has shown that this can, in some cases, result in an increase in domestic violence (DV). It is comparatively seldom that programming on WEE builds in programme components designed to track the impact of WEE activities on VAW, or to minimise the potential for violence. Addressing WEE and VAW in isolation from each other[1] potentially results in different threads of women's rights programming working at cross-purposes (Vyas 2013).

In this chapter, we highlight the impact of WEE programming on women's risk of DV. It is critical for development policymakers and practitioners to develop greater awareness of why and how WEE initiatives contribute to raising or lowering women's risk of DV. More economically empowered women may be less vulnerable to abuse on account of their enhanced financial contributions to their households (Vyas and Watts 2009), while on the other hand, WEE programmes 'could unintentionally increase their chances of being somehow abused by their partners' (García Aísa 2014, 10), especially if women's increased earning power results in 'atypical roles within the household such as the woman being the main income earners' (Hidrobo and Fernald 2013, 305). However, recognition that WEE programming can potentially increase violence should not call WEE into question; it is clearly in women's interests to raise incomes and promote gender equality, and many women are keen to be involved in these programmes. Therefore, as we argue in this chapter, interventions aimed at economically empowering women must incorporate strategies to minimise unintended negative impacts on women, including risks of increased DV, and promote the empowerment of women from a holistic perspective.

Our chapter presents the findings of a study we undertook into WEE and DV, which drew on extensive sources – both published and unpublished – and which is rooted in the knowledge, experiences, and perspectives of staff within the Oxfam confederation. It specifically draws on work done by Value for Women and Oxfam in Latin America to build conceptual and practical tools into WEE programming (Fries and Finigan 2014). Oxfam is an international NGO that has committed to putting women's rights at the heart of everything it does (Oxfam International 2013), but still grapples with the challenges of better connecting economic justice and gender justice work.

The chapter begins by looking more closely at understandings of WEE, DV, and our methodology. It then offers some useful insights from published and unpublished sources, and makes recommendations for practitioners. The conclusion suggests directions for further research. In terms of this books theme of inequalities, we aim to contribute to better understanding how to address, in mutually reinforcing ways, gender inequality that manifests both through economic disadvantage and through violence.

Women's economic empowerment: Oxfam's approach

Poverty and economic insecurity have an intrinsic relationship to gender inequality. From Oxfam's perspective, gender inequality is of particular significance as a driver of wider inequalities and poverty: 'systematic discrimination against women and girls is the most pervasive cause, and consequence, of the inequality in power relations that drives poverty' (Wakefield 2014, 4). Increased emphasis therefore has been devoted to addressing poverty through economically empowering women. Oxfam defines WEE as a process through which women 'enjoy their rights to control and benefit from resources, assets, income and their own time, and ... have the ability to manage risk and improve their economic status and wellbeing' (Reference Group, Oxfam WEE in Agriculture Knowledge Hub 2014, 1).

Oxfam-supported WEE programming currently occurs in over 40 countries around the world, and includes both gender-mainstreamed approaches that increase women's inclusion and participation in livelihoods, and standalone programming centred specifically on women's economic rights.[2] The elements and indicators of WEE are understood as multi-faceted and interconnected: personal economic security, control over assets and income, spending autonomy, greater contribution to household expenses, and a fairer balance of market-oriented opportunities for women and men. However, more holistic WEE incorporates related issues of enhanced self-worth, agency in personal and household decision-making, equal rights to men, and (critically for our concerns in this chapter), freedom from domination in the household, including freedom from violence (Hashemi *et al.* 1996). WEE programming incorporates a broad spectrum of approaches and tools, including livelihoods, enterprise development, microfinance, and women's economic leadership programmes.

When analysing WEE initiatives, we consider it important not only to focus narrowly on their economic successes and failures, but on the extent to which they help deliver more holistic empowerment, due to the potential WEE offers to shift gender roles and social norms. Our chapter builds on a strong body of research on how WEE interventions impact household gender dynamics, including the division of labour, decision-making, control of assets, and other expressions of power (for example, Goetz and Gupta 1996; Hashemi *et al.* 1996; Kabeer 2001). Research on the impact of microfinance in particular has shown contradictory evidence: the potential to increase financial independence of women, improve family relationships, and decrease DV (Cheston and Kuhn 2002; Haile *et al.* 2012; Kabeer 2001; UNESCAP 2007), but also to increase household tension and conflict around shifting roles and tasks, and increased assertion of household authority by men (Kabeer 1997; Kulkarni

2011; Rahman 1999). For this chapter, we reviewed the literature on various types of WEE interventions for their impact specifically on DV against women.

Domestic violence against women: defining the concept

Violence against women (VAW) is a serious violation of human rights and a pervasive problem worldwide. Globally, 35 per cent of women have experienced physical or sexual violence (WHO 2013, 2) and rates of intimate-partner VAW surpass 50 per cent in some countries (Kabeer 2014, 5). For the purposes of this paper, we define violence against women as: any act of gender-based violence (GBV) that results in, or is likely to result in, physical, sexual, or psychological harm or suffering to women, including threats of such acts, coercion, or arbitrary deprivation of liberty, whether occurring in public or in private life (United Nations 1993). GBV can be understood as the use of power to enforce gender norms (Raab 2012). While not intending to minimise other forms of GBV,[3] we focus in this paper on men's DV against women,[4] meaning physical, emotional, psychological, or sexual violence that occurs in the same family, household, or intimate relationship.

VAW is increasingly recognised as an obstacle to development (Raab 2012) because of its profound economic, social, and political costs to society (Duvvury *et al.* 2013). These persuasive views have put VAW on financial institutions' agendas (e.g. Klugman *et al.* 2014). However, as feminists working in development, we stress that VAW must be eliminated first and foremost because it is a violation of women's human rights that profoundly affects their health and life potential.[5] From a feminist perspective, violence against women is most fundamentally based in unequal gender power relations notwithstanding other forms of identity and disadvantage – such as ethnicity, class, and age, among others – that intersect with gender to put some women at greater risk than others (Rosche 2014). From this perspective, men perpetuate DV against women as an expression of power and control. What we are interested in investigating is how WEE potentially alters the contours of gender relations at the household level, thereby keeping with the understanding of DV as rooted in unequal gender power relations.

Our study

Ours is a literature-based study, informed by the preliminary yet trail-blazing work on better integrating VAW considerations into women's economic leadership initiatives (for example, Fries and Finigan 2014) and informed by colleagues within the Oxfam confederation. Approximately 75 resources were consulted, including academic chapters, organisational reports, programme evaluations, and internal Oxfam documents. Over two-thirds of these reported on original empirical research while secondary materials (for example, literature reviews) accounted for the remainder. The vast majority focused on the global South, but we cannot claim that each region was represented proportionately. Interspersed throughout the chapter, we present some of the insights we received from nine Oxfam colleagues with many years of experience in implementing and evaluating WEE or VAW programmes in Latin America, Africa, and Asia-Pacific. These insights were intended to make our literature-based research relevant to practitioners' perspectives and needs.

Explanations of the impacts of WEE on DV

Understanding why WEE may increase or decrease DV risk is important for planning how to address those links. Much of the literature discussing this draws on economic theory for explanations, while emphasising the socio-cultural impacts on gender power relations. The first economic explanation focuses on *bargaining* (Kabeer 1994), where the household or conjugal relationship is seen as a site of negotiation over resources (Agarwal 1997). DV is understood to be an outcome of gender inequality and lack of women's rights. It is linked to gendered poverty in the sense that women who are economically dependent on men are unable to escape abusive relationships, and may be forced to tolerate some level of violence in return for men's economic support (Farmer and Tiefenthaler 1997). A woman's economic empowerment can, therefore, potentially contribute to decreasing her male partner's violence by improving her bargaining power: she is financially more able to leave the relationship or use income transfers as bargaining resources of her own (Perova 2010).

A second strand of the literature examining violence through the lens of economics looks at violence in *instrumental or extractive* terms, where it is used to control others' behaviour or the allocation of resources (Anderberg and Rainer 2011). As women become increasingly economically empowered, the risk of DV may increase because men may use violence as an instrument to disrupt women's market-oriented activity, exert authority over managing women's income, or seize it (Schuler *et al.* 1996), sometimes withholding it in blackmail schemes to demand better dowries (Bloch and Rao 2002).

A third strand of the literature addresses DV in *expressive terms*, as a way to express frustration or dissatisfaction, or improve self-esteem. If WEE makes households better off, men may feel less economic stress, which they might otherwise express through violence (Vyas and Watts 2009). Or, a man may feel his economic and household status or roles threatened, which can lead to violence as a way of expressing those feelings (Jewkes 2002). In short, 'backlash' may result from economic status inconsistencies that challenge the status quo (Macmillan and Gartner 1999).

Although these economic explanations are illuminating, they tend to isolate economic concerns from important socio-cultural or ideological considerations and impacts (Vyas and Watts 2009). For instance, DV is more likely in contexts where gender roles are more rigidly defined (Heise 1998) and less likely in relationships that adhere more to principles of gender equality (Vyas and Watts 2009). Schuler *et al.* (1996) show that the financial component may not always be the most significant aspect of how WEE affects DV, pointing to socio-cultural implications. WEE often disrupts or challenges existing gender norms and roles by facilitating new models of behaviour. For instance, livelihoods programmes may include awareness-raising about gender issues (for example, Haneef *et al.* 2014), and make women's lives more public and their struggles more collective (Schuler *et al.* 1996). However, as WEE increases awareness and promotes changes to gender roles, men may respond with a backlash as patriarchal systems are challenged, a tendency that our Oxfam colleagues emphasised. Overall, WEE can reduce the risk of DV by increasing women's economic and social power, but can also provoke DV by giving men reason and opportunity to (re-)assert their dominance.

Evidence and examples – how WEE outcomes may decrease DV risk and help survivors

We began our research for this study by looking at sources that document a reduction in DV attributable in part to WEE outcomes. We organised these by type of economic empowerment intervention or indicator: livelihood and microfinance programmes, conditional cash transfers, and property ownership. We extract just a few of the insights offered by individual studies in this very large and complex literature in the four paragraphs below.

In rural Bangladesh, a study of women's participation in a livelihoods programme found that it contributed to reducing DV through household poverty reduction, women's independent income generation, and education (Haneef *et al.* 2014). Poverty reduction decreased the conflict that tended to result from women having to ask husbands for money, women's independent income encouraged husbands to better recognise women's financial contributions to the household – thereby raising their respect for women and belief in women's abilities. Such elevation of status was summarised as follows by an Oxfam colleague we surveyed: 'women are seen as positive contributors to the household, not just carers – their contributions are appreciated by everyone in the family'. In rural Bangladesh, the livelihood programme's education and training components also raised women's and men's awareness of the negative consequences of VAW; one woman commented: '[violence] will stop if we become conscious and if our husbands become conscious' (Haneef *et al.* 2014, 14).

The findings on microfinance and its impact on DV also offer a rich and varied picture of context-specific effects. After participating for two years in one microfinance programme in South Africa, women's risk for physical and sexual violence by an intimate partner fell significantly, compared to no reductions for the control group in the study (Kim *et al.* 2007). The authors attributed these reductions to enabling women to challenge the acceptability of violence, expect and receive better treatment from partners, leave violent relationships, and raise community awareness about the need to address violence.

In apparent contrast, a very well-known and influential study in Bangladesh by Sidney Ruth Schuler *et al.* examined the impacts of the Grameen Bank and Bangladesh Rural Advancement Committee (BRAC) credit programmes on DV. They found that in comparison to women living in villages without credit programmes, prevalence of physical DV was lower for both women participating in either programme and for non-participant women in a Grameen Bank community. To explain this, the authors argued that, for many women, 'other aspects of credit programs [than the loan components] are more important for reducing VAW' (1996, 1737), such as shifting ideas about violence, presence of outsiders, increased visibility of women, training, and social networks, all of which can benefit non-participant women.

A few studies examining the effects of *conditional cash transfer* (CCT) programmes in Latin America clearly document a decrease in DV among recipient women (García Aísa 2014; Perova 2010). CCT programmes provide parents – typically mothers – in poor households with regular government funds as long as they meet set obligations, usually concerning health care and/or education for their children (Perova 2010). For example, Perova found that the *Juntos* programme in Peru contributed to reductions in the percentage of recipient women experiencing domestic physical and emotional violence, an effect that can be attributed to increases in women's household status, autonomy, and bargaining power alongside a reduction in household poverty.

Property ownership accounts for the last WEE measure we analysed for its relation to DV risk. These studies focused on the potential of property ownership (land and/or house) to both deter DV and offer an escape option for survivors. Focusing on both of these potentials, Panda *et al.* (2006) found in India that property ownership helped to prevent DV by enhancing women's status and respect in their marital families, increasing their confidence and household decision-making roles, and raising the potential for future financial independence, As well, women with property – especially a house – who faced violence were more likely to permanently escape (Swaminathan *et al.* 2008). Based on studies such as these, international organisations like the UNDP and UNWomen are promoting the potential in property ownership to reduce the risk of DV and to help women exit situations of violence (e.g. UN Women and OCHCR 2013).

Evidence and examples – how WEE outcomes may increase the risk of DV

Next, we briefly discuss some of the empirical studies that have apparently demonstrated the opposite effect, suggesting an increase in DV in the context of economic empowerment programmes directed at women. Beginning with microfinance programmes, two studies of microfinance programming in Bangladesh indicated that women's participation in these schemes contributed to raising their risk of DV. Syed Masud Ahmed (2005) demonstrated that in the absence of other complementary interventions (such as training, capacity building, and work on behaviour change) microfinance increased women's exposure to DV. Compared to non-members, female members in the programme faced a greater level of DV upon receipt of the credit. In Aminur Rahman's (1999, 74) study, 70 per cent of women participating in a microfinance initiative reported an increase in violence in their households because of their involvement in the programme. Explanations advanced focus on conflict over women's control of funds, and male anger over women's inability to secure new loans.

In studies centring on CCTs, Gustavo Bobonis *et al.* (2013) showed that the *Oportunidades* programme in Mexico contributed to decreasing the incidence of physical violence against women, but also to increasing the number of violent threats they received from their husbands. Manuela Angelucci (2008) found that *Oportunidades* increased DV in households where husbands held traditional gender roles, suggesting that the increased income in the hands of their wives threatened their identity. This finding is consistent with the observations of Oxfam staff, who have noted that WEE programmes that encourage an independent source of income for women can cause jealousy among men and lead to conflict, especially where household gender roles were highly unequal and men felt their status threatened.

Some studies have suggested that women's employment outside the home can also increase exposure to DV. A study in one community in Peru (Flake 2005) revealed that women who were employed in agricultural, service, or professional jobs were significantly more likely to be abused by partners than are unemployed women. Suneeta Krishnan *et al.* (2010) echoed this finding with their health-focused study in India, where women who moved from unemployment to employment over a two-year period were 80 per cent more likely to have experienced DV compared to women who maintained their unemployed status (employment was defined as working for money outside the home in the past six months). Oxfam staff noted that often men are not in support of women going to public places – such as the market, group meetings, or to a job – and that household conflict can arise from women having an independent source of income.

Differentiated results and the importance of context

The studies reviewed and discussed here show that shifts in dynamics of economic inequality have varied implications for household gender inequality as manifested in DV against women. Enhanced economic security in some cases supports while in other cases impedes women's right to live free of violence. Further illustrating the lack of straightforward correlations, several resources suggested different outcomes within the same study (an example is Vyas and Watts 2009). Here, we highlight four sets of factors that influence how WEE–DV relationships play out to produce these differences: socio-cultural contexts of households, characteristics of households, characteristics of individuals, and particularities of WEE processes themselves.

DV rates vary greatly both across countries and within them (WHO 2013), and where rates and acceptance of DV are high, the risk of WEE programming contributing to DV is likely to be greater. The same can be said of more patriarchal contexts more generally: Michael Koenig *et al.* (2003) found in Bangladesh that increased female empowerment through savings or credit groups led to conflict and increased DV in the more culturally conservative settings, but not in the less conservative ones. Cultural conservatism often maps onto rural areas: selected studies of conditional cash transfer (CCT) programmes show that among rural compared to urban women, CCT income is more likely to be a risk factor than a protective factor for DV (García Aísa 2014). Relatedly, we need to consider how a socio-cultural context shapes a woman's options should she be economically able to escape a violent relationship (Sen 1999). Limitations on a woman's status and opportunities outside of marriage make it less likely that she can leave a violent situation, thereby reducing the bargaining power that increased economic resources might otherwise give her.

Among household-level factors, we emphasise the *relative* status of women and men in terms of decision-making, employment or income-generation, and education, that is, how their power and resources compare to one another. The literature suggests that WEE is more likely to increase than decrease DV if: before WEE interventions women already have much less decision-making power than men (Hidrobo *et al.* 2013); WEE contributes to women arriving at a higher economic status than their husbands (Agarwal and Panda 2007); or women have education levels equal to, or higher than, their partners (Hidrobo and Fernald 2013).

This last point brings us to individual-level factors. Others found in our review merit mention for their influence. Although not necessarily generalisable across contexts, studies suggest that the following circumstances lowered the incidence or risk of DV for women in the context of their participation in WEE programming: non-indigenous ethno-cultural identity (Hidrobo *et al.* 2013), higher age at marriage (Heath 2014), and having cash-paying jobs and fewer children (in the case of CCTs) (Perova 2010), strong social networks (Sen 1999), and control over their earnings (Sen 1999).

Finally, we identified a handful of factors from the sources we studied concerning WEE processes themselves, especially certain combinations of interventions. For instance, the inclusion of skills training and awareness-raising – for both women and men – in microfinance schemes have had a protective influence versus cash or credit alone; these components increase women's 'ability to negotiate conflict and avoid violent situations with greater confidence, knowledge, and information' (Ahmed 2005, 99). Finally, time-frames of WEE programming influence DV risk. Overall, the risk of increased DV may decline over time as both men's individual and broader social attitudes become more accepting of women's increased market-oriented activity (Ahmed 2005), and as women's economic activities become more profitable. These sets of influential factors reinforce the point made by several authors about the importance of context and heterogeneity when understanding DV, including in the context of WEE.

Recommendations for practitioners: strategies to enhance programme integration

Awareness of the potential links between WEE processes and DV risks puts development practitioners in a position of ethical responsibility to do their best to minimise unintended negative consequences and to maximise the positive potential implications that our literature review has illuminated. To that end, we provide recommendations for WEE and VAW practitioners contained in the literature and emerging from our assessment of the empirical evidence.

First, awareness on the part of both WEE and VAW practitioners and the development community at large about the correlations between WEE and DV is necessary. WEE programmes led by development institutions need a clear mandate for considering VAW risk mitigation as part of the planned interventions.

Second, WEE practitioners need to be prepared to handle situations of VAW (domestic or other types) among programme participants. This does not necessarily mean that they must become experts on VAW or offer services to survivors. At the least, however, they should understand the reasons WEE might increase the risk of violence, put in place confidential spaces where participants can disclose their experiences, know where survivors can seek help, and provide that information to women participants at the outset of any programme.

Our third set of recommendations supports enhanced communication and collaboration between teams working on a WEE initiative, and VAW practitioners, social workers, and other gender justice experts. WEE–VAW alliances could be in the same development organisation, or in other development or women's organisations working in the same context. VAW practitioners in particular could provide insights on what they see as links between WEE processes and DV, offer DV-awareness and risk-mitigation training and resources, and provide information on local support services. They themselves would also benefit from knowing more about the WEE initiatives underway in communities they work in: WEE programming could contribute to shifts in local VAW incidence, and they could refer survivors of violence to economic empowerment programmes or integrate WEE into their support services in order to boost survivors' financial independence.

Our fourth set of recommendations concerns the design and implementation of WEE programmes. They should be consciously designed as holistic in scope and multi-disciplinary, and be based on risk assessments. They need to include components to minimise risk of DV, monitor its occurrence, and respond to incidents with safety and referral plans. To start, risk assessments and baseline assessments of DV prevalence should be undertaken, either at the community level or among potential WEE initiative participants themselves

(Fries and Finigan 2014). Ideally, these would be complemented by existing data on VAW incidence in a given country or community. Baseline assessments are particularly important to properly differentiate the existence of DV before the programme from how the programme itself affects DV (Heath 2014). From baseline assessments, WEE programme design should include the monitoring of impacts on DV – both on actual incidents, and the change in DV overall compared to baseline analyses – as well as specific procedures to follow in the case of DV detection. Assessments and monitoring need to be done in an expert, safe, and ethical manner. To assist with strategies such as these, Oxfam and Value for Women recently developed a toolkit that provides guidance on participatory mapping of local resources, local risk assessment of VAW, and risk reduction planning for WEE programmes (Fries and Finigan 2014).

Design and implementation of programmes should also include non-technical skill development and awareness-raising, and ways to enhance women's collective supports and involve male stakeholders. Programmes should foster women's leadership, negotiation power, self-confidence, and communication skills, which can decrease the occurrence of violence by strengthening their abilities to negotiate conflict and avoid violent situations (Ahmed 2005). Awareness-raising work should include topics like women's rights, household gender relations, and DV specifically, and information about local prevention and attention resources. Practitioners can also foster the creation of women-only, safe, peer spaces where women can discuss challenges, form networks of support, and get referrals for services. Finally, programmes should provide information and training to men, right from the design phase, especially male partners of female participants as well as community leaders. This can help to generate 'buy-in' and prevent backlash at the household or community level (CARE 2010), and raise awareness of violence against women and girls and gender power relations more generally (Fries and Finigan 2014).

Our fifth set of recommendations centres on community-level initiatives aimed at defeating the widespread acceptance of GBV and ensuring a facilitating environment for WEE initiatives (World Vision Australia 2011). As Christina Haneef and colleagues (2014, 13) note, '[E]ducation and unity of all villagers is important. When all people become conscious and unite to remove it from society, only at that time will [gender-based violence] reduce'. To these ends, both WEE and VAW practitioners – in concert with other gender justice allies – should raise awareness of the negative consequences of GBV in communities, and DV against women in particular. Awareness-raising should also take place to ensure men and community leaders are better aware of the positive impacts of gender equality and inclusion, and of violence-free homes and communities. Activities can include communications campaigns, targeted gender-sensitivity training, and commemorations of important women's rights dates. A targeted community support base (including elders and recognised leaders) can help with these community-level activities, by setting positive examples and raising their voices (Haneef *et al.* 2014). These community-level initiatives also reinforce the value in collaboration among WEE, VAW, and other gender justice practitioners.

We saw examples of some of these recommendations after a tragic case in which a participant in an Oxfam-supported WEE initiative was murdered by her spouse in Colombia. Although her husband's motive could not be linked to her participation in the WEE programme, her death nevertheless underlines the urgent need for such programmes to address VAW, and indeed prompted the programme team to take responsive action. They liaised with local VAW experts to pilot innovative strategies aimed at violence prevention and mitigation, and provision of services to WEE participants who experienced violence. They worked to increase community awareness about VAW, and began assessing and monitoring risk of VAW throughout the WEE programme, and providing psycho-social support. More information can be found in the toolkit mentioned above (Fries and Finigan 2014).

Conclusion

This chapter has presented theoretical perspectives and insights from empirical studies focused on how microfinance schemes, conditional cash transfers, and women's employment may alter gender power relations at the household level with implications for DV. We have seen that the links between WEE processes and DV risk are complex – flowing through both socio-cultural and economic avenues, sometimes contradictory, and always dependent on context and the particularities of WEE processes. We do not wish to call into question the excellent, life-changing results that WEE practitioners facilitate through their initiatives, but rather to raise awareness about possible unforeseen implications for DV of WEE programming, and to thereby foster changes in thinking and practice toward making programming more integrated and holistic.

We see several possible avenues for future research and monitoring, evaluation, and learning (MEL) arising from our study. More primary research is needed on the links between WEE and VAW – including both domestic and other forms[6] – in contexts where development organisations like Oxfam support programmes. We also see a need for more and better monitoring, evaluation, and learning (MEL) on WEE initiatives that have integrated DV risk reduction and mitigation into programme design and implementation. MEL should be long-term, to see if and why potential backlash dissipates over time. It should also investigate the questions of whether holistic and gender-based approaches to WEE result in better economic success for women; and generate recommendations for key actors other than practitioners, such as policymakers and international financial institutions.

Overall, we hope this study offers a particular programmatic perspective to the wider literature on WEE and its impact on gender equality in the household and wider society. More broadly, we hope we have contributed to better understanding the complex and sometimes contradictory ways that shifts in dynamics of economic inequality can impact changes in gender-based inequality expressed as violence against women. Most importantly, we hope our chapter generates further discussion, research, and good practice to better connect WEE and VAW practitioners for the mutual benefit of the women whose rights and empowerment they promote.

Acknowledgements

We express profound thanks to our reference group for their encouragement and direction, and excellent feedback on an earlier draft of this paper. The group included gender justice experts in Oxfam – Ines Smyth, Alivelu Ramisetty, Caroline Marrs, Thalia Kidder, and Robert Silverman – and Lynn Pikholz from CapitalPlus Exchange and the Small Business Banking Network (SBBN). We also gratefully acknowledge the excellent contributions during the literature review phase of this project of two interns at Oxfam America, Faustino Mora and Faria Rashid.

Notes

1. For instance, only 43 per cent of WEE practitioners in the Oxfam confederation currently expect to link their work to anti-violence programming (Morcillo-Espina 2014).
2. For more information on Oxfam-supported WEE programmes, see for instance http://growsellthrive.org/
3. GBV includes some forms of violence against men and boys perpetrated based on perceptions that they are not enacting or living up to normative masculine identities.
4. Women are much more likely to experience GBV than men (Raab 2012), women are most likely to experience violence in the domestic sphere or conjugal relationships (Heise 2011), and most of the literature we reviewed examined WEE in relation to domestic forms of violence. We did however encounter some limited discussion of the risk of public violence against economically active women (e.g. Fries and Finigan 2014).
5. These two perspectives on VAW – sometimes labelled 'instrumentalist' versus 'human rights' – differ in their dominant understanding of why VAW is a development concern. We acknowledge and see value in both perspectives.
6. Although DV is the type of violence against women most often considered and researched in relation to WEE, other, more public forms of violence may result from women's increased market-oriented activity and public presence (Fries and Finigan 2014).

References

Agarwal, Bina (1997) '"Bargaining" and gender relations: within and beyond the house-hold', *Feminist Economics* 3(1): 1–51, available at http://www.binaagarwal.com/downloads/apapers/bagaining_and_gender_relations.pdf (last checked by the authors 23 June 2015)

Agarwal, Bina and Pradeep Panda (2007) 'Toward freedom from domestic violence: the neglected obvious', *Journal of Human Development* 8(3): 359–88

Ahmed, Syed Masud (2005) 'Intimate partner violence against women: experiences from a woman-focused development programme in matlab, Bangladesh', *Journal of Health Population and Nutrition* 23(1): 95–101, available at http://www.researchgate.net/profile/Syed_Masud_Ahmed/publication/7855925_Intimate_partner_violence_against_women_experiences_from_a_woman-focused_development_programme_in_Matlab_Bangladesh/links/0c96051ef396435021000000 (last checked by the authors 23 June 2015)

Anderberg, Dan and Helmut Rainer (2011) 'Domestic abuse: instrumental violence and Economic Incentives', CESifo Working Paper No. 3673. Munich: Ifo Institute, Centre for Economic Studies (CES), available at http://www.cesifo-group.de/DocDL/cesifo1_wp3673.pdf (last checked by the authors 23 June 2015)

Angelucci, Manuela (2008) 'Love on the rocks: domestic violence and alcohol abuse in rural Mexico', *The B.E. Journal of Economic Analysis & Policy* 8(1): Article 43, available at http://www-personal.umich.edu/~mangeluc/Angelucci_violence.pdf (last checked by the authors 23 June 2015)

Bloch, Francis and Vijayendra Rao (2002) 'Terror as a bargaining instrument: a case study of dowry violence in rural India', *American Economic Review* 92(4): 1029–43, available at http://elibrary.worldbank.org/doi/pdf/10.1596/1813-9450-2347 (last checked by the authors 23 June 2015)

Bobonis, Gustavo, Melissa González-Brenes, and Robert Castro (2013) 'Public transfers and domestic violence: the roles of private information and spousal control', *American Economic Journal: Economic Policy* 5(1): 179–205

CARE (2010) *Strong Women, Strong Communities: CARE's Holistic Approach to Empowering Women and Girls in the Fight against Poverty*, Atlanta, GA: CARE, available at http://www.care.org/sites/default/files/documents/PSJ-2010-Womens-Empowerment-Report.pdf (last checked by the authors 23 June 2015)

Cheston, Susy and Lisa Kuhn (2002) *Empowering Women through Microfinance*, New York: United Nations Development Fund for Women. http://www.seepnetwork.org/empowering-women-through-microfinance-resources-444.php (last checked by the authors 23 June 2015)

Duvvury, Nata, Aoife Callan, Patricia Carney, and Srinivas Raghavendra (2013) *Intimate Partner Violence: Economic Costs and Implications for Growth and Development. Women's Voice, Agency & Participation Research Series 2013 No. 3*. New York: World Bank Group, available at http://www.worldbank.org/content/dam/Worldbank/document/Gender/Duvvury%20et%20al.%202013%20Intimate%20Partner%20Violence.%20Economic%20costs%20and%20implications%20for%20growth%20and%20development%20VAP%20No.3%20Nov%202013.pdf (last checked by the authors 23 June 2015)

Farmer, Amy and Jill Tiefenthaler (1997) 'An economic analysis of domestic violence.' *Review of Social Economy* 55(3): 337–58

Flake, Dallan (2005) 'Individual, family, and community risk markers for domestic violence in Peru', *Violence against Women* 11(3): 353–73

Fries, Rebecca and Stephanie Finigan (2014) 'Women's economic leadership in LAC, book 3: prevention of violence against women in the context of programmes', *A Training Pack*, Oxford: Oxfam Great Britain and Value for Women, available at http://policy-practice.oxfam.org.uk/publications/womens-economic-leadership-in-lac-book-3-prevention-of-violence-against-women-i-344039 (last checked by the authors 23 June 2015)

García Aísa, Martina (2014) 'Conditional cash transfers and intimate partner violence among Mexican couples: the impact of oportunidades on psychological abuse prevalence', Master's Degree Thesis, Lund University, available at http://lup.lub.lu.se/luur/download?func=downloadFile&recordOId=4499414&fileOId=4499425 (last checked by the authors 23 June 2015)

Goetz, Anne Marie and Rina Sen Gupta (1996) 'Who takes the credit? Gender, power, and control over loan use in rural credit programs in Bangladesh', *World Development* 24(1): 45–63

Haile, Hirut Bekele, Bettina Bock, and Henk Folmer (2012) 'Microfinance and female empowerment: do institutions matter?', *Women's Studies International Forum* 35: 256–65

Haneef, Christina, Stuart Kenward, Muhammad Maksudul Hannan, Mohammad Mizanur Rahman, and Tarit Mohan Halder (2014) 'CLP's influence on dowry and violence against women on the chars', Chars Livelihood Programmes, available at http://clp-bangladesh.org/wp-content/uploads/2014/10/2014-10-13b-CLPs-influence-on-dowry-and-violence-against-women-on-the-chars_final1.pdf (last checked by the authors 23 June 2015)

Hashemi, Syed M., Sidney Ruth Schuler, and Ann P. Riley (1996) 'Rural credit programs and women's empowerment in Bangladesh', *World Development* 24(4): 635–53, available at http://siteresources.worldbank.org/INTEMPOWERMENT/Resources/13314_hashemi_etal.pdf (last checked by the authors 23 June 2015)

Heath, Rachel (2014) 'Women's access to labor market opportunities, control of household resources, and domestic violence: evidence from Bangladesh', *World Development* 57: 32–46, available at http://faculty.washington.edu/rmheath/dvpaper_Heath.pdf (last checked by the authors 23 June 2015)

Heise, Lori L. (1998) 'Violence against women: an integrated, ecological framework', *Violence against Women* 4(3): 262–90, available at http://gbvaor.net/wp-content/uploads/sites/3/2012/10/Violence-Against-Women-An-Integrated-Ecological-Framework-Heise-1998.pdf (last checked by the authors 23 June 2015)

Heise, Lori L. (2011) 'What works to prevent partner violence: an evidence overview', Working Paper, available at http://www.oecd.org/derec/49872444.pdf (last checked by the authors 23 June 2015)

Hidrobo, Melissa and Lia Fernald (2013) 'Cash transfers and domestic violence', *Journal of Health, Economics* 32(1): 304–19

Hidrobo, Melissa, Amber Peterman, and Lori Heise (2013) 'The effect of cash, vouchers and food transfers on intimate partner violence: evidence from a randomized experiment in Northern Ecuador', Working Paper, available at https://www.wfp.org/sites/default/files/IPV-Hidrobo-Peterman_Heise_IPV%20Ecuador%203%2028%2014.pdf (last checked by the authors 23 June 2015)

Jewkes, Rachel (2002) 'Intimate partner violence: causes and prevention', *The Lancet* 359 (9315): 1423–29, available at http://www.ayamm.org/english/Violence%20against%20 women%201.pdf (last checked by the authors 23 June 2015)

Kabeer, Naila (1994) *Reversed Realities: Gender Hierarchies in Development Thought*, Brooklyn: Verso

Kabeer, Naila (1997) *'Can Buy Me Love'? Re-evaluating the Empowerment Potential of Loans to Women in Rural Bangladesh*, IDS discussion paper 363. Sussex: Institute for Development Studies, available at http://www.ids.ac.uk/files/Dp363.pdf (last checked by the authors 23 June 2015)

Kabeer, Naila (2001) 'Conflicts over credit: re-evaluating the empowerment potential of loans to women in rural Bangladesh', *World Development* 29(1): 63–84

Kabeer, Naila (2014) 'Violence against women as "relational" vulnerability: engendering the sustainable human development agenda', Occasional Paper, available at http://hdr.undp.org/sites/default/files/kabeer_hdr14.pdf (last checked by the authors 23 June 2015)

Kim, Julia C., Charlotte H. Watts, James R. Hargreaves, Luceth X. Ndhlovu, Godfrey Phetla, Linda A. Morison, Joanna Busza, John D.H. Porter, and Paul Pronyk (2007) 'Understanding the impact of a microfinance-based intervention on women's empowerment and the reduction of intimate partner violence in South Africa', *American Journal of Public Health* 97(10): 1794–1802, available at http://www.ncbi.nlm.nih.gov/pmc/articles/PMC1994170/ (last checked by the authors 23 June 2015)

Klugman, Jeni, Lucia Hanmer, Sarah Twigg, Tazeen Hasan, Jennifer McCleary-Sills, and Julieth Santamaria (2014) *Voice and Agency: Empowering Women and Girls for Shared Prosperity*, Washington, DC: International Bank for Reconstruction and Development / The World Bank, available at https://openknowledge.worldbank.org/bitstream/handle/10986/19036/9781464803598.pdf?sequence=5 (last checked by the authors 23 June 2015)

Koenig, Michael A., Saifuddin Ahmed, Mian Bazle Hossain, and A.B.M. Khorshed Alam Mozumder (2003) 'Women's status and domestic violence in rural Bangladesh: individual- and community-level effects', *Demography* 40(2): 269–88, available at ib. scnu.edu.cn/ngw/ngw/xwbk/Women%A1%AFs%20status%20and%20domestic%20violence%20in%20 rural%20Bangladesh%20Individual%20and%20community%20level%20 effects. pdf (last checked by the authors 23 June 2015)

Krishnan, Suneeta, Corinne H. Rocca, Alan E. Hubbard, Kalyani Subbiah, Jeffrey Edmeades, and Nancy S. Padian (2010) 'Do changes in spousal employment status lead to domestic violence? Insights from a prospective study in Bangalore, India', *Social Science & Medicine* 70(1): 136–43, available at http://www.ncbi.nlm.nih.gov/pmc/articles/PMC2791993/ (last checked by the authors 23 June 2015)

Kulkarni, Vani (2011) *Women's Empowerment and Microfinance: An Asian perspective study*. Occasional Paper 13, Knowledge for development effectiveness. Rome: International Fund for Agricultural Development, available at http://www.ifad.org/operations/projects/regions/pi/paper/13.pdf (last checked by the authors 23 June 2015)

Macmillan, Ross and Rosemary Gartner (1999) 'When she brings home the Bacon: labor-force participation and the risk of spousal violence against women', *Journal of Marriage and Family* 61(4): 947–58

Morcillo-Espina, Álvaro (2014) 'The Case of the Women's Economic Empowerment (WEE) in Agriculture Knowledge Hub: Key Points to Maximize Value for Programme Teams' Oxfam Internal Document

Oxfam International (2013) *The Power of People against Poverty: Oxfam Strategic Plan, 2013–2019*, Oxford: Oxfam International Secretariat, available at https://www.oxfam.org/sites/ www.oxfam.org/files/file_attachments/story/ oxfam-strategic-plan-2013-2019_0.pdf (last checked by the authors 23 June 2015)

Panda, Pradeep, Jayoti Gupa, Indika Bulankulame, Nandita Bhatla, Swati Chakraborty, and Nata Duvvury (2006) *Property Ownership and Inheritance Rights of Women for Social Protection – The South Asia Experience: Synthesis Report of Three Studies*, Washington, DC: International Centre for Research on Women, available at http://www.icrw.org/files/publications/Property-Ownership-and-Inheritance-Rights-of-Women-for-Social-Protection-The-South-Asia-Experience.pdf (last checked by the authors 23 June 2015)

Perova, Elizaveta (2010) 'Three Essays on Intended and Not Intended Impacts of Conditional Cash Transfers', Doctoral Dissertation, University of California, Berkeley, available at http://gradworks.umi.com/34/49/3449054.html (last checked by the authors 23 June 2015)

Raab, Michaela (2012) 'Ending Violence against Women: A Guide for Oxfam Staff', Oxfam International, available at http://www.oxfam.org/sites/www.oxfam.org/files/ending-violence-against-women-oxfam-guide-nov2012.pdf (last checked by the authors 23 June 2015)

Rahman, Aminur (1999) 'Micro-credit initiatives for equitable and sustainable development: who pays?' *World Development* 27(1): 67–82, available at http://www.academia.edu/8324940/Microcredit_initiatives_for_equitable_and_sustainable_development_Who_pays (last checked by the authors 23 June 2015)

Reference Group, Women's Economic Empowerment (WEE) in Agriculture Knowledge Hub (2014) 'Definition of Women's Economic Empowerment', Internal Oxfam document

Rosche, Daniela (2014) 'Close the gap: how to eliminate violence against women beyond 2015', Briefing Note, available at http://www.oxfam.org/sites/www.oxfam.org/files/file_attachments/bn-close-gap-violence-women-2015-110314-en_0_0.pdf (last checked by the authors 23 June 2015)

Schuler, Sidney Ruth, Syed Hashemi, Ann P. Riley, and Shireen Akhter (1996) 'Credit programs, patriarchy and men's violence against women in rural Bangladesh', *Social Science & Medicine* 43(12): 1729–42

Sen, Purna (1999) 'Enhancing women's choices in responding to domestic violence in Calcutta: a comparison of employment and education', *The European Journal of Development Research* 11(2): 65–86

Swaminathan, Hema, Kimberly Ashburn, Aslihan Kes, Nata Duvvury, Cherryl Walker, Michael Aliber, Busi Nkosi, Margaret A. Rugadya, and Kamusiime Herbert (2008) 'Women's Property Rights, HIV and AIDS and Domestic Violence: Research Findings from Two Rural Districts in South Africa and Uganda', Report, available at http://www.hivhousingsummit.org/

BriefingBook/FactSheetsAndReports/International%20Center%20for%20 Research%20on%20Women_Womens%20Property%20Rights%20HIV%20 and%20AIDS%20and%20Domestic%20Violence.pdf (last checked by the authors 23 June 2015)

UN Women and United Nations Human Rights Office of the High Commissioner (OCHCR) (2013) *Realizing Women's Rights to Land and Other Productive Resources*, New York: United Nations, available at http://www. ohchr.org/documents/publications/realizingwomensrightstoland.pdf (last checked by the authors 23 June 2015)

UNESCAP (United Nations Economic and Social Commission for Asia and the Pacific) (2007) *Economic and Social Survey: Asia and the Pacific 2007*, New York: UNESCAP, available at http://www.unescap.org/resources/economic-and-social-survey-asia-and-pacific-2007 (last checked by the authors 23 June 2015)

United Nations (1993) 'Declaration on the Elimination of Violence against Women', UN Declaration, available at http://www.un.org/documents/ga/ res/48/a48r104.htm (last checked by the authors 23 June 2015)

United Nations (2014) 'The Millennium Development Goals Report of 2014', New York: United Nations, available at http://www.un.org/millenni-umgoals/2014%20MDG%20report/MDG%202014%20English%20web.pdf (last checked by the authors 23 June 2015)

Vyas, Seema (2013) 'Estimating the association between women's earnings and partner violence: evidence from the 2008–2009 Tanzania national panel survey', *Women's Voice, Agency, & Participation Research Series* No.2, available at http://www-wds.worldbank.org/external/default/WDSContentServer/ WDSP/IB/2013/11/07/000456286_20131107124736/Rendered/PDF/82535 0WP0Estim0379862B00PUBLIC0.pdf.pdf (last checked by the authors 23 June 2015)

Vyas, Seema and Charlotte Watts (2009) 'How does economic empower-ment affect women's' risk of intimate partners violence in low and middle income countries? A systematic review of published evidence', *Journal of International Development* 21: 577–602

Wakefield, Shawna (2014) 'The G20 and gender equality', Oxfam Briefing Paper 183, Oxford: Oxfam Great Britain, available at http://www.oxfam. org/sites/www.oxfam.org/files/file_attachments/the_g20_and_gender_ equality_en.pdf (last checked by the authors 23 June 2015)

World Bank / International Bank for Reconstruction and Development (2011) 'World Development Report 2012: Gender, Equality and Development', available at http://siteresources.worldbank.org/INTWDR2012/Resour ces/7778105-1299699968583/7786210-1315936222006/Complete-Report. pdf (last checked by the authors 23 June 2015)

World Health Organization (2013) 'WHO Global and Regional Estimates of Violence against Women: Prevalence and Health Effects of Intimate Partner Violence and Non-partner Sexual Violence', Geneva: World Health Organization, available at http://apps.who.int/iris/bitstr eam/10665/85239/1/9789241564625_eng.pdf (last checked by the authors 23 June 2015)

World Vision Australia (2011) 'Tackling Gender-based Violence by Empowering Women', *Case Study*, available at http://www.svri.org/CaseStudyGBV.pdf (last checked by the authors 23 June 2015)

About the Authors

Christine Hughes is Women's Rights Knowledge Specialist. Email: christine.hughes@oxfam.ca
Mara Bolis is Associate Director, Women's Economic Empowerment, Oxfam America. Email: MBolis@OxfamAmerica.org
Rebecca Fries is Director, Value for Women, Mexico. Email: rfries@v4w.org
Stephanie Finigan is Director of Operations, Prosperity Catalyst. Email: stephanie@prosperitycatalyst.org

CHAPTER 8

The food insecurity–obesity paradox as a vicious cycle for women: inequalities and health

Andrea S. Papan and Barbara Clow

Abstract

Poverty and income inequality undermine women's health in a myriad of ways. This chapter discusses findings from the Full Plate Project, which addressed women's experience of food security, obesity, and chronic disease in Atlantic Canada. Through first-hand accounts, it identifies a vicious cycle surrounding the food insecurity–obesity paradox. The cycle's core elements included experiences of poverty, food insecurity and nutritional deprivation, weight gain leading to obesity, stress, and experiences of chronic illness. These mainly qualitative findings provide a vivid and multi-layered analysis of the effects of inequalities on health. A majority of Full Plate participants were lone mothers and unattached women, and existing outside of a two-adult member household framework. The vicious cycles experienced are intertwined and cannot be addressed by compartmentalising elements of health or social services. Evidence indicates that policies must respond fully to the social determinants of health and multiple inequalities related to poverty, gender, age, mobility, disability, location, culture, coping skills, and other dynamics.

Keywords: gender; women; food insecurity; obesity; poverty; chronic disease

Introduction

But the way it is right now, you don't have enough money for food, and that's the reason why a majority of the people have a lot of health problems? They're sick, they're stressed. They're worrying because when you don't have adequate food, and healthy and balanced food on the table for your family, then the stress, the illness sets in. And yes, the weight is up and down. It fluctuates. Because if you don't have the proper food, then you're going to plan a meal that, as long as a child or yourself has something to eat and is going to fill your stomach but [it] is not always the best meal, so then you gain all this weight and you start having all kinds of health problems. And then before, back to what this lady's saying, you can't sleep at night because it's all different issues that take place, and it goes back again to how you are eating …. And because we don't eat healthy, we end up with all these health

http://dx.doi.org/10.3362/9781780447278.008

problems. And before you know it, people are chronic sick? And then before you know it, your body is just deteriorating because you haven't had the proper food from the beginning. And we're not saying that you have to have a lot of money, but you need enough money that's going to be standard with the cost of living, so that you can go to the grocery store and you can buy groceries. You can come home and you can plan a healthy meal.

This chapter examines the effects of inequalities on women's health in relation to food security, obesity, and chronic disease for predominantly female headed households in Atlantic Canada. Through first-hand accounts, it identifies a vicious cycle surrounding the food insecurity–obesity paradox. William H. Dietz (1995) was the first to recognise that 'because obesity connotes excessive energy intake, and hunger reflects an inadequate food supply, the increased prevalence of obesity and hunger in the same population seems paradoxical' (766). As outlined by the participant above, the cycle's core elements include experiences of poverty, food insecurity and nutritional deprivation, weight gain leading to obesity, stress, and experiences of chronic illness.

The chapter summarises findings from the Full Plate Project on Women, Obesity and Food Security,[1] which aimed to investigate the food insecurity–obesity paradox. We were intrigued with the question of moderate food insecurity[2] being linked to overweight rather than low body weight, and that this was the case only for women. This type of food insecurity is at the other end of the malnutrition scale. In other words, if food insecurity is typically associated with hunger and low body weight, this paradox is concerned with the link between moderate food insecurity, nutritional deprivation, and obesity.

This chapter starts by exploring synergies between the key areas of this research case of women in Atlantic Canada, and global transitions in nutrition and dietary patterns; the growth of health inequalities, especially with regard to obesity and chronic disease; and the effects of intra-household inequality and 'fall-back positions' on food consumption and food security. An explanation of research methods used, and the role of community-based organisations in the project process, are also discussed. Findings and analysis on five areas of participants' experiences relating to: (1) poverty; (2) gaining access to sufficient, nutritious, socially acceptable food; (3) linkages to food insecurity, obesity, and chronic diseases; (4) gendered constructs of maternal deprivation, that is, eating less and last; and (5) experiences of social isolation, vulnerability, stress as well as experiences they identified as 'dark times' and depression are examined. The last section offers conclusions.

Nutrition transitions, health inequalities, and 'fall-back positions'

You have no control. You have to buy what is close to what you think is nutritional or do without. That's the truth. (Participant)
The social determinants of health are the circumstances in which people are born, grow up, live, work and age, and the systems put in place to deal with

illness. These circumstances are in turn shaped by a wider set of forces: economics, social policies, and politics. (WHO 2013b, 1)

From a global perspective, research on 'nutrition transitions' (Hansford 2010) in which accelerated shifts in dietary patterns (due to an increase in energy dense, but nutrient poor foods) and reductions in physical activity (due to factors including urbanisation, technological, economic changes) have led to rises in overweight and obesity in low- and middle-income countries is of particular relevance. Barry Popkin *et al.* (2012) write that:

> *[t]he general impression has been that in higher-income countries we often find greater obesity rates in rural areas and among the poor – the reverse of what is seen in lower-income countries. However, new evidence suggests that these patterns are changing, and the increasing rate of obesity among the poor has important implications for the distribution of health inequalities. (Popkin et al. 2012, 2)*

The World Health Organization (WHO) identifies a 'double burden' of disease in which '[i]t is not uncommon to find under-nutrition and obesity existing side-by-side within the same country, the same community and the same household' (WHO 2015, 1). This is in keeping with research by Adam Drewnowski and Petra Eicheldoefer: 'Obesity-promoting foods are – in a word – cheap, whereas foods that may stem the obesity epidemic are likely to be more expensive. Choosing healthful versus unhealthful food is an economic decision, especially for people with limited resources' (Drewnowski and Eichelsdoerfer 2010, 728).

Globally, nearly three-quarters of chronic disease or non-communicable disease (NCD) deaths occur in low- and middle-income countries (WHO 2015). Obesity is associated with a number of health conditions or morbidities including incidence of type 2 diabetes, asthma, gallbladder disease, osteoarthritis, chronic back pain, several types of cancers (colorectal, kidney, breast, endometrial, ovarian, and pancreatic cancers) and major types of cardiovascular disease (hypertension, stroke, congestive heart failure, and coronary artery disease) (PHAC and CIHI 2011). Moreover, with regard to maternal and newborn health, other risks may include gestational diabetes (GDM), preeclampsia, pregnancy-induced hypertension, or stillbirths (WHO 2013a, 3).

The WHO (2011) asserts: 'Issues such as whether households get enough food, how it is distributed within the household and whether that food fulfils the nutrition needs of all members of the household show that food security is clearly linked to health'. In the US, Europe, and Australia, studies have consistently shown that for women the risk of obesity is 20 per cent to 40 per cent higher among individuals who are food insecure (Burns 2004, 15). An intra-household inequalities lens provides strong challenges to a household unity that models a behaviour of equal consumption (Lise and Seitz 2011) and equitable sharing of resources between two adults. For our research, intra-household inequalities were visible. Participants noted expectations of greater food allocations from their male partners. Also, as detailed in our findings, many women expressed experiences of what can be described as 'maternal deprivation', 'in which mothers sacrifice their intake so that their children will be less affected' (Dinour *et al.* 2007, 1956). Canada still has not introduced universal, affordable, quality childcare, a key social policy important to sharing care responsibilities in two-adult households as well as in alleviating the poverty of lone mothers (CCPA 2014). However, as our chapter primarily focuses on female headed households, and includes participants who were unattached women living alone and lone mothers, elements of 'bargaining power' and/ or 'fall-back position' as they relate to women 'whether directly through welfare benefits and divorce settlements, or enabling them to realise their labour market potential' (de Henau and Himmelweit 2013, 6) were proven key in shaping dimensions that extended beyond the intra-household lens. As one participant asserted:

> *My husband and I have been separated for 14 years and all I've been doing is falling in between the cracks .... I've asked four times [for a divorce] and the answer was no, because of control issues, I imagine, ah.*

Some of the highest rates of food insecurity for females are experienced by those living as a lone parent with a child or children, or living alone. CCHS collected in 2007/2008 found food insecurity was twice as likely among households led by female lone parents, and four times that of households led by couples. The prevalence of severe food insecurity in households led by female lone parents was six times that led by couples (Health Canada 2010, 1). Brandi Franklin *et al.* (2011) in their review of 19 studies on the food insecurity–obesity paradox, confirmed that 'low-income, ethnic minority, and female-headed households exhibit the greatest risk for food insecurity, which often results in higher prevalence of diet-related disease' (1). In Canada, 'women's poverty continues to be concentrated in populations of women who face systemic barriers of discrimination and colonial legacies as well as unaddressed social policy gaps' (CCPA 2014, 18).

Research methods

The Full Plate Project was co-ordinated by the Atlantic Centre of Excellence for Women's Health, which, until its closure in 2013 due to federal government budget cuts, was funded by Health Canada through the Women's Health Contribution Program. The project took approximately 18 months, involved six focus groups conducted between November 2011 and February 2012 in the four Atlantic Canadian provinces, New Brunswick (NB), Newfoundland and Labrador (NL), Nova Scotia (NS), and Prince Edward Island (PEI), and included Aboriginal women, bilingual Franco-phone women, and those living in urban, rural, and/or remote locales. Atlantic provinces have some of the highest rates of food insecurity in Canada. Similar to other countries in the global North and global South, in Canada wealth inequality plays a significant role in the social and economic determinants of health. Historically, this region has been identified as the so-called 'have-not' provinces or provinces that receive equal-isation payments from the federal government, and Canada-wide, only 3.4 per cent of the top 1 per cent of tax filers combined are found in the Atlantic region. As Christine Saulnier (2013) explains, within the region itself, wealth is also unevenly distributed: 'To be in the 1 per cent in Atlantic Canada, you need to have an income of at least $151,900 [US$151,105], with an average income of $259,300 [US$257,943]. The average income of the bottom 90 per cent of tax filers in contrast is $26,700 [US$26,560]' (CCPA, 30 January 2013).

This research project was supported by an Advisory Committee, which comprised representatives from all four provinces, and included provincial food security networks, government departments of health, community-based organisations, researchers, and poverty and social justice organisations. Prior to conducting the study, ethical approval was received from the Dalhousie University Health Sciences Research Ethics Board. The Advisory Committee provided input and feedback on the research design and members were, together with associated community-based partners, the local contacts for logistical co-ordination and participant recruitment. A monetary honorarium and reimbursements for transportation and/or childcare were offered to all participants.

Participants had to satisfy four criteria to be included: self-identify as a woman, be at least 18 years old, have self-reported weight and height that resulted in a Body Mass Index (BMI) over 25, indicating overweight or obesity, and identify as being food insecure based on a positive response to either one of two food security screening questions. These were: (1) *In the past 12 months, have you worried that you would not be able to access sufficient, nutritious and personally acceptable food through normal food channels?* (2) *In the past 12 months, have you been unable to obtain sufficient, nutritious and personally acceptable food through normal food channels?* While participants self-identified as experiencing food insecurity and weight challenges, local organisations played a key role in recruitment. We found that participants who were already part of a community-based programme were more likely to become involved in the project because they trusted the host organisation, which could address any apprehensions by introducing the researchers, explaining more about the focus groups, and bridging the process for us.

The Full Plate Project used three methods to collect data and gather insights: a demographic questionnaire, a food security questionnaire, and six focus groups. Twenty-seven participants took part in the Full Plate Project. For all but two of the participants who were lower, each woman's BMI was measured at 30 or above (classifying in the obese range) based on self-reported height and weight information. The average age of participants was 51–52 years old; the age range was 26–73.

The majority of women involved were living in poverty, located in the lowest income quintile of Canadian society. Eighty-one per cent of partici-pants surveyed had children, and one-third were lone mothers, and 41 per cent of participants identified as unattached/living alone. Two-thirds of participants reported an annual household income of less than CA$15,000 or US$14,530 and the balance of those surveyed reported an income ranging from CA$15,000 to CA$24,999 or the equivalent of US $14,530 to US$24,200, notably lower than the 91 per cent of tax filers above.

Income sources varied among Full Plate Project participants. Over half (55 per cent) were receiving income support through social assistance. In addition, nearly one-quarter noted income from pension (22 per cent), and child tax benefit (22 per cent). Others cited disability benefits (15 per cent), employment insurance (11 per cent), old age security (4 per cent) as well as savings (4 per cent), friends (7 per cent), and room rental (7 per cent). Fifteen per cent of those surveyed worked part-time and indicated income from wages or salary. Eighty-five per cent of those surveyed did not do paid work. The highest level of formal education for 41 per cent of those surveyed was high school; 15 per cent had less than high school; 37 per cent had some post-secondary, some vocational, or some trade school; and 22 per cent surveyed had some graduate or post-graduate training.

The food security questionnaire completed by participants included questions from the Canadian Community Health Survey (CCHS) (Cycle 2.2, Nutrition, 2004 and Cycle 3.1, 2005) and the First Nations Regional Longitudinal Health Survey (RHS) (Adult Questionnaire, 2008), to gauge the degree of food insecurity they had experienced in the preceding 12 months. Ninety-three per cent of participants indicated that they often (52 per cent) or sometimes (41 per cent) could not afford to eat balanced meals. Two-thirds (67 per cent) of participants responded that they had enough, but not always the kinds of food they wanted to eat; 15 per cent said sometimes they did not have enough to eat, and the remaining 15 per cent said they often did not have enough to eat. In response to the question, *'Do you or other household members worry that food would run out before you got money to buy more?'*, 37 per cent said this was often true, and a further 48 per cent said this was sometimes true. In response to the statement: *'The food we bought just didn't last, or there wasn't any money to get more'*, 30 per cent said this was often true, and 48 per cent said it was sometimes true.

The focus group discussions were extremely rich. Our study focused heavily on the opportunity to hear from and document what food insecure women living with weight challenges had to say. Premised on feminist, Indigenous and participatory methodological frameworks, this paper uses multiple quotations from focus groups to give space to a diversity of women's narratives. In the sections which follow, all quotations come from the participants. The women who participated were open, willing to discuss all the questions asked, and had very thorough knowledge of and ability to express what food insecurity meant to them and how it had affected their weight and health. The direct feedback from participants to us and to our partners was excellent and many noted 'relief', being 'thankful for having the chance to talk about these issues', and even 'a sense of release' in having a chance to discuss their obstacles and coping strategies in detail. The participants framed their comments, experiences, and potential solutions within the context of living in poverty (i.e. an increased income would make things better). When participants began to assess their experiences with a health lens, in particular by observing their experiences with food insecurity as something that had negatively affected their health, this opened up the discussion and allowed for new dialogues to be included, in turn, peeling back layers and revealing some valuable insights. Even for us as researchers the overlaps between obesity, poverty, and food insecurity were at times blurred; discussions with participants moved readily between discourses framed around health to those framed around poverty to those again framed by other dimensions. It became clear very quickly during the project that the concepts we were looking at were extremely fluid, and required flexibility in data collection and data analysis.

Findings from the project

Participants' stories reveal the food insecurity–obesity paradox as a vicious cycle for women. Figure 1 captures this in graphic form. The diagram is purposely off-centre and asymmetrical, to suggest the varying experiences of participants; yet, throughout the interviews, the core elements remained the same. These included experiences of poverty, often in childhood, as well as adulthood; food insecurity and nutritional deprivation caused by an inability to purchase healthy foods; weight gain in the context of food insecurity, eventually becoming obesity; ongoing and increasing stress due to a myriad of factors, including lone parenting and social isolation; reduction in well-being; and experiences of chronic illness.

Figure 1 Food insecurity–obesity paradox as a vicious cycle for women

Five key themes emerged from the focus group discussions: (1) poverty; (2) gaining access to sufficient, nutritious, socially acceptable food; (3) linkages to food insecurity, obesity, and chronic diseases; (4) gendered constructs of maternal deprivation: eating less and last; and (5) experiences of social isolation, vulnerability, stress, dark times, and depression.

Poverty

The choices of participants regarding food and nutrition were frequently embedded in poverty. When asked about the connection between food insecurity and their weight challenges, one participant stated succinctly: '*We don't have enough money to buy healthy food*'. Another participant agreed, stating: '*When I go to the grocery store, I only have "x" amount to spend … when that's spent, there's no more money to spend*'. When asked what key changes they would prioritise to address these issues, a respondent answered firmly: '*Cost of food. Well that would be the number one factor*'. Another respondent quickly added on behalf of the rest of the group members: '*That would be the number one factor from the whole group*'.

According to another research project, the Nova Scotia Participatory Food Costing Project, 'having an adequate income to purchase a healthy diet is the most important factor in determining food security' (Williams 2009, 9). In Nova Scotia, using the National Nutritious Food Basket (NNFB) as a standardised food costing tool,

> *a basic nutritious diet for a female led lone parent household with three children between the ages of 7 and 12 years costs … would have a deficit of at least $393.49 each month, assuming the family is receiving full transportation and childcare allowances. (Williams 2009, 12)*

What is important to understand about the NNFB and the deficit mentioned above is that 'in this household there would be no money to spare for out of pocket healthcare expenses, food purchased outside the home, costs associated with physical activities and recreation, education expenses, emergencies or savings for unexpected expenses' (Williams 2009, 12). Participants in our own study talked about the challenge of deciding where food costs should come in a long list of household expenses. One participant broke down her spending, and laid out how she prioritised and calculated her food choices:

> *So I know that when I only had the two [hundred and] eighty-five and I paid two [hundred and] sixty for rent, and I only had twenty-five dollars to buy food and whatever else I needed, well, guess what came first? Toilet paper, shampoo. Forget the food. I didn't have any money for food. I did go, sometimes I had a few bucks left to go and buy Mr. Noodles at the Dollar Store, because then there was like, six for a buck. Okay? So if you had five bucks, that's thirty. At least one meal a day.*

Participants framed their choices in terms of a 'rock and a hard place', whereby the balance between two options was determined according to which was less likely to do immediate harm. One participant put this way:

> *So it's like, people make choices. Medicines or food.*

> *(Participant 1) Because what we really need is the cost of living lined up with the amount of the cost that we're living with today. And if they done that then people would have enough money for their food, and for their medical, and for transportation.*

> *(Participant 2, strongly agreeing)* Wouldn't that be a miracle!

These findings and those of the next sections support Valerie Tarasuk *et al.*'s (2007) argument:

> *The declines in intake in women experiencing moderate or severe food insecurity suggests that they live tenuously in need of their next income infusion. Anything that threatens those funds, or the use of those funds for food purchases, must threaten their nutritional health. (1986)*

Reliance on irregular and low income or social support payments leads to irregular patterns of consumption. Women in poverty are prone to developing disordered eating patterns (Sarlio-Lähteenkorva and Lahelma 2001), such as bingeing and fasting. In this way, patterns of distribution of social assistance shape women's spending power and food choices.

Gaining access to sufficient, nutritious, socially acceptable food

Participants were asked what they ate, and where they got their food. Their feedback clustered into at least three themes: firstly, participants' limited ability to buy food staples, and some of the strategies they used to try to purchase them; secondly, the accessibility of food, especially relating to food deserts, transportation, and mobility; and, thirdly, their experience with food banks and other charitable food programmes.

Participants talked repeatedly about increasing food costs and price hikes in food staples, such as bread, milk, and meat. These were due to a variety of 'macro, sector and domestic drivers' such as currency shifts, trade environments, retail distribution as well as climate change (Charlebois *et al.* 2015, 6).

One participant explained the impasse she faced when selecting food:

> *They say eat fruits and vegetables – have you seen the price of them? Unless you have a garden and you grow it, it's virtually impossible to do. So you're eating all of the unhealthy things just to stay alive, and the healthy things go, well, that's just a luxury that, that's for someone else. But you just can't do it.*

Many participants outlined intricate strategies for survival. They talked about the exact use of their money and how to get the best bargains at multiple stores including buying less nutritious items, or products close to or past their expiry date, co-ordinating purchases with neighbours and friends, participating in community gardens, skipping meals, and sharing meals. One person described some of her strategies:

> But I buy a lot of stuff that's reduced for clearance or on half-price. I don't buy fresh fruit because it's just too expensive, so I'll buy like the canned fruit, and again, the heavy syrups and all that, but I can divide that up and make it last a little longer .... But lots of rice, lots of macaroni, ground beef is the biggest staple. If I have a piece of chicken, it's like a big celebration at my house. So if I have a chicken breast, going in with rice or whatever, I dice it up so small just so you get a little bit. And same if I make a stew, the beef is so small you can barely see it, but at least that way I know there's something's going in it, but.

A second issue discussed was accessibility and availability of food. In particular, participants talked about a lack of proximity to healthy food and/or grocery stores. Many people living in poverty live in so-called 'food deserts' – that is, urban neighbourhoods with low household income that do not have nearby grocery stores, or remote areas where fresh food is not easily accessible or affordable. As a result, residents may be forced to rely more often on the food available at convenience stores, which tends to be packaged, processed, sodium-rich, and energy-dense, or to visit fast-food restaurants (Larsen and Gilliland 2008). This problem is made worse by the absence of affordable, reliable transportation. One participant discussed the impact of her mobility challenges with regard to obtaining food:

> Costs ten bucks to get there, ten bucks to go home, that's twenty bucks that I can't spend on groceries because I've got to spend it on a cab because I can't walk that distance. Because of my weight, because of my mobility issues, I just can't do it.

A third issue participants talked about was their experience with food banks or other charitable food programmes. In 2010, Food Banks Canada reported that '[o]ver the last two years, food bank use in Canada has risen by 28% – an unprecedented rate of growth' (Food Banks Canada 2010, 2). A 'large percentage of those needing support (40%) [were] single-person households, many of them counting social assistance as their primary source of income' (Food Banks Canada 2010, 1).

In practical terms, focus group participants' experiences of charitable food programmes were mixed. They were appreciative of the added food resources, and (in the instance of soup kitchens) the chance to socialise with others. However, some participants highlighted distinct and significant concerns. These included poor food quality and freshness, and limited types of healthy food available, particularly to individuals without children. Foods are often high in carbohydrates and/or sodium, and inconsistent distribution of vegetables, fruits, and proteins, especially to users without children. Participants also talked about feeling a sense of stigma or embarrassment associated with going to food banks.

Comments from many participants detailed their frustrations with having to depend on charitable food programmes in a wealthy nation like Canada. One participant voiced her concerns:

> *And the stigma – going to the food bank is an awful stigma in itself. Standing out there in a line and having somebody determine when you're poor .... This is ridiculous. Me and my friend go to university, we've discussed this a hundred times. There should not be, in a country like Canada, food banks. There should be enough food for everybody.*

Links between food insecurity, obesity, and chronic diseases

For participants, the challenge of affording and being able to prioritise healthy food that would aid in conventional weight loss or maintenance strategies was a central obstacle. This is a particularly important and interesting finding, since the discourse around the food insecurity–obesity paradox is grounded in conventional understandings of obesity as an imbalance of energy intake and expenditure. In their chapter, 'The economics of obesity: why are poor people fat?', Drewnowski and Eicheldoefer bring attention to a dynamic that we witnessed in our research: health promotion literature generally emphasises the psychosocial aspects of food selection, and 'underlying this is the unspoken middle-class premise' (Drewnowski and Eichelsdoerfer 2010, 729) on building awareness and motivation among obese individuals to make better choices. As they put it, 'Consideration of food prices and diet costs has been notably absent from the research literature' (Drewnowski and Eichelsdoerfer 2010, 729).

In conversation, participants frequently identified a 'catch-22' in relation to knowing how to choose better food options, but being unable to do so due to cost.

> *Participant 1: It's the type of food that you're eating that's causing your overweight. Starchy food.*

> *Participant 2: Chips and pop .... You can get a bottle of pop for ninety-nine cents, two-litres. How much are you paying for two litres of milk?*

> *Participant 3: Three eighty-nine.*

Moreover, being able to maintain and regulate diets and plan meals play a fundamental role in disease management (Terrell 2009, S3-3), with one woman stating clearly: 'Personally, my fear is if I don't gain control of my eating is that I will be dealing with diabetes'.

Many participants were exasperated by the lack of understanding from health care providers. One woman discussed her experience with her doctor and the presumption that she must be seemingly making 'bad choices':

> *And I have diabetes and I have heart trouble, and I have asthma, and I have high cholesterol. I mean, they tell you to have these fruit and vegetables but I*

*can't afford them! I can just barely afford eggs sometimes. After I pay every-
thing, and the light bill, there's nothing left! They tell you this and that, and
how easy it is. You go to the doctor, [who says:] 'Oh it's really easy to keep your
sugar down' and this and that, but everything without sugar in costs more!
And the fruits and vegetables cost more. And they just tell you: 'Well, you must
be drinking'. I don't drink and I don't smoke. And I live in a very tiny, tiny,
tiny, small apartment. And I still have to pay my light bill. And I have to eat.
And there's not much left.*

Gendered constructs of maternal deprivation: eating less and last

As Molly Martin and Adam Lippert (2012) observe:

*[F]ood insecurity is a 'managed process', meaning that families strategize and
diligently work to avoid hunger. That responsibility, however, falls more heavily on women given the traditional discourses about family life and 'women's
work' that place greater expectations on women for feeding and nurturing their
family, especially when children are present. (1754)*

In our discussions, many participants spoke intensely about prioritising their
child or children's needs and about their willingness to sacrifice their food
intake. Participants' comments repeated the same sentiment over and over
again:

*I feed them and then I eat. It's just that, you know what I mean, I just make
sure. I mean, they're more important than I am.*

I feed my daughter first.

In my house, it goes youngest to oldest.

When discussing their compromises, participants also seemed to mask some
of the discomfort by making light of the issue, frequently laughing or joking.
One participant remarked how her male partner prioritised food distribution
differently. Intra-household dynamics were evident as participants stated that
gender norms about men as household heads and main breadwinners might
be invoked to justify men eating before children:

*Participant 1: Always my children. Make sure they were looked after there. I
think everybody [reckons] God made women especially with a different kind of
an instinct than he gave to men. Participant 2: Men will eat first before their
[children].*

*Participant 1: Yeah. They think they should be, even after they have children
of their own, they think that they should be the first ones. Oh no. See the
children get fed first. You'll get fed afterwards. So he thought because he was
the head of the household and he was the bread-winner – well we were both
bread-winners, but – because he was the head of the household, he should get*

fed first and the children could eat [after]. No, no, you don't! These children, God only gives you your children for a very short time. They're a gift. And you look after them first.

One other parent talked about balancing her needs as a diabetic with those of her son, who is also a diabetic:

I'm diabetic. My son is diabetic. And I just can't go out and afford to buy all the proper foods that we're both supposed to eat .... And I'll do without because I know he needs it more than I do.

Yvonne Hanson argues that when public health strategies relating to well-being and nutrition for example are examined through a 'combined gender and food insecurity lens', and family structures are viewed in terms of individual units rather than part of larger social cohesion (such as within determinants of health), then women as caregivers become targets to blame for the impact of food insecurity on children and other dependents, rather than the state. Women commonly internalise this caregiving role to the extent that they assume blame for the poor health of individual family members (Hanson 2011, 33).

Social isolation, vulnerability, stress, dark times, depression

Intersecting inequalities arising from poverty, gender, and other aspects of identity can cause what Mariana Chilton and Sue Booth (2007) termed 'hunger of the mind' (119), in research on low-income African-American women, 'related to trauma, encompassing feelings of depression and hopelessness' (116). Participants in our research regularly referred to depression, 'dark times', and loneliness, and discussed treatment and care for sleeplessness and mental health issues. This might in turn contribute to further weight gain:

When you get depressed, you don't really think about all the [rest of the] month. You're going to eat. If that's what you do when you get depressed, you're going to eat. No matter, you don't really think. You're depressed; you're going to eat.

As evidenced by numerous comments throughout this paper, participants regularly talked about feeling socially isolated, stigmatised, and vulnerable. They spoke about this in the context of being poor, of being lone mothers, of being unattached women living alone, of going to food banks, of being overweight and obese, of being disabled or immobile, of dealing with chronic diseases, of coping with mental health issues, and when dealing with bureaucratic hoops related to government assistance programmes, among other things. Throughout the focus groups, participants regularly spoke about obstacles they were experiencing, and the impact these stressors had on their abilities to cope with day-to-day life. They discussed a complex web of feelings that included depression, isolation, guilt, and humiliation. One participant discussed her feelings of social isolation:

> *I pretty much have nobody to talk to about it. Because I don't go out very much. I don't have much a social circle anymore, because [of the] … mobility issue. I just don't go to the soup kitchens anymore, because the food's not that good. And I just have nobody.*

Participants also talked about their relationships or lack thereof. Others spoke about sleeplessness and being unattached:

> *No, I don't sleep much. I go to bed and I worry most of the time. Yeah. Cause there's a lot to worry about. Even though I'm only one, in fact, just being one person sometimes is harder. Because you know … I mean I can't turn around, I'm disabled so I can't turn around and really go and live with someone else, a male friend, because they'll cut me off.*

In addition to mental health challenges, participants also talked about forms of resilience and in doing so, the positive changes they were undertaking including returning to school, joining walking groups and nutritional training programmes, and engaging in community activities.

Conclusion

In Canada, the agriculture and agrifood system is a key pillar of the country's economy, accounting for 8.1 per cent of national GDP and employing 2.1 million Canadians, roughly 13 per cent of all employment in the country (UNHCHR 2012). Participants spoke frequently about their frustrations of being poor, food insecure, and trying to managing their weight and associated chronic diseases while living in a country of such abundance.

The women we spoke with from New Brunswick, Newfoundland and Labrador, Nova Scotia, and Prince Edward Island living with food insecurity and weight challenges were heavily burdened by a cycle of overlapping factors that were threaded together by poverty and complex inequalities. The project focused on the experiences of women from marginalised communities who are expected to cope with the challenges of low income and overcome the challenges of food insecurity for themselves and their dependents. These women, who lived primarily on income support, simply did not have enough money for the day-to-day costs of living in Canada. The daily obstacles participants faced in trying to obtain sufficient and nutritious food for themselves and their children were numerous. The effects of poor-quality diets and constant stress on their physical and mental well-being were significant. These women felt like they did not have control over their lives in many ways. The vicious cycles they are experiencing are intertwined and cannot be addressed by compartmentalising elements of health or social services. The vicious cycle associated with the food insecurity–obesity paradox encompasses a myriad of challenges for women that need to be further understood and addressed by policymakers.

Participants spoke about lifelong challenges with weight; they remembered childhood experiences of feast and famine and reflected on the impact this had on their relationship to food as adults. They talked about making food choices based not on a lack of understanding, but rather based on strategic choices that reflected the limitations of their income, and especially as relating to their choices as lone mothers. They also talked about feeling isolated, stigmatised, and vulnerable, which left them feeling highly stressed and often depressed, which in turn contributed to further weight gain. They talked about their experiences of chronic diseases and the effect food insecurity had on managing illness. Participants framed their choices in terms of a 'rock and a hard place', whereby the balance between options would leave them pitting one need, such as rent or medication, against another and leaving food very low on the list of priorities. Our evidence showed that rather than an absence of knowledge around how to live in healthy ways, there was an absence of choice to do so.

To respond to food insecurity issues, especially for lone mothers and unattached women, social and economic policy needs to be rooted in a commitment to address women's fall-back and bargaining positions. As Sharon Kirkpatrick and Valerie Tarasuk observe in their writings on food insecurity in Canada, 'the existing evidence points very strongly to the need for adequate incomes, suggesting that improvements to the adequacy of welfare rates and minimum wage levels, for example, would be useful in ameliorating food insecurity' (Kirkpatrick and Tarasuk 2008, 26). Women in the Full Plate Project challenged decision-makers in government to increase social protections. The women challenged decision-makers in government to *live in our shoes and see first-hand what it is like to live like this'.*

Notes

1. The full report including a comprehensive bibliography can be found here: http://www.dal.ca/diff/Atlantic-Centre-of-Excellence-for-Womens-Health/projects-and-publications/obesity/food-insecurity–obesity-and-chronic-disease.html (last checked by the authors 29 April 2015). This project was funded by Health Canada. The views represented in this chapter are those of the authors and do not necessarily represent the views of Health Canada.
2. 'In food insecure households without hunger, all members feel anxious about running out of food or compromise on the quality of foods they eat by choosing less expensive option, little or no reduction in the household members' food intake is reported. In food insecure households with moderate hunger, food intake for adults in the household has been reduced to an extent that implies that adults have repeatedly experienced the physical sensation of hunger. In most (but not all) food insecure households with children, such reductions are not observed at this stage for children. In food insecure households with severe hunger at this level, all households with children have reduced the children's food intake to

an extent indicating that the children have experienced hunger, adults in households with and without children have repeatedly experienced more extensive reductions in food intake.' Statistics Canada, *Table 104-2004*, Canadian Community Health Survey, Cycle 2.2, Government of Canada, http://www5.statcan.gc.ca/cansim/pick-choisir?lang=eng&p2=33&id=1052004, (last checked by the authors 21 April 2015).

References

Burns, Cate (2004) 'A review of the literature describing the link between poverty, food insecurity and obesity with specific reference to Australia', Carlton, Vic: VicHealth

Chilton, Mariana and Sue Booth (2007) 'Hunger of the body and hunger of the mind: African American Women's perceptions of food insecurity, health and violence', *Journal of Nutrition Education and Behavior* 39(3): 116–25

Canadian Centre for Policy Alternatives (2014) 'Progress on women's rights: missing in action a shadow report on Canada's implementation of the Beijing declaration and platform for action prepared by a network of NGOs, trade unions and independent experts', *Canadian Centre for Policy Alternatives*: 1–88, https://www.policyalternatives.ca/sites/default/files/uploads/publications/National%20Office/2014/11/Progress_Women_Beijing20.pdf (last checked by the authors 30 March 2015)

Charlebois,Sylvain,Michael von Massow,Francis Tapon, Erna van Duren,Paul Uys,Warren Pinto, and Amit Summan (2015). The food price report. University of Guelph. https://www.uoguelph.ca/foodinstitute/system/files/Food%20Price%20Report%202015.pdf (last checked by the authors 21 April 2015)

De Henau, Jerome and Susan Himmelweit (2013) 'Examining Public Policy from a Gendered Intra-Household Perspective: Changes in Family-Related Policies in the UK, Australia and Germany since the Mid-Nineties', *Oñati Socio-Legal Series* 3(7): 1222–1248

Dietz, William (1995) 'Does hunger cause obesity?', *Pediatrics* 95(5): 766–7

Dinour, Lauren M., Dara Bergen, and Ming-Chin Yeh (2007) 'The food insecurity-obesity paradox: a review of the literature and the role food stamps may play', *Journal of the American Dietetic Association* 107(11): 1952–61

Drewnowski, Adam, and Petra Eichelsdoerfer (2010) 'Chapter 58: the economics of obesity: why are poor people fat?', in L. Dubé, A. Bechara, A. Dagher, A. Drewnowski, J. Lebel, P. James, and R.Y. Yada (eds.) *Obesity Prevention: The Role of Brain and Society in Individual Behavior*, San Diego, CA: Academic Press, pp. 727–43

First Nations Information Governance Centre (2008) *First Nations Regional Longitudinal Health Survey, Adult Questionnaire*, Akwesasne, On: FNIGC

Franklin, Brandi, Ashley Jones, Dejuan Love, Stephane Puckett, Justin Macklin, and Shelley White (2011) 'Exploring Mediators of Food Insecurity and Obesity: A Review of Recent Literature', *Journal of Community Health* 37(1): 253–264

Food Banks Canada (2010) *Hunger Count 2010*, 1–46, Toronto: Food Banks Canada

Hansford, Frances (2010) 'The nutrition transition: a gender perspective with reference to Brazil', *Gender and Development* 18(3): 439–52

Hanson, Yvonne (2011) *Recipes for Food Insecurity: Women's Stories from Saskatchewan. Project #238*, 1–64, Winnipeg: Prairie Women's Health Centre of Excellence

Health Canada (2010) Household Food Insecurity in Canada in 2007–2008: Key Statistics and Graphics. http://www.hc-sc.gc.ca/fn-an/surveill/nutrition/ commun/insecurit/key-stats-cles-2007-2008-eng.php#fnb6 (last checked by the authors 30 April 2015)

Kirkpatrick, Sharon I. and Valerie Tarasuk (2008) 'Food insecurity in Canada: considerations for monitoring', *Canadian Journal of Public Health* 99: 324–7

Larsen, Kristian and Jason Gilliland (2008) 'Mapping the evolution of "food deserts" in a Canadian city: supermarket accessibility in London, Ontario, 1961–2005', *International Journal of Health Geographics* 7: 1–16

Lise, Jeremy and Shannon Seitz (2011) 'Consumption Inequality and Intra-Household Allocations', *Review of Economic Studies* 78(1): 328–355

Martin, Molly A. and Adam M. Lippert (2012) 'Feeding her children, but risking her health: the intersection of gender, household food insecurity and obesity', *Social Science & Medicine* 74(11): 1754–64

Popkin, Barry M., Linda S. Adair, and Shu Wen Ng (2012) 'Global nutrition transition and the pandemic of obesity in developing countries', *Nutrition Reviews* 70(1): 3–21

Public Health Agency of Canada (PHAC) and Canadian Institute for Health Information (CIHI) (2011) *Obesity in Canada: Health and Economic Implications*, Ottawa. http://www.phac-aspc.gc.ca/hp-ps/hl-mvs/oic-oac/ assets/pdf/oic-oac-eng.pdf (last checked by the authors 22 June 2015)

Sarlio-Lähteenkorva, Sirpa, and Eero Lahelma (2001) 'Food insecurity is associated with past and present economic disadvantage and body mass index', *Journal of Nutrition* 131: 2880–4

Saulnier, Christine (2013) 'Atlantic Canada's story of inequality', *Behind the Numbers: a Blog from the Canadian Centre for Policy Alternatives*. January 30th, CCPA-NS. http://behindthenumbers.ca/2013/01/30/atlantic-cana-das-story-of-inequality/ (last checked by the authors 20 April 2015)

Statistics Canada. Table 105-2004 - level of household food insecurity, by age group and sex, household population, Canadian Community Health Survey cycle 2.2, Canada and provinces, occasional, CANSIM (database). http:// www5.statcan.gc.ca/cansim/pick-choisir?lang=eng&p2=33&id=1052004 (last checked by the authors 2 May 2015)

Tarasuk, Valerie, Lynn McIntyre, and Jinguang Li (2007) 'Low-income women's dietary intakes are sensitive to the depletion of household resources in one month', *Journal of Nutrition* 137(8): 1980–7

Terrell, Ashley (2009) 'Is food insecurity associated with chronic disease and chronic disease control?', *Ethnicity and Disease* 19 (2): S3-3–S3-6

UNHCHR (2012) 'Olivier De Schutter, United Nations special rapporteur on the right to food: visit to Canada from 6 to 16 May 2012 – end-of-mission statement', http://www.ohchr.org/EN/NewsEvents/Pages/DisplayNews. aspx?NewsID=12159&LangID=E (last checked by the authors 22 June 2015)

Williams, Patty (2009) *Cost and Affordability of a Nutritious Diet in Nova Scotia: Report on 2008 Participatory Food Costing*, Halifax: Nova Scotia Participatory Food Costing Project, Mount Saint Vincent University

World Health Organization (2011) *Trade, Foreign Policy, Diplomacy and Health: Food Security*. http://www.who.int/trade/glossary/story028/en/ (last checked by the authors 2 May 2015)

World Health Organization (2013a) *PMNCH Knowledge Summary #15 Non-Communicable Diseases*, http://www.who.int/pmnch/knowledge/publications/summaries/ks15/en/ (last checked by the authors 30 April 2015)

World Health Organization (2013b) *Backgrounder 3: Key Concepts.* http://www.who.int/social_determinants/final_report/key_concepts_en.pdf?ua=1 (last checked by the authors 30 April 2015)

World Health Organization (2015) *Obesity and overweight Fact sheet N°311.* http://www.who.int/mediacentre/factsheets/fs311/en/ (last checked by the authors 2 May 2015)

About the Authors

Andrea S. Papan is the Technical Advisor, Gender and Behaviour Change at Nutrition International, Canada and previously worked at Malmö University in Sweden. She specialises on human rights-based approaches to gender and development. Email: a.papan@outlook.com

Barbara Clow is a researcher, writer, and educator on women's health and well-being and Principal Consultant at Barbara Clow Consulting. Email: barbara.clow@eastlink.ca

CHAPTER 9

Measuring the drivers of gender inequality and their impact on development: the role of discriminatory social institutions

Gaëlle Ferrant and Keiko Nowacka

Abstract

This paper highlights the key role of discriminatory social institutions – formal and informal laws, social norms, and practices – as the underlying drivers of gender inequality. Using the Social Institutions and Gender Index (SIGI) from the OECD Development Centre, this paper assesses the cost of gender-based discrimination in social institutions for economic and human development. Quantifying such complex issues is a powerful lever for advocacy, where rights-based arguments have tended to gain less traction. The paper provides evidence that measuring the invisible is feasible and critical to position social norms on the policy radar. It demonstrates that any truly transformative post-2015 development agenda must take into account how such inequalities impact the development pathways of women and girls across their entire life course, limiting their rights and empowerment opportunities.

Keywords: social institutions; measurement; post-2015

Introduction

The ongoing discussions on the new development framework that will replace the Millennium Development Goals (MDGs) have put the concepts of social transformation and gender equality under the magnifying lens. What does social transformation look like, and what are the implications for gender equality? Gender equality is now recognised as a human right, as well as smart economics – both essential for sustainable development, and a pillar of social transformation (World Bank 2012).

Gender equality advocates have actively campaigned for a stand-alone goal on gender equality and women's empowerment in the post-2015 framework, partly in recognition of the beneficial effect of focusing development resources to this universal challenge, but also based on the growing evidence linking reduction of gender inequalities to social transformation (Ferrant *et al.* 2015). The benefits of sustained investments and commitments to gender equality

http://dx.doi.org/10.3362/9781780447278.009

and women's empowerment over the past four decades, and in particular over the past 15 years, are incontestable. Narrowing gender gaps in education, employment, and health mean that in 2015, more women and girls than ever before are able to enjoy their rights and access empowerment opportunities.

Yet, the process of selecting targets and indicators that can inspire and track social transformation and gender equality by 2030 has put into question the effectiveness of current development approaches. Social institutions have emerged as a 'missing link' that explains why certain inequalities persist, after years of being invisible to development practitioners and researchers. Institutions create, formulate, and challenge the formal and informal laws, norms, attitudes, and practices in society which impact on inequality and bring about development. However, recognising the importance of institutions is just the first step. There remains the significant challenge of quantifying the impact of institutions. Without numbers and data, social institutions as a concern remain on the development periphery (Morrisson and Jütting 2005).

In 2009, the OECD Development Centre launched the first index to measure the impact of discrimination against women in social institutions: the Social Institutions and Gender Index (SIGI). It measures discrimination against women in five areas: family code, physical integrity, son bias, secure access to land and assets, and civil liberties. Over the past five years, the SIGI experience of data collection and measuring discriminatory social institutions has contributed to advancing understanding of the underlying drivers of gender-based inequalities and the consequences for development (OECD Development Centre 2014).

This chapter will first present the SIGI's conceptual framework and methodology. It will then provide some preliminary results, drawing on data from the latest 2014 edition of the SIGI, which help development policymakers, researchers, and practitioners to better understand how and why discrimination against women represents a development cost.

The Social Institution and Gender Index

Why do discriminatory social institutions matter for gender inequalities?

Measuring gender discrimination in social institutions draws attention to the role of 'culture' or social relations in limiting or enabling individual or collective agency. Douglas C. North (1990) describes institutions as 'the humanly devised constraints that structure political, economic and social interaction. They consist of both informal constraints (sanctions, taboos, customs, traditions, and codes of conduct), and formal rules (constitutions, laws, property rights)' (97). Formal and informal laws can co-exist in different types of legal systems including civil or common law, customary law, and religious laws. The social aspect of institutions refers to the way they influence social relations and shape the decisions, choices, and behaviours of groups, communities, and individuals (Jütting *et al.* 2008), determining what is deemed acceptable or unacceptable in a society. Social institutions therefore, play a key role in defining and influencing gender roles, power, and relations. They determine whether women have an opportunity to forge their own pathway to empowerment.

Social institutions operate and exert influence at micro-, meso-, and macro-levels (Kabeer 1994). For example, social institutions regarding women's status in the family play out at a household (micro-) level in behaviours and attitudes, such as unequal financial decision-making power between men and women; at community (meso-) level in specific beliefs or sanctioned practices, such as discrimination against widows; and at a country (macro-) level in terms of broader social norms or laws which allow discrimination, such as discriminatory laws in relation to inheritance.

Gender discriminations in social institutions affect the whole female life-cycle; for example, by ascribing greater social value to sons over daughters, by preventing women from owning land, or by restricting widow's inheritance rights.

How does the SIGI measure gender inequalities in social institutions?

The full methodology of the SIGI can be found at www.genderindex.org (last checked by the authors 18 May 2015). Briefly, the SIGI is composed of five sub-indices, each representing a distinct dimension of discrimination against women in social institutions: discriminatory family code, restricted physical integrity, son bias, restricted resources and assets, and restricted civil liberties. Figure 1 sets out the theoretical justification for the SIGI sub-indices, explaining what each sub-index aims to capture and why.

The 2014 edition of the SIGI expanded its country coverage to include OECD economies,[1] an innovation on the 2009 and 2012 editions which measured levels of discrimination in social institutions only in non-OECD economies. The same conceptual framework was applied to OECD economies based on two assumptions. Firstly, no country has achieved gender equality; and secondly, social institutions that discriminate against women cut across all economies irrespective of levels of economic development, with the obvious caveat that their manifestation differ according to geography, culture, religion

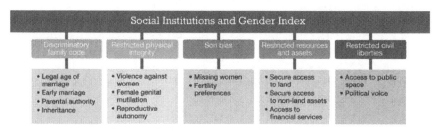

Figure1 The composition of the SIGI

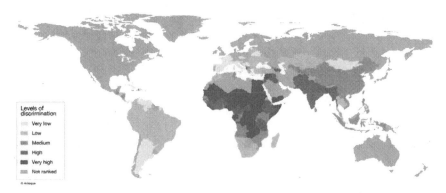

Figure 2 SIGI results for 2014. For a colour rendition of this chart, please see the online version of this chapter
Source: OECD (2014), Gender, Institutions and Development Database, http://stats.oecd.org

as well as other factors. This inclusion of OECD economies within the 2014 edition put the spotlight on these two factors, showing, for example, the universal challenge of violence against women, women's political participation, unpaid care work, or women's land and economic rights. It also raised conceptual questions around the relevance of indicators that were more pertinent for some countries or regions. For example, female genital mutilation (FGM) is practised in 28 out of the 160 countries covered by the SIGI, while 'missing women' is of significant concern in South and Central Asia, and less so in others.

The SIGI scores 108 countries according to their level of discrimination in social institutions. The variables are shown in Figure 1.

The SIGI classifies countries into five groups, from very low levels of discrimination in social institutions (15 per cent of the countries), to very high levels (16 per cent of the countries). This classification groups countries where women experience a similar level of discrimination in the SIGI by minimising differences between countries' SIGI scores in the same class, and maximising the differences between classes.

Below, the results for 2014 are discussed, to show the SIGI in action.

The 2014 SIGI results

Among the 108 countries included in the 2014 SIGI, Argentina, Belgium, Mongolia, and Trinidad and Tobago have the lowest levels of gender inequality in social institutions. On the other side of the spectrum, the highest levels of gender inequality in social institutions are found in Bangladesh, Egypt, Niger, and Yemen, among others.

Countries which have very low levels of gender discrimination in social institutions (SIGI<0.04) are characterised by robust legal frameworks, and measures that provide equal rights in the family code and in access to resources and assets and that promote women's civil liberties. In most of these countries, women and men have equal parental and inheritance rights, and early marriage is not a common practice. Women do not face restrictions on their access to public space or their participation in politics. Neither 'missing women' nor FGM are concerns. However, these countries commonly still lack laws to protect women from violence and measures to implement them, and women need better access to justice. On average, 20 per cent of women in these countries have been victims of domestic violence in their lifetime.

Countries which have low levels of gender discrimination in social institutions (0.04<SIGI<0.12) are characterised by strong laws providing equal rights for women and men in the family code, in access to resources and assets, and in civil liberties. Both sexes enjoy equal opportunities to own and make decisions over land and other resources. Female genital mutilation is not practised, and most women have reproductive autonomy.[2] In respect to violence against women, legal frameworks are either inadequate or there are reported issues of implementation. On average, almost one-third (31 per cent) of women have been victims of domestic violence in their lifetime, and more than 29 per cent of women agree that domestic violence is justified under certain circumstances.

Countries with medium levels of gender discrimination in social institutions (0.12<SIGI<0.22) are characterised by inconsistent or conflicting legal frameworks covering the family code, women's access to resources and assets, and civil liberties. Religious and/or customary laws and practices perpetuate discrimination in these areas. Specifically, women face discrimination in terms of the legal age of marriage, parental authority, inheritance, and rights to land and financial services. Women are restricted in their access to public space, as well as in their participation in political life due to the absence of quotas at the national and/or sub-national levels. Legal frameworks addressing violence against women are inadequate (for example, certain types of violence may not be included). On average, 39 per cent of women in these countries agree that domestic violence is justified under certain circumstances.

Countries having high levels of gender discrimination in social institutions (0.22<SIGI<0.35) are characterised by discrimination in customary laws, social norms and practices, and by inappropriate legal protections against gender discrimination in all dimensions of social institutions. The legal frameworks and/ or the customary laws and practices discriminate against women in respect to the legal age of marriage, parental authority, and inheritance. Women's physical integrity is restricted due to inadequate legal frameworks to address violence against women, and high levels of acceptance of domestic violence. Moreover, FGM is a common practice in many of these countries, depending on cultural and religious factors. Most of the South Asian countries in this category have medium to very high levels of devaluation of daughters and preference for sons, as shown by the numbers of missing women or the unbalanced sex ratios at last birth. Finally, women's access to public space and resources is limited in all these countries. On average, 32 per cent of women have been victims of domestic violence in their lifetime, and more than 49 per cent of women agree that domestic violence is justified under certain circumstances.

Countries having very high levels of gender discrimination in social institutions (SIGI>0.35) are characterised by very high levels of discrimination in legal frameworks and customary practices across most sub-indices, and by very poor implementation measures. The family code greatly discriminates against women: almost one-third of girls younger than 19 are married, and women face severe discrimination in their parental authority and inheritance rights. Women's rights to own and control land and other resources and to access public space are extremely limited. There are serious infringements on their physical integrity matched by high levels of acceptance and prevalence of domestic violence: 44 per cent of women have been victims of domestic violence, and 59 per cent accept that it is justified under certain circumstances.

The adverse impact of gender inequality in social institutions

In this section, we highlight the implications of gender discrimination and inequality in social institutions for a range of development outcomes. These preliminary avenues of research consider two discriminatory social institutions focused on in the SIGI, highlighting them as underlying drivers of gender equality, and assume that such persistent discrimination against women negatively affects economic and human development (Ferrant 2015). First, the unequal distribution of unpaid care work between women and men represents an infringement of women's rights (Sepulveda Carmona 2013), and is also a brake on their economic empowerment. Second, the practice of early marriage violates girls' right to education, and prevents them taking advantage of empowerment opportunities.

Discriminatory social institutions, unpaid care work, and gender gaps in the labour market

Despite significant progress in recent decades, women's participation in productive work in the formal economy remains far below its potential. Female labour-force participation remains lower than male participation (55 per cent versus 82 per cent in 2012 [World Bank n.d.]). In addition, when women are employed in paid work, they are paid less than men for equal work, over-represented in the informal sector, and relegated to low-skill and low-wage jobs. Gender gaps in the labour market have serious macro-economic consequences (Klasen and Lamanna 2009) and account for GDP per capita losses of up to 27 per cent in the Middle East and North Africa, 23 per cent in South Asia, and around 15 per cent in the rest of the world (Cuberes and Teignier 2012, 1). Moreover, women's economic empowerment is critical for their own well-being as well as for the well-being of their families and communities, for poverty reduction, and for inclusive growth (World Bank 2012).

The key roles of unpaid care work and social institutions have been neglected in the analysis of gender gaps in labour outcomes, even though this is critical to understand gender inequalities. Women typically bear the bulk of caring responsibilities spending disproportionately more time on unpaid care work than men (two to ten times more per day on average [OECD 2014]). This is in addition to their paid activities, thus creating the 'double burden' of work for women. On account of gendered social norms that view unpaid care work as a female prerogative, women across different regions, socioeconomic classes, and cultures spend an important part of their day on meeting the expectations of their domestic and reproductive roles. This has significant implications for women's ability to actively take part in the labour market and the type/quality of employment opportunities available to them.

The unequal distribution of unpaid care work between women and men represents a brake on women's economic empowerment and influences gender gaps in labour outcomes. Time is a limited resource, which is divided between labour and leisure, productive and reproductive activities, paid and unpaid work. Every minute more that a woman spends on unpaid care work represents one minute less that she could be potentially spending on market-related activities, investing in her educational and vocational skills, or leisure.

When gender inequality in time devoted to unpaid care work increases, women's experience of employment worsens, both in absolute terms, and in comparison to the experience of men. Gender inequalities in unpaid care work are linked to gender gaps in labour-force participation: the higher the inequality in distribution of care responsibilities between women and men, the higher the gender gaps in labour-force participation. In countries where women spend almost eight times the amount of time on unpaid care activities than men, they represent only just over one-third (35 per cent) of the active working population. However, when the difference drops to less than twice the amount, women's labour-force participation increases to 50 per cent for a given level of GDP per capita, fertility rate, urbanisation rate, maternity leave, gender inequality in unemployment and education, and regional characteristics (Ferrant *et al.* 2014, 5–6).

Unpaid care activities constitute a time and energy-consuming occupation (Elson 2000) that limits women's access to the labour market, relegating them to low-income and insecure employment. The struggle for women to reconcile care responsibilities with paid employment can lead to 'occupational downgrading', where women choose employment below their skills level and accept poorer conditions. Alternatively, this struggle results in part-time employment, and informal work, which both have negative long-term implications for women workers who are forced to accept this work in countries where governments and employers make provision for old age via employee contributions, either in the form of taxation or as pension contributions.

Discriminatory social norms can also explain gender inequalities in unpaid care work and thus in labour outcomes. Some of these gender disparities in time-use may be explained by socio-demographic and economic factors, such as levels of education and wealth, but discriminatory social attitudes are also to blame. By defining which behaviours are deemed acceptable or unacceptable in a society, social institutions influence gender roles: in most societies, working for pay is considered a masculine task, while unpaid care work is seen as women's domain. Gender norms and gender stereotypes 'feminise' caregiving, and prevent men from assuming equal caring responsibilities.

The unequal gender distribution of caring responsibilities also provides an important clue to understanding why reduced gender gaps in education have not led to reduced gender gaps in employment in certain countries. Women living in countries where women have a high responsibility for unpaid care work are less likely to be able to take up paid employment. Even if these countries have managed to decrease the gender gap in education, the fact that adult women are still required to shoulder the majority of the unpaid care work burden means there will still be persistent gender gaps in employment outcomes. In contrast, countries with family-friendly policies that promote better work–family life balance for both parents see a higher female participation rate in the formal labour market.

Early marriage, early pregnancies, and the gender gap in education

Gender inequalities in social institutions affect a woman through her whole life-cycle, including influencing her marital decisions. Social norms, customary laws, and practices can strongly determine whether she has an opportunity to make her own decisions on when she gets married, and to whom. Across the world, close to 250 million girls before the age of 15 have been subject to early marriage (UNICEF 2014, 2).

Despite improvements in some countries such as Malawi, where the number of early marriages decreased from 36 per cent in 2004 to 26 per cent in 2010 (OECD 2014), early marriage and adolescent pregnancy remain common. Despite legislative measures, globally 39,000 girls marry every day: one in three marries before the age of 19, and one in nine before the age of 15 (UNFPA 2014, 9). Early marriage is closely linked to early motherhood: 90 per cent of the 16 million adolescents who give birth each year across the globe are already married (UNFPA 2013, 4).

Decreasing and eliminating both early marriage and adolescent pregnancies is critical for protecting girls' rights and enabling them to take advantage of empowerment opportunities. These practices are not only violations of girls' human rights, but also expose them to higher rates of maternal mortality, domestic violence, and reduced decision-making power within her new family. Even if child marriage affects girls in far greater numbers than boys (156 million men aged 18 years and older were married or in union before turning 18, against 720 million women), early marriage also diminishes boys' education and future income-earning prospects (UNICEF 2014, 2).

Early marriage and pregnancy affect girl's empowerment and education opportunities: there are more than 35 million girls in the world whose education is cut short by child marriage (Watson *et al.* 2013). Social expectations and heavy domestic workloads force many married girls to abandon their education. In Nigeria, marriage and childbearing account for 15–20 per cent of girls dropping out of school (Nguyen and Wodon 2012, 3).

By cutting short girls' education, early pregnancy also explains persistent gender gaps at the secondary school level. In countries where adolescent fertility rates are high, fewer girls enrol in secondary school, thereby increasing the gender gap in enrolment and completion rates. Hence, a higher prevalence of adolescent pregnancy is linked to greater inequality in secondary school enrolment (for a given country's level of poverty, GDP per capita, share of female teachers, government expenditures in education, gender gap in unemployment rates, urbanisation rates, and controlling for regional and year characteristics).

Likewise, higher gender gaps in early marriage are related to higher gender gaps in secondary school completion rates: in countries where more girls aged 15–19 marry than boys, fewer girls complete secondary school, thus increasing the gender gap in secondary completion rates (OECD Development Centre 2014). This is the case regardless of other factors such as the country's level of poverty, share of female teachers, government expenditures in education, female unemployment rates, urbanisation rates, and region-specific characteristics.

Hence when the prevalence of both early marriage and early pregnancy increases, gender inequality in secondary school enrolment rates and completion rates increases, reducing the women's contribution to the well-being of their families and communities. In a union, young girls have significantly reduced bargaining power to make decisions over their own well-being, household incomes, and key life choices for their children. The greater school achievement of mothers has a positive effect on those of their children and the importance the latter attach to schooling. In the United States, each additional year of mother 's schooling before the birth of a child adds 1.6 points to the child's math and reading scores, 2.1 points to the vocabulary score, and increases the probability of going on to higher education (Rosenzweig and Wolpin 1994, 1121); in India, children whose mothers are better educated study almost two hours more per day than do the children of women with no formal education (Behrman *et al.* 1999, 707).

In conclusion, delaying marriage and pregnancy means that girls have greater chances to complete their education and is thus a key step towards gender equality. This will have positive consequences for themselves and their communities, and their development pathway does not abruptly stall at age of marriage.

Conclusion

These preliminary analyses of the 2014 edition of the SIGI confirm that gender inequalities in social institutions are not, therefore, innocuous for national or global development goals. They have direct and indirect consequences for inclusive economic growth and human capital, *inter alia*. For this reason, any truly transformative post-2015 development agenda must take into account how such inequalities impact the development pathways of women and girls across their entire life course, limiting their rights and empowerment opportunities.

Measuring the impact of discriminatory social institutions has never been more necessary or timely in the age of 'data revolutions',[3] and calls for social transformation. Quantifying such complex issues is a powerful lever for advocacy, where rights-based arguments have tended to gain less traction. As a data exercise, the SIGI has proved that measuring the invisible is feasible and critical to position social norms on the policy radar. The SIGI has benefited from the improvements in data availability and quality over the past decade but lacunae remain which will require governments and statistical agencies to prioritise gender statistics and sex-disaggregation of data in order to better understand the impact of inequalities for development.

However, measuring the impact of discriminatory social institutions on gender inequality and development is only half the journey: the data-gathering and analysis are only as useful as the policies and actions they inspire or inform. The SIGI's evidence base offers insights into policies that have helped transform or reduce gender inequalities and provides a monitoring benchmark for future investments in these areas. The 2014 edition of the SIGI is a reminder that gender inequalities in social institutions are not a 'women's issue', or an issue of relevance only to developing countries, but instead a universal phenomenon with widespread implications for communities and economies.

Acknowledgement

The authors would like to thank Mario Pezzini, Nicola Harrington and Alexandre Kolev (OECD Development Centre) for their comments on previous versions of this chapter.

Notes

1. The OECD economies include Australia, Austria, Belgium, Canada, Chile, Czech Republic, Denmark, Estonia, Finland, France, Germany, Greece, Hungary, Iceland, Ireland, Israel, Italy, Japan, Korea, Luxembourg, Mexico, Netherlands, New Zealand, Norway, Poland, Portugal, Slovak Republic, Slovenia, Spain, Sweden, Switzerland, Turkey, United Kingdom, and United States.
2. Reproductive autonomy refers to women's ability to participate to the couple's decision-making regarding the number, spacing, and timing of their children, and to have the information and means to do so. We measure it using the percentage of women having met needs for family planning.
3. New technologies are leading to an exponential increase in the volume and types of data available, creating unprecedented possibilities for informing development. Governments, companies, researchers, and citizen groups are in a ferment of experimentation, innovation, and adaptation to the

new world of data, a world in which data are bigger, faster, and more detailed than ever before. This is the data revolution.

References

Bantebya, Grace, Florence Muhanguzi and Carol Watson (2013) 'Good Policies Versus Daily Discrimination: Adolescent Girls and Gender Justice in Uganda', London: Overseas Development Institute, available at http://www.odi.org/sites/odi.org.uk/files/odi-assets/publications-opinion-files/8649.pdf (last checked by the authors 23 June 2015)

Behrman, Jere R., Andrew D. Foster, Mark R. Andrew D., Rosenzweig, Mark R., and Vashishtha, Prem (1999) 'Women's schooling, home teaching, and economic growth', *Journal of Political Economy* 107(4): 682–714

Cuberes, David and Marc Teignier (2012) 'Gender gaps in the labor market and aggregate productivity', *Sheffield Economic Research Paper SERP 2012017*, Sheffield, Department of Economics, University of Sheffield

Elson, Diane (2000) 'Progress of the World's Women 2000, UNIFEM Biennial report', New York: United Nations Development Fund for Women

Ferrant, Gaëlle, Luca Maria Pesando, and Keiko Nowacka (2014) 'Unpaid Care Work: The missing link in the analysis of gender gaps in labour outcomes', *Issues paper*, Issy-les-Moulineaux: OECD Development Centre, available at http://www.oecd.org/dev/development-gender/Unpaid_care_work.pdf (last checked by the authors 23 June 2015)

Ferrant, Gaëlle (2015) 'How do gender inequalities hinder development? Cross-country evidence', *Annals of Economics and Statistics*, Number 117/118, January/June 2015

Ferrant, Gaëlle, Keiko Nowacka, and Annelise Thim (2015) 'Living up to Beijing's vision of gender equality: Social norms and transformative change', Issues paper, Issy-les-Moulineaux: OECD Development Centre, available at http://www.oecd.org/dev/development-gender/BeijingPolicyBrief_Final_wreferences.pdf (last checked by the authors 23 June 2015)

Jütting, Johannes, Christian Morrison, Jeff Dayton-Johnson, and Denis Drechsler (2008) 'Measuring gender (In)Equality: The OECD gender, institutions and development data base', *Journal of Human Development and Capabilities* 9(1): 65–86

Kabeer, Naila (1994) *Reversed Realities: Gender Hierarchies in Development thought.* London, New York: Verso

Klasen, Stephan and Francesca Lamanna (2009) 'The impact of gender inequality in education and employment on economic growth: New evidence for a panel of countries', *Feminist Economics* 15(3): 91–132

Morrisson, Christian and Johannes Jütting (2005) 'Women's discrimination in developing countries: A new data set for better policies', *World Development* 33(7): 1065–1081

Nguyen, Minh Cong and Quentin Wodon (2012) *Child Marriage, Pregnancies, and the Gender Gap in Education Attainment: An Analysis Based on the Reasons for Dropping Out of School*, Mimeo, Washington, DC: World Bank

North, Douglass C. (1990) 'Institutions', *The Journal of Economic Perspectives* 5(1): (Winter, 1991): 97–112, available at http://pubs.aeaweb.org/doi/pdfplus/10.1257/jep.5.1.97 (last checked by the authors 23 June 2015)

OECD Development Centre (2014) 'Social Institutions and Gender Index (SIGI) 2014 Synthesis Report', Issy-les-Moulineaux: OECD Development Centre, available at http://www.oecd.org/dev/development-gender/BrochureSIGI2015-web.pdf (last checked by the authors 7 July 2015)

OECD (2014) *Gender, Institutions and Development Database*, http://stats.oecd.org/Index.aspx?DatasetCode=GID2 (last checked by the authors 7 July 2015)

Rosenzweig, Mark R. and Kenneth I. Wolpin (1994) 'Inequality among young adult siblings, public assistance programs, and intergenerational living arrangements', *Journal of Human Resources* 29(4): 1101–1125

Sepulveda Carmona, Magdalena (2013) 'Report of the Special Rapporteur on Extreme Poverty and Human Rights: Unpaid Care Work and Women's Human Rights', New York: United Nations, available at http://daccess-dds-ny.un.org/doc/UNDOC/GEN/N13/422/71/PDF/N1342271.pdf?OpenElement (last checked by the authors 23 June 2015)

UNFPA (2013) 'Adult pregnancy: a review of the evidence', New York: UNPFA, available at http://www.unfpa.org/sites/default/files/pub-pdf/ADOLESCENT%20PREGNANCY_UNFPA.pdf (last checked by the authors 26 June 2015)

UNFPA (2014) 'The Power of 18 Billion. Adolescents, Youth and the Transformation of the Future. State of World Population 2014', New York: UNPFA, available at http://www.unfpa.org/sites/default/files/pub-pdf/EN-SWOP14-Report_FINAL-web.pdf (last checked by the authors 26 June 2015)

UNICEF (2014) *Ending Child Marriage. Progress and Prospects*, http://data.unicef.org/corecode/uploads/document6/uploaded_pdfs/corecode/Child-Marriage-Brochure-HR_164.pdf (last checked by the authors 23 June 2015)

World Bank (2012) 'World Development Report 2012: Gender Equality and Development', Washington, DC: World Bank

World Bank (n.d.) *World Development Indicators* (database), Washington, DC: World Bank, http://data.worldbank.org/data-catalog/world-development-indicators (last checked by the authors 23 June 2015)

About the Authors

Gaëlle Ferrant works as an Economist, OECD Development Centre, and is corresponding author for this chapter. Email: gaelle.ferrant@oecd.org.

Keiko Nowacka works as Gender Coordinator, OECD Development Centre. Email: keiko.nowacka@oecd.org.

CHAPTER 10

Addressing multiple dimensions of gender inequality: the experience of the BRAC Gender Quality Action Learning (GQAL) programme in Bangladesh

Sheepa Hafiza, Mohammed Kamruzzaman and Hasne Ara Begum

Abstract

Recent analyses have highlighted that poverty reduction in Bangladesh has been accompanied by growing inequality in society, measured by household income. This chapter considers what the implications are for development actors who are concerned with empowering the poor in society, and who understand poverty from a gender and women's rights perspective. We draw on experience from BRAC's work to address these issues, focusing on the Gender Quality Action Learning (GQAL) programme. A focus on women's self-employment alone does not result in challenging the structures of patriarchal inequalities. Gender inequality and its link to economic inequality needs to be much more centrally positioned than it currently is in development discourse. Currently economic empowerment is widely seen as a potential route to gender equality, but the GQAL programme shows work to challenge gender inequality is necessary as an entry-point to ensure effective economic empowerment.

Keywords: gender inequality; economic empowerment; domestic violence; GQAL; BRAC; Bangladesh

Introduction

Bangladesh has transitioned from a period of extreme poverty in the 1970s, to a period of steady growth and a steady reduction of poverty. Development strategies in Bangladesh have focused on poverty eradication and national development, using income-generation as the main strategy to achieve this. This approach has often invoked the phrase 'economic empowerment' (Hossain *et al.* 2011; Sukaj 2014). However, recent analyses have highlighted that poverty reduction in Bangladesh has been accompanied by growing inequality in society, measured by household income (Ferdousi and Dehai

http://dx.doi.org/10.3362/9781780447278.010

2014). This pattern holds true across the sub-continent. It may seem a paradox that the poor can become less poor, but society as a whole can simultaneously become less equal.

This chapter considers the implications of this trend, and considers what the implications are for development actors who are concerned with empowering the poor in society, and who understand poverty from a gender and women's rights perspective. It focuses on BRAC's Gender Quality Action Learning (GQAL) initiative, which was launched in 1995 in response to these concerns. What started as an initiative to build on gender training for staff and effect transformation within BRAC itself was then developed into a programme element for use with communities.

In the next section, we briefly explore changing gender relations in Bangladesh. We then outline BRAC's response to poverty and gender inequality, and relate how GQAL was developed, before exploring its impact on women in communities.

Gender relations in Bangladesh

When BRAC was founded in 1972, the women of Bangladesh faced restrictions on their mobility, and there was a rigid division of labour based on gender. The differences between male and female education were among the highest in the world. Bangladesh was one of the few countries in the world where the ratio of women to men was lower; this indicates the prevalence of female infanticide, malnutrition, spousal violence, and lack of access to health care. Women's subjugation was a social norm and formalised in law. Patriarchal values shaped the work environment (World Bank 2008). The values that shaped both the broader social context and BRAC's environment produced BRAC programmes that were designed to change women's socioeconomic condition, without placing any emphasis on changing gender power relations.

Since then, change has taken place across the country. The female labour force has increased from 10.3 million in 2002–2003 to 17.2 million in 2010 (BBS 2011, 1). The female labour force participation rate increased from 29.2 per cent in 2005–2006, to 36 per cent in 2010 (BBS 2011, 6). In the garment-manufacturing sector, women make up 85 per cent or more of the labour force (Titumir 2013, 6). Parallel to this, women of Bangladesh have become increasingly engaged in the politics of empowerment, and now have representation in different spaces – from the national parliament to rural local government. The Global Gender Gap Report of 2014 ranks Bangladesh 111th out of 136 countries in girls' educational attainment; its comes 68th out of 142 countries (WEF 2014, 114). Enrolment in secondary education for females is now 51 per cent (WEF 2014, 71). BANBEIS (2013) data reveal that 32.61 per cent of students at the university level are women.

In spite of the above progress, there is of course the other side of the coin. The economic empowerment of women is incomplete; female employment rates are still very low, even by South Asian standards. Despite growth in employment, the labour market is highly segmented along lines of gender, consigning women to lower-paid jobs with poorer and less secure working conditions (World Bank 2008). Women are still concentrated in domestic services and home-based work, much of it unpaid (World Bank 2008). Social indicators on empowerment highlight continuing gender inequality. Violence against women also is an increasing concern in the country (BBS 2013). A very recent national survey reveals that 65 per cent of married women have experienced physical violence at the hands of their current husbands (BBS 2013, 29). Increasing women's self-employment and their contribution to household income can in some circumstances lead to increased violence against them, due to the threat that this represents to norms concerning gender roles and power relations (Ahmed and Khatun 2008; Solotaroff and Pande 2014).

In this context, it is clear that a programme working to support women in self-employment needs to focus beyond economic empowerment through earning income, to a holistic understanding of empowerment as concerned with both economic inequality and gender inequality. In the next section, we explore how BRAC has responded to gender inequality and how it has understood its role in supporting women in poverty to raise their incomes through self-employment, but also to address the gender dimensions of poverty.

BRAC and its approach to gender inequality

BRAC is the world's largest NGO, currently reaching an estimated 135 million people. It has become globally known for its innovative approaches to providing services to the poor including micro-finance. Over the years, it has provided women with access to livelihoods through programmes supporting various modes of self-employment (Halder 2003). BRAC's programme rationale has been to support women's self-employment as an entry-point to the broader empowerment of women.

BRAC's experience has been that micro-finance and self-employment have particular benefits for specific categories of women. One key group of projects benefit extremely poor women. This group benefits from economic empowerment projects where in many cases the male breadwinner is unable to contribute (Matin 2004). Women whose husbands are unable to contribute are also sole breadwinners. Some women in this category may also find the experience of self-employment empowering due to changing attitudes on the part of communities and extended family perceiving the woman as capable of supporting her household on her own, which challenges gender norms. However, to ensure micro-finance for self-employment is empowering for women in mixed-sex households where men are also earning money, programmes should include components which transform attitudes and beliefs about women, their role in the household and society, and the worth of their economic contribution to the family.

BRAC developed an initial Gender Awareness and Analysis Course (GAAC) for staff members in 1993. The GQAL initiative, on which we focus in this chapter, began in 1995. It was a response to an intensive needs assessment process, including field visits and field-level learning, involving 2,000 staff. GQAL created a new space for addressing gender equality issues within the organisation and fostering a more respectful relationship between staff, not only between women and men but also between those who occupied different positions in the hierarchy. From 1996 to 2003, GQAL expanded to involve more than 14,000 BRAC staff members, about 90 per cent out of a then total of approximately 21,000 (Ghuznavi 2008, 8).

GQAL gained wide acceptance among BRAC leaders as well as staff members, for helping change BRAC's work environment, as well as the organisation culture (Rao and Kelleher 1998). GQAL had clear potential to be adapted for use at the community level, as a means of addressing gender inequality as it intersects with poverty, and in particular to reduce domestic violence in households. GQAL's aim was to address the intra-household dimensions of economic inequality which are related to gender inequality, ensuring that the women participating in BRAC's programming benefited as fully as possible from self-employment, and crucially did not experience increased risk of violence as a result of their role in income-generation.

In the rest of the chapter, we focus on GQAL's use at the community level, and draw on a number of sources for our information. Different internal and external evaluations used in writing this chapter include Adair *et al.* (2011), Alim (2012), Ghuznavi (2008) and Huq *et al.* (2012).

Using GQAL at the community level

From 1999, GQAL was incorporated as a pilot in BRAC's Challenging the Frontiers of Poverty Reduction – Targeting the Ultra Poor (CFPR-TUP) programme. The CFPR-TUP programme aimed to improve the economic and social situation of extremely deprived women and their households. However, there had been a focus on the practical needs of women and no emphasis on addressing gender equality via awareness-raising or activism among ultra-poor female participants, and the wider community.

During that period, GQAL was used to help men and women from ultra-poor households involved with the CFPR-TUP programme to recognise gender-based discrimination, help them develop more gender-sensitive and equitable relations, give women more of an equal voice in personal as well as family affairs, and enable women to exert greater control over resources and decisions within households. It aimed to target gender inequality by addressing the power dynamics between the sexes, through working with ultra-poor men in order to raise their awareness, to encourage their participation in ending gender-based violence, and also alter unequal distribution of food within households, which left women and girls malnourished. The ultra-poor women and men involved in GQAL were trained to become gender justice educators, taking on the role of front-line equality promoters. As a grassroots development organisation, BRAC engages thousands of community volunteers, most of them women, in its different programmes. They are front-level change-makers in GQAL (BRAC 2014).[1]

GQAL also involved women and men from other classes – local influentials, organised social groups, and non-poor groups. The reason behind involving different classes and sexes was to strengthen the support that needed to be given to ultra-poor women, in order to bring about community-wide changes in gender relations.

Following a pilot phase, which took place in four rural areas of the country, GQAL was integrated into CFPR on an expanded basis, in 50 sub-districts in 12 districts from 2004 to 2011 and covered 30,000 ultra-poor households (Huq *et al.* 2012). Since 2012, GQAL has been implemented at a large scale in at least 390,000 households, 1,062 villages and 40 unions in eight *upazilas* (sub-districts) of eight districts across Bangladesh (BRAC 2012, 8). GQAL works with every household in the area, irrespective of class, caste, religion, ethnicity, and sex.

Taking account of recommendations of various evaluations, the new phase of GQAL that started in 2012 has two specific focal points for intervention. One is to increase the capacity of targeted women to influence decisions that are affecting their lives and their well-being. The other is to support men and women working together to change gender relations and reduce violence against women. Even though GQAL largely focuses on gender relations and (in)equality at the household level, it also considers these in the context of wider household–community–state dynamics.

This new post-2012 phase is yet to be evaluated by any independent body, but the programme in its earlier phase was evaluated both internally and externally. An internal BRAC study (Alim 2012) assessed changes in knowledge, attitude, and practices, regarding women's access to and control over assets, in selected samples. Around 35 per cent of respondents in the baseline felt that both the husband and the wife should engage in collective decision-making in the purchase of land, livestock, trees, and ornaments. Midline, around 90 per cent of them believed the same. Similar changes were also observed in respondents' perception of who should decide about sale of household assets, and how to spend the money derived from such sales.

The GQAL programme has a vast database on the households it works with, and can track and measure the changes in household gender relations. The internal monitoring process of GQAL captures changes through the application of a range of tools and techniques that are both quantitative and qualitative. A baseline study was carried out in 2012 (Alim and Khatun unpublished). It used quasi-experimental design, and employed quantitative methods of data collection and analysis in areas in which GQAL activities were operating, and control areas where they were not. Baseline data were collected in 2012 and data collected one year later enabled us to see the trends and explore these further via case studies of individual participants. Those included in the next section are taken from the internal monitoring progress report for 2013 (BRAC GJD 2015).

Addressing gender inequality: evidence from the field

Supporting gender equality and economic equality through focusing on VAWC

As stated earlier, the core area of GQAL intervention is to reduce domestic violence in households. The data show that the prevalence of domestic violence is less than before. In the last six months, 83 per cent of women had not been slapped nor pushed away, 95 per cent had not been beaten, and 91 per cent had not been forced out of the house. Over one-third (36 per cent) of women said that in the last six months, their husbands had not put up resistance to their wishes to visit their relatives.

Qualitative research into individuals reveals the links between economic activities, VAWC, and the role of an intervention like GQAL in supporting couples to negotiate changes to gender roles and relations. An example is Tania, 32, who lives in Kalopota village of Madhukhali sub-district in Faridpur, a district in the southern region. In an in-depth interview (15 November 2014), she gave an account of empowerment which attributed much to economic opportunities (both as part of development interventions, and as part of a process of industrial development in which garment factories offer employment to women, as described earlier in this chapter).

Tania's story. Tania's account of her life began with her marriage, aged 15, to a farmer, who was keen to improve his family's financial situation, and therefore also started working as a mason. In 2001, Tania learnt about a BRAC programme that aimed to train women like her in income-generating activities. She decided to join the programme to support her family. Upon finding out, her husband protested because no women in his family had ever been involved with NGO-related work. Despite such protests, Tania with a neighbour went to BRAC's office in Madhukhali town, 7km away from her village, Kalopota, to receive training in sewing. When her husband found out, he physically assaulted her. Tania silently bore the torture. Even her parents told her to be silent, and to negotiate a compromise with her husband.

Unable to withstand her husband's violence, Tania ultimately fled from home, and went to one of her cousins in Savar, an industrial town near the Bangladeshi capital Dhaka. There she tried to find a job in order to be financially independent. After several unsuccessful attempts she finally got a job in a garment factory. However, her job did not last long; her husband found out about her whereabouts, tracked her down and brought her home. At this point, his violent behaviour towards her remained unchanged. However, Tania's dream to earn her own income still burnt strongly within her as the numerous financially independent women in Savar 's garments' factories had greatly inspired her. Therefore, despite being fearful of her husband's behaviour, she joined BRAC's GQAL programme in 2012 when BRAC staff members approached her.

Tania became a member of SAMPRITI, a women's collective instigated by GQAL, which supports and mobilises women's collective action, and provides access to various state and non-state services (including the government's allowance for poor women, skill training) to women like Tania. As a member, she also received training on issues such as women's empowerment and equality. Tania's husband refused to join the programme when he was also approached by BRAC. However, this time he did not object to his wife's decision. Tania also attended a BRAC primary school.[2] Here, she learnt painting. With her first income – from a painting she did for SAMPRITI – in 2013 she bought a sewing machine. She discussed this with her husband and gained agreement. He sold a cow to pay for the machine, as he thought that Tania's work could increase the family income. She started to earn TK.500–600 ($7–8) per month, and earned TK.2,000 ($26) during Eid and other festivals. To do business, she now travels to Madhukhali town alone.

As a member of SAMPRITI, Tania also now participates in various local meetings, where she advocates on poor women's rights, and earns on average TK.300 per meeting per month for this from the organisers (the local government authority and NGOs). Tania is known to other poor women, who see her as someone dedicated towards bargaining for their rights. Even her husband supports her, runs chores for her, and no longer hits her. Now she spends her income on her children, mainly for the sake of their education. She reports that this in turn makes her husband very happy.

Throughout this account of Tania's marriage and her evolving livelihood strategy, we can see the links and connections between economic poverty and gender inequality. It is clear how gender inequality, and in particular violence against women, constrains women's economic decisions, and the need for activities which enable men and boys to see the value of changes to the gender division of labour, and to gender norms which underestimate the importance of women's actual and potential contribution.

This reduction in marital violence is associated with a change in men's and women's perception of VAWC, including the recognition of it as a crime. Since GQAL targets men and boys as well as women and girls, both men and women have recognised that violence against women and children is a crime. About 94 per cent of men who had participated in GQAL over a six month period reported that discrimination based on gender among children is not right. About 93 per cent of men recognised that financial discrimination and emotional violence against women were crimes; 81 per cent of men stated that physical torture or violence against women was a crime.

Transfer of economic assets to women as an indicator of increasing gender equality

Along with the reduction in violence against women, GQAL has also aimed to increase men's awareness of the value of their partners and other female family members. GQAL recorded a total of 1,792 husbands who gave property, land in some cases, to their wives. This valuation is reflected in the transfer of assets in the woman's name. Earlier evaluation also carried out by Huq *et al.* (2012) explored this valuation in GQAL. This asset transfer to women by husbands, particularly land, is significant in the Bangladeshi society where men have traditionally inherited property.

In an in-depth interview, in Gazipur sub-district, a town in central Bangladesh, (10 November 2014) Nandita, a married woman aged 30, gave an account of property transfer from her husband.

Nandita's story. Nandita is from the Mirzapur union (sub-sub-district) of Gazipur sub-district. She stated that she was satisfied in general with her marriage prior to involvement with GQAL, because, she reported, her husband treated her well and was non-violent, and her in-laws' family was affluent and offered economic security. However, underneath the surface she was unhappy, because she was not entitled to control any family assets, and could not spend money by her choice. Her husband also believed that a woman did not have any need for her own money. Moreover, she did all the household chores without any assistance from her husband.

Nandita's account was that when the couple was invited to the GQAL programme training, it dramatically affected them. Nandita's husband realised that he was treating her wrongly, and was underestimating and undermining her contribution to his life. Upon attending meetings for men in his neighbourhood, he came to understand that he was discriminating against his wife and that a happy, peaceful conjugal life depended on partnership and mutual respect. He started to change his attitude, and presented Nandita with ten decimals of land from his property, as a symbol of respect and commitment to change. Nandita stated that such an action had filled her with a sense of dignity and confidence as she felt that her husband had finally recognised her existence, and had acknowledged her contribution to the family. Nandita also understood that women needed something of their own to feel confident.

Ensuring increased economic contribution leads to growing gender equality in marriage

GQAL aims to help women to raise their voices, to increase their mobility and to rise their participation in household decisions. In assessing the impact of the programme, women were asked questions about gender relations over the past six months. Forty-five per cent of women said that in the last six months their husbands have always asked for their opinion on decisions in family matters and have listened to them if they opposed their own view. Forty-six per cent of women said that their husbands had not silenced them from speaking. Thirty-five per cent said they had immediately protested or spoken out if there was any injustice in their families.

In the case of mobility, GQAL appeared to have had a positive impact. Echoing the story of Tania, above, many women said they could now travel alone when they needed to, without waiting for their husbands' permission, or for someone to escort them. In the last six months, 36 per cent of women had visited relatives' homes by themselves; 29 per cent of women had been able to visit spectacular places when they wanted to; and 61 per cent of women said that they had been able to attend social gatherings or enjoy cultural events.

Over two-thirds (68 per cent) of women knew about their husbands' income levels and expenditure. Sixty-seven per cent of women said that their husbands shared all household issues with them. It is clear from GQAL that if there is an economic rationale to deviate from norms about the gender division of labour within marriage and the family, this can start a process of growing economic and gender equality within marriage, if there is support to a couple to negotiate a way through these changes.

Fatema's story. Before GQAL, Fatema, a married woman aged 35 who had studied up to primary level only, did not contribute any income to the family. She was confined to doing unpaid household chores, while her husband worked as a share-cropper. The family did not have sufficient income. After she and her husband participated in GQAL, Fatema reported that her life had changed drastically. Fatema's husband no longer shouted at her, but became more caring. She became confident, and started to believe that women can accomplish anything that a man can. With her new-found confidence, she decided to start a ladies' cosmetic shop, and told her husband about her desire to earn her own income. Her husband helped her in getting her own shop in a local Baleshor market by seeking help from the market's secretary, who was also a relative of theirs.

Fatema started her business in 2013 with a loan of TK.10,000 ($130) and TK.10,000 from her parents. She sourced products from both far-off and nearby markets. As her business grew, she realised that she could double her profit if she could take her goods to the capital city of Dhaka (nearly 100km from her home). Initially her husband accompanied her, but now she goes alone. She faced challenges in running a business amidst 150 other shops that were run by men. Moreover, people gossiped about her and tried to influence her husband. However, Fatema reported that she did not care about the public's opinion. Her husband now asks for her advice and consults her at times. Sometimes he also helps in shop keeping. Other women also come to her for advice about starting their own personal business (in-depth interview, Madhukhali, Faridpur, 16 November 2014).

This change to Fatema's economic role in her marriage and the household came about after changes in attitudes about gender roles and relations: gender inequality shifted before economic inequality. Changing gender roles in households fully involves men moving into unpaid care work, and this is also quite common in GQAL intervention areas. This is interesting since often it seems that persuading men to take over unpaid care responsibilities is much harder than advocating for wives to earn more income. Data collected in 2013 revealed that one-third (36 per cent) of husbands of women involved also assisted them in household chores, in contrast to just 0.71 per cent reporting this at the time of collecting baseline data in 2012.[3]

The data show that 72 per cent of husbands were fetching water from outside for household work and over one-third (36 per cent) of husbands cooked sometimes. Sixty-eight per cent of husbands also started hanging mosquito nets. Husbands also took care of their children. They understood that it was also their duty to look after their children. Forty per cent of husbands are now taking care of their children regularly; they feed them, clean them up, supervise their education, and take them to the doctor.

The changes have an inter-generational dimension as well. Once the rural women become members of the GQAL programme and take part in different activities, it positively influences their younger children. A change in perception is also developing among the younger generation.

Changes in wider society to support gender equality at all levels

GQAL is informed by an awareness that changing gender relations within the family is not enough until and unless wider society and state services come forward in favour of such changes. Thus, it facilitates community-based collective action to ensure women's increasing access to different state and non-state services.

Kolpona Rani Sarker is a GQAL-led SAMPRITI member at Ramrail village in Brahmanbaria, an eastern district of Bangladesh. As a SAMPRITI member, she bargains with Union Parishad (UP), the lowest tier of local government, to gain access to different services. Kolpona also came to know about gender-based rights, discrimination, violence etc. One day, she, along with other SAMPRITI members, went to Ramrail Union Parishad to bargain with the UP member in order to receive training on the operation of sewing machines and to obtain some guidance for production. They asked the chairman and other UP members about services for income-generation. After collective lobbying, Kolpona received a 15 day long training course in sewing, and was able to engage in income-generating activities (in-depth interview, Brahmanbaria Sadar, 22 October 2014).

Such community actions also address the need for women and girls to gain control of valuable assets beyond economic income, which will enable them to challenge both economic inequality and gender inequality. Education is the most powerful of these. The following story is about a young girl who could pursue her education due to the support from GQAL. With four other siblings, Sabina, aged 12, came from a poverty stricken family. Her father was ill and her mother was unable to bear the household expenses (that also included Sabina's tuition). Thus, her schooling was discontinued and it was decided that she would be married off to her cousin in the hope of easing the financial burden. Sabina knew about GQAL and she went to her neighbour, a member of GQAL-led SAMPRITI about her problem. SAMPRITI along with BRAC's gender-equality promoters came forth, convinced her parents to call off the marriage, urged the school committee to grant Sabina a full free studentship, and enabled her to return to school (in-depth interview, Brahmanbaria Sadar, 20 October 2014).

Finally, the GQAL approach is inclusive, aiming to meet the interests and needs of women facing complex inequalities, including women with disabilities. There is some evidence of some success in supporting disabled women to build their own self-confidence, at the community level as well as within the household. An example is the story of Sabina Khatun, aged 25, who had lost the ability to walk normally as a child. Extreme poverty had meant that she had to drop out of school. Her disability caused her to be viewed as a burden and she was neglected. However, she wanted to help people and contribute to society. Now she works as a gender justice educator, raising community awareness about issues like the importance of equal education among boys and girls, elimination of gender-based discrimination and child marriages etc. She is now appreciated by her community. She no longer thinks of herself as inferior; in fact, she is now a confident woman (in-depth interview, Royganj, Sirajgonj, 18 October 2014).

Conclusion

There is a growing global debate on the relationship between gender equality, economic growth, and economic equality in society (Kabeer 2012; Kabeer and Natali 2013). States and development organisations have often used economic empowerment as an entry-point to working with women on wider issues of gender inequality and women's rights. However, critiques by feminists have stressed the limitations of focusing on women's economic activities as a route to gender equality. A key argument is that this focus on women as agents of development leaves the structural subordination of women by institutions including the state, the market, and the household intact. This makes economic interventions much less useful and effective to poverty eradication, as well as potentially harming women who face a backlash. To gain structural transformation in the wake of economic empowerment projects, sufficient women need to become successful entrepreneurs to bring about change on a scale to challenge attitudes and beliefs about gender roles in the family and community. This model of change relies on male relatives, families, and wider society perceiving the worth of women's increased economic contribution to household income and national development (Kabeer 2012). It also assumes women can cope with the risk of violence and resistance while longer-term change occurs.

BRAC has evolved a method of working which aims to overcome these concerns, via the GQAL programming which works on gender equality in its own right, via activities which run parallel to self-employment promotion. While the organisation contributed significantly to poverty reduction and women's economic empowerment since the 1980s, our experience is that women's self-employment on its own does not necessarily bring vast numbers of women out of poverty (whether we understand women's poverty either in relation to intra-household poverty, or in relation to household income levels, which are the focus of current concerns about growing inequality in society). A focus on self-employment alone did not result in challenges to the structures of patriarchal inequality. However, programmes like GQAL which take a gender equality approach to poverty alleviation are employing a gender analysis of poverty and the linkages between gender inequality and economic inequality and these are showing success. In the GQAL experience we can see that addressing gender equality within households can be a first and essential step to women's economic empowerment, rather than the other way around. Attitudinal change among women and men can lead on to changes in gender roles, including women taking up self-employment. Gender inequality and its link to economic inequality needs to be much more centrally positioned than it currently is in development debates.

Notes

1. For example, Sasthay Sebika (health volunteer) in Health Nutrition and Population Programme, Ain Sebika (legal volunteer) in Human Rights and Legal Services Programme, Kishori Netri (adolescent leader) in Adolescent Development Programme. The GQAL programme facilitates more than 47,000 community volunteers, familiar as Gender Justice Educator (GJE), Volunteer Youth Educator (VYE), SAMPRITI members.
2. BRAC has provided basic education to around 10 million students in Bangladesh, with graduates from its non-formal primary schools numbering nearly five million. For more about this, please visit: http://education. brac.net/ (last checked by the authors 22 June 2015).
3. However, this is not the common practice, especially in rural Bangladesh. The GQAL training, which includes the spouse, intends to sensitise men enough in favour of changing gender roles. It, therefore, encourages men to be braver in reporting the household work they do in the family. Thus, they become able to remove the sense of shame surrounding such household chores in this particular cultural context.

References

Adair, Mike, Michael Samson, and Tahera Yasmin (2011) (unpublished) *CFPR Joint Review*, Dhaka: BRAC

Ahmed, Sharmeen and Mahmuda Khatun (2008) 'Gender relations in post-modern societies: Impact of globalization on women's position', *Journal of Knowledge Globalization* 1(2): 109–25

Alim, Md. Abdul (2012) *Shaking Embedded Gender Roles and Relations: An Evaluation of GenderQuality Action Learning Program*, Dhaka: Research and Evaluation Division, BRAC

Alim, Md. Abdul and Fathema Zhura Khatoon (unpublished) *Determining the Existing Gender Discrimination and Violence and Sexual Harassment against Women in Selected Districts: A Baseline Survey of GQAL Programme*, Dhaka: Research and Evaluation Division, BRAC

BANBEIS (2013) Bangladesh Bureau of Educational Information and Statistics, http://banbeis.gov.bd/data/index.php?option=com_content&view=articl

e&id=979:table-81-number-of-university-teacher-and-enrolment-by-type-and-gender-2012&catid=147:university-education-2011&Itemid=231 (last checked by the authors 14 May 2015)

BBS (2011) 'Report on Labour Force Survey 2010', Dhaka: Bangladesh Bureau of Statistics

BBS (2013) 'Report on Violence against Women Survey 2011', Dhaka: Bangladesh Bureau of Statistics

BRAC (2012) *The GQAL Project Proposal, Gender Justice and Diversity*, Dhaka: BRAC

BRAC (2014) 'BRAC Bangladesh Report 2013', Dhaka: BRAC

BRAC GJD (2015) 'Gender Quality Action Learning Programme – Annual Progress Report, January to December 2014', Dhaka: Gender, Justice and Diversity, BRAC

Ferdousi, Samiya and Wang Dehai (2014) 'Economic growth, poverty and inequality trend in Bangladesh', *Asian Journal of Social Sciences and Humanities* 3:1

Ghuznavi, Farah (2008) 'From Action Learning, to Learning to Act: Lessons from GQAL', Dhaka: Gender Justice and Diversity, BRAC

Halder, Shantana (2003) *Poverty Outreach and BRAC's Microfinance Interventions: Programme Impact and Sustainability*, Dhaka: BRAC

Hossain, Naomi, Sohela Nazneen, and Maheen Sultan (2011) National Discourses on Women's Empowerment in Bangladesh: Continuities and Change, BDI Working Paper 03, Dhaka: BRAC Development Institute, BRAC University, July 2011

Huq, Lopita, Simeen Mahmud, and Maheen Sultan (2012) *Assessing the Performance of GQAL in Changing Gender Norms and Behaviour*, Dhaka: BRAC Development Institute, BRAC University

Kabeer, Naila (2012) Women's Economic Empowerment and Inclusive Growth: Labour Market and Enterprise Development, SIG Working Paper 2012/1, paper prepared for DFID and IDRC, London: DFID and Ottawa: IDRC

Kabeer, Naila and Luisa Natali (2013) Gender Equality and Economic Growth: Is there a Win-Win? IDS Working Paper 2013: 417, Brighton: Institute of Development Studies, University of Sussex

Matin, Imran (2004) *The Very Poor Who Participate In Microfinance Institutions and Those Who Never Did: A Comparative Analysis*, Dhaka: BRAC, August 2004

Rao, Aruna and David Kelleher (1998) 'Gender lost and gender found: BRAC's gender quality action-learning programme.' *Development in Practice* 8(2): 173–85

Solotaroff, Jennifer L. and Rohini P. Pande (2014) *Violence against Women and Girls: Lessons from South Asia*, Washington, DC: The World Bank

Sukaj, Rubena (2014) Priority Areas for Bangladesh's Future Development: Inequality, Employment and Poverty, Bangladesh Development Research Working Paper Series 21, Falls Church, VA: BDRC, January 2014

Titumir, Rashed Al Mahmud (2013) *Institutions Matters: State of Women in Bangladesh 2013*, Dhaka: Shrabon Prokashani

WEF (2014) 'The Global Gender Gap Report 2014', Cologny/Geneva: World Economic Forum

World Bank (2008) Whispers to Voices: Gender and Social Transformation in
Bangladesh, Bangladesh Development Series, paper No. 22, Washington,
DC: The World Bank

About the Authors

Sheepa Hafiza works as executive director of Ain O Salish Kendra - ASK Law
and meditation centre, a national legal aid and human rights organization.
Email: sheepa.h@gmail.com

Mohammed Kamruzzaman is Research Investigator Health Systems and
Population Studies Division, icddr,b, Dhaka, Bangladesh. Email: linktapan@
hotmail.com

Hasne Ara Begum works as Programme Manager for Gender Justice and
Diversity programme of BRAC in Bangladesh. Email: aradalia@yahoo.com

CHAPTER 11

Bridging inequalities through inclusion: women's rights organisations as the 'missing link' in donor government-led participatory policy development and practice

Abigail Hunt, Hannah Bond and Ruth Ojiambo Ochieng

Abstract

This chapter focuses on women's rights organisations and their role in challenging inequality within the development process. Women in poverty are excluded as a result of their unequal societal position, geographic location, and the predominance of 'top-down' and piecemeal policymaking processes carried out by donor governments. We argue that in-country women's rights organisations provide the 'missing link' to bridge the disconnect between grassroots, marginalised women and donor decision-makers. This chapter focuses on the UK government's approach to developing policy and practice aimed at furthering international women's rights, focusing on the Women, Peace and Security agenda. Engaging with women's rights organisations not only ensures that donor policy and practice responds fully to the interests and needs of the poorest and most marginalised women in the global South, but renders the decision-making process itself empowering to the women involved.

Keywords: women's rights organisations; policy; participation; women, peace and security; inclusion; decision-making

Introduction

There is an increasing recognition among the community of actors and institutions working to support global development, including bilateral and international development and humanitarian donors,[1] of the 'participatory approach'[2] as the ideal foundation of policy development in the inter-related spheres of international development, conflict prevention and resolution and post-conflict recovery, reconstruction, and peace-building. This important

http://dx.doi.org/10.3362/9781780447278.011

turn towards the involvement of women and men in conflict-affected environments in policy processes has been broadly welcomed by women's rights activists and organisations working in countries affected by armed conflict. Full implementation of participatory approaches would contribute substantially to the implementation of post-conflict peace and security commitments, and the realisation of women's rights. There are many challenges in addressing inherently unequal power relations between ruling global, regional, and national elites – the majority of whom are men – and the women affected directly by conflict who live in poverty in many countries in the global South. Women's participation offers opportunities for increased national and local 'buy-in' to policies led or instigated by international actors, making it far more likely that these will fit with women's realities, and that they will be effective, responding to the full range of women's and girls' experiences, locally-identified priorities, needs, challenges, and opportunities.

The focus on participation as a key factor in policy processes has been flanked by an emphasis on integrating gender equality and women's rights concerns into conflict resolution and peace-building. The well-known UN Security Council Resolution (UNSCR) 1325 was adopted unanimously in October 2000. It, and associated resolutions, signal an intent to place gender concerns at the centre of peace-building processes. UNSCR 1325 has four 'pillars', one of which is commonly known as the 'participation pillar ' and calls for increased participation of women at all levels of decision-making, in mechanisms for the prevention, management, and resolution of conflict, in peace negotiations, and in peace operations.[3]

However, despite acknowledgement of the need for women's participation and the integration of gender concerns into post-conflict and peace-building, progress has been painfully slow. Many post-conflict reconstruction agendas neglect entirely the experiences of women during conflict, simultaneously side-lining their most basic needs during the aftermath. In Africa, many post-conflict, transition, and reconstruction policy processes have been driven by international institutions, emphasising legislation and governance amidst a stream of recommendations highlighting the need to improve the rule of law, hold free and fair elections, combat corruption, and hold perpetrators of violence responsible for their actions (Englebert and Tull 2008). This agenda reflects the priorities of dominant actors in conflict resolution and post-conflict reconstruction. However, it has not been put together with the full and meaningful participation of women, and hence may reflect their priorities to some extent, but cannot claim to be informed and shaped by the gendered experiences and voices of women.

The continued absence of women from policy processes is acknowledged by many development and humanitarian actors as a problem. It represents, and perpetuates, a de-politicisation of women's experiences during conflict, turning women into victims of violence and abuse, and objects of charity, rather than political actors (Chigudu 2014). This results in policies which do not respond to gender concerns, and hence do not fully meet the interests and needs of women. For example, in Democratic Republic of the Congo, despite the reports of the extent of violence against women and girls (VAWG), 54 per cent of projects were judged to be gender-blind (CARE International 2014, 7) – that is, to be planned and implemented without a gender analysis, and without gender-disaggregated aims and objectives – and of 585 peace agreements from 1990 to 2010, only 92 contained any references to women (Bell and O'Rourke 2010).

What solutions can be proposed to ensure women's full and meaningful participation in post-conflict and peace-building policy processes? In this chapter, we draw on our own first-hand experiences, and on research from organisations including our own – that is, Womankind Worldwide, Gender Action for Peace and Security (GAPS), and Isis-Women's International Cross Cultural Exchange (Isis-WICCE) – to argue that women's rights organisations could be the missing link. The participation of women's rights organisations offers huge potential for equalising power-imbalanced relations between donors and people they often view as 'beneficiaries'; and, more widely, between the elites who dominate development, and the women and men whose lives are shaped by the laws, agreements, policies, and practices they design, legislate, and implement. This would represent a concerted attempt to redefine the donor–'beneficiary' power relationship by placing in-country women's rights organisations at the centre of policymaking.

Because we see this problem as fundamentally concerning class, race, and gender-based inequalities between donors and beneficiaries, we advanced the idea of writing this chapter for inclusion in *Gender and Inequalities*. Development and humanitarian workers are often focused on the ideal of 'partnership' between themselves and the people they seek to support and help, but this masks an inherently unequal relationship in which power and resources are often held on one side. Working with in-country women's rights organisations should be both a key to challenging this, and provide a model of a different way of working in which the politics of (in)equality are visible and acknowledged, and all actors involved consciously work to dismantle unequal power relations.

In the next section, we focus on participation. After that, we set the scene by reviewing the qualities and attributes of women's rights organisations, which enable them to be uniquely useful in bridging the gap between development donors and the women whose lives they aim to improve via policies and practices. We then shift to review the United Kingdom (UK) government's approach to developing policy and practice aimed at furthering international women's rights, focusing on the Women, Peace and Security agenda. We conclude by outlining a number of concrete steps, which if taken by donors would contribute significantly to ensuring their policy development process and practice is participatory and more inclusive of marginalised women.

As suggested above, this chapter draws on various sources, including personal learning about the issues, gained from our different experience as expert policy and programming practitioners in the thematic area of participation as related to Women, Peace and Security. It also draws on findings from the literature on participation and the role of women's rights organisations in development and humanitarian work, including a research project undertaken by ActionAid, Institute of Development Studies and Womankind Worldwide (2012) to examine women's roles in local peace-building in Afghanistan, Liberia, Nepal, Pakistan, and Sierra Leone and the role of women's rights organisations in supporting women and bridging the disconnect between local peace-building and national and international policy processes.

Towards participatory policy development and practice in conflict-affected environments

Given the vast range of conflict-affected environments, an 'ideal' participatory process will vary depending on the specific context; there can never be a 'one-size-fits-all' approach. However, as the following sections demonstrate, both research and our own extensive experience of participation from a gender perspective can be drawn on to identify certain core elements that are important to consider in any participatory initiative.

First, the scope and nature of interaction between donors and women participants is of key importance. Women's participation needs to be systematically planned throughout the policy and programme cycle; instead, it is often introduced into the process in the form of ad hoc consultation, as a means of incorporating 'women's voices' and claiming the initiative has the buy-in and support of women, once the initiative is well underway. While it is often important for donors to set parameters within which processes will operate as a first step, a failure to engage in-country stakeholders at the earliest opportunity means any subsequent dialogue can be interpreted as a 'tick-box' instrument designed to increase the donor 's own credibility rather than fostering meaningful participation and empowerment of the targets of their interventions.

As Harry Jones *et al.* (2012, 103) state:

> *Participatory approaches have been incorporated into processes without altering the associated ways of working; in fact, they are often seen as a set of measures to be used after the scope and objectives of a project have been defined, in order to help meet its predefined goals. Poor and vulnerable people rarely have the chance to question project objectives or scope.*

There is a big difference between participation and consultation, although these are often apparently understood to be synonymous. Consultation often entails stakeholder views being collected without any commitment to act upon them, or as a means of simply informing programme participants, community members, or stakeholders about upcoming or ongoing projects (Jones *et al.* 2012, 103). Although this form of consultation can at times offer some tangible opportunity for participants to influence donor actions, and is arguably preferable to a total absence of communication, it often involves a piecemeal, non-sustained approach, in which women are provided with or asked to provide information relating to a pre-defined framework or agenda.

Similarly, if not more problematic is the even less clearly defined notion of 'stakeholder/beneficiary engagement', the terms of which can also be set by the donor and limit women's *de facto* influence. Indeed, research into women's substantive participation at the regional and international level following conflict reveals women's limited effectiveness at influencing outcomes within such 'invited spaces' (Isis-WICCE 2014a).

Therefore, although good participatory processes will inevitably be varied and context-specific, they will be based on a principle of sustained inclusion of women from the earliest stage possible. This will include principles of two-way communication, empowering participants to reflect and share their views and priorities on the conceptualisation and design of policy and programming, through to their implementation, delivery, monitoring, and evaluation. Furthermore, by ensuring equal decision-making powers with participants, donors can become enablers of the transformative change many women's rights organisations are working to achieve, instead of these same organisations being brought in to implement a pre-defined, top-down agenda.

There are three additional core elements upon which participatory donor-facilitated processes will ideally be based. First, the country or local context is crucial in determining the approach and, in line with established development principles, the role and position of the country's government will have implications for donor engagement with women. Notably, 'bottom-up' development approaches rely on supportive measures by government authorities, meaning that participatory development can be difficult where governments are unwilling to reform social and political systems (Nunnenkamp 1995, cited in Jad 2007). While established political processes in-country cannot and should not be bypassed, it is important that donors do not use challenging country-contexts as an excuse to weaken their own efforts towards ensuring women's full and meaningful participation.

Second, feminist methodologies have posited for many years that only by foregrounding women's own lived experiences will comprehension of the complex realities that shape women's lives emerge (Knight 2000). This understanding is an essential precursor to locally-relevant, sustainable, and impactful donor action. Useful lessons in this regard can be drawn from Uganda, where women had developed a locally-relevant conceptualisation of participation, rights promotion, prevention of violence against women, and conflict recovery long before UNSCR 1325 and related resolutions. The long experience of Isis-WICCE of working in Uganda has led to an understanding within the organisation that an unintended effect of the establishment of the global Women, Peace and Security framework is that these established and home-grown theories of women's rights and empowerment and the specific concerns of Ugandan women were subsumed into the international architecture.

Another notable lesson on the way in which women's rights organisations have reconciled their locally-relevant understandings of women's experiences of conflict with the UNSCR 1325 framework comes from Libya, where despite international acceptance of the Convention on the Elimination of All Forms of Discrimination Against Women (CEDAW) as a universal benchmark on gender equality, women rarely advocate for policy and legislative change using CEDAW because it is seen as synonymous with a rights-based approach and is therefore widely rejected by conservative elements of government and society. However, in a context where security-related discourse holds significant political resonance, activists cite UNSCR 1325 and related resolutions as more useful framing tools for policy-related advocacy (personal communication with Rida Al Tubuly, Libyan activist and Director of Maan Nabneeha ['Together we build it'], 4 December 2014).

Despite the recurring emphasis within dominant international development discourse on embracing local solutions and knowledge, donors have often tended to use mainstream, 'internationalised' knowledge and content, or, at best, knowledge gathered from stakeholders based in capital cities, to determine and shape their policies. Alternative approaches and knowledge provided by in-country women's rights organisations, such as in the Libyan and Ugandan examples cited above, is often disregarded because it does not clearly resonate with the global frameworks to which donors subscribe. In this context, interventions will inevitably remain 'top-down' and paternalistic until indigenous women's knowledge is prioritised and validated as a primary evidence base for development interventions.

Third, ensuring wide-reaching representation and diversity of the women taking part in participatory processes cannot be overlooked, even when involving only the most easily accessible groups of women is often quicker, easier, and requires fewer resources. Basing knowledge and understanding in development on close and collaborative relationships with marginalised communities has been advocated for many years (for example, see Chambers 1997). However, this has not always been translated into practice. Women are not a homogenous group, yet women are often conceived as a single entity with little account paid to intersectional markers such as age, social class, caste, disability, geographic location, ethnicity, and marital status including widowhood. To reach the most marginalised women, whom development often purports to be concerned with, processes must at a minimum ensure the participation of diverse groups, including those outside urban areas and in other difficult to access locations, such as prisons.

Some promising practice in these areas can be identified, for example some women's rights organisations have welcomed the approach taken by the government of the Netherlands under its current National Action Plan on Women, Peace and Security (Hunt and Cansfield 2014). Positively, this government supports inclusive accountability spaces and engages in some meaningful discussion with civil society and women's organisations, particularly with regard to implementation of the NAP, as well as working with women's rights organisations and communities in long-term partnerships. In addition, feminist activists from conflict-affected countries have been invited to the Netherlands to engage in public discussion on the importance of overseas development assistance in post-conflict contexts. Such participation of women not only increases donor-government understanding of the role of aid in supporting women's inclusion in post-conflict reconstruction, but can also benefit donor governments where political will is present but they struggle to justify overseas development assistance spending to their country's public. Another example of promising practice includes the Norwegian Ministry of Foreign Affairs, which has invited in-country women's rights organisations to address its ministers and officials.

Bridging inequality between donors and beneficiaries: the role of women's rights organisations

Women's rights organisations – which we will define for the purposes of this chapter as women-led organisations working to advance gender equality and women's rights (Esplen 2013) – are diverse in form, and operate at multiple levels and in many arenas, from grassroots to international levels. An advantage for international donors and organisations of working with in-country women-led organisations is that these are usually strongly rooted in the communities with whom they work (O'Connell 2013). Evidence from a study carried out in 2013 which included a review of key findings from research and practice as well as semi-structured interviews with African women's rights organisations in receipt of Comic Relief grants suggested they offer added value to donors, by adopting the innovative approaches they take to achieving their objectives, as well as their relevance and connectedness to women's and girls' lives (O'Connell 2012).

Women's rights organisations are frequently to be found working in highly challenging environments, during conflict and its aftermath. From this, they are well-placed to understand the realities of women's lives on the ground, and their local connections potentially allow for context-specific insights which can be difficult for outsider organisations to grasp. In-country women's rights organisations can play a full role in peace processes to represent the interests and concerns of women in their constituencies, rooted in their concrete experience of offering support to women during conflict and post-conflict. By supporting grassroots, marginalised women to create spaces to organise collectively, build skills, and share information, women's rights organisations play a vital role in fostering women's empowerment in a range of spheres, as well as contributing to local-level peace-building (ActionAid *et al.* 2012). They may also adopt roles in training more women leaders in the skills of peace-building and advocacy, and act as key connectors between local-level peace processes and national priorities.

As a result of this connection to, and understanding of, grassroots women's lives, in-country women's rights organisations are a key connector between local-level peace processes and priorities, and those at the national and international level (ActionAid *et al.* 2012). This connection flows in two directions, and has an effect at multiple levels. Translating global norms into domestic policy and practice is conditional on the presence of strong, vibrant in-country women's rights organisations and movements, meaning that these organisations are crucial for locally-relevant implementation of international frameworks (Htun and Weldon 2012). They also play a key role in sharing knowledge to raise women's awareness of how policy issues affect their lives, which can be particularly important for marginalised groups (Tembo and Wells 2007).

Equally importantly, women's rights organisations can help fill the gap between women and the institutions governing their lives (Gaventa 2003), by representing knowledge and perspectives of women's lived realities in the policy process, as well as empowering marginalised women themselves to participate in these processes. For example, in Uganda, at the national level, Isis-WICCE facilitated the formation of a Women's Task Force in 2009 to advocate for the integration of gender perspectives in the country's Peace, Recovery and Development Plan (PDRP) and the National Action Plan on Women, Peace and Security and to ensure the government's accountability on the implementation of these policies. A key priority of the Task Force was to ensure the meaningful participation of a diverse constituency of women, including rurally-based, marginalised women, leading to their successful influencing of the implementation of the PRDP and its later revision to better respond to their priorities and concerns. In this context, we can infer that by recognising and involving in-country women's rights organisations as the 'missing link' between themselves and grassroots women, international donors can make tangible steps towards ensuring relevant and impactful policy and practice.

Barriers encountered by women's rights organisations

However, despite their multi-faceted role at the forefront of protection and promotion of women's rights, and as connectors between the grassroots and national and international levels, in-country women's rights organisations face a multitude of barriers to their participation in the policy and practice of development processes.

The context in which these organisations operate is constantly changing. When there is an expansion of regressive legislation dictating the role and operations of civil society, the scope of women's rights organisations whose rights-based and socially transformative agendas are unsupported is narrowed substantially, or in some cases overtly restricted, by the national regime. The effect of this is that international government donors often limit the offer and availability of financial, technical, and political support to women's rights organisations based in such countries. In addition, there is a real and current risk in some contexts of reprisals against civil society representatives who participate in or collaborate with international donors on their projects, especially in countries where freedom of assembly is restricted by the government, and security services, and where women's rights are under threat from 'extremist' views.

More widely, the current environment has been conceptualised as a 'perfect storm', in which donor language and thinking, increased role and influence of the private sector, and the expansion of many international non-governmental organisations to become global corporate actors in development combine to limit the participation of the poor and of many Southern women's rights organisations in donor government-led processes (Wallace *et al.* 2013). One important consequence of this is that access to donor resources is becoming increasingly difficult for many women's rights organisations which are unused to operating in the large-scale partnerships currently proliferating and favoured by international government donors. This severely limits the capacity of both donors and women's rights organisations to push forward progress on gender equality and women's rights over multiple spheres and levels and genuinely incorporate the voices and experiences of women into policy and practice (Wallace *et al.* 2013).

Our own experience of working in networks and with partners located in conflict-affected countries has led us to directly observe a range of specific barriers limiting the meaningful participation of a diverse range of women's rights organisations in policy and practice development. These barriers are common across numerous contexts. Perhaps most significantly, the tendency of donors to consult only with organisations already known to them leads to the exclusion of others. Organisations with resources, whose access to donors is already established (for example through programme funding arrangements or other partnerships), and who are familiar with donor working methods are often more likely to be approached by governments to participate in consultations, or to take advantage of open consultation or engagement processes. Of concern is that these spaces are increasingly inhabited by large, multi-mandate international development agencies, while locally-based women's rights organisations without these characteristics remain marginalised from these processes.

Such selection methods can significantly compromise the integrity of processes vaunted as participatory by the donors leading them. Inviting only selected women's rights organisations can in some cases exclude organisations deemed to be 'problematic', whether intentionally or not. Such organisations can include those not familiar with donor working methods, but also those critical of the donor and/or its working methods, or those not aligned with the donor's approach or even its political framework (Kiai 2014). In the worst-case scenario, donors can use their discretion to encourage the participation of civil society organisations predisposed to support their favoured policy or programmatic approach, meaning that organisations whose mission is aligned with their pre-defined agenda may find it easier to engage in certain discussions (Stone 2004).

Following the Adoption of the Paris Declaration in 2005 and Accra Agenda for Action in 2008 many international statutory donors have increasingly initiated new policies and programmes through recipient country government structures, including those focusing on women's rights and gender equality (Alemany *et al.* 2008). However, as this approach is focused on delivery through national governments, it side-lines civil society organisations including women's rights organisations and their role in advancing gender equality, making it difficult for interventions to address the concerns of the women on whom donors and governments should most focus (Alemany *et al.* 2008).

Logistical barriers are no less relevant: holding meetings in capital cities or major urban areas, neglecting to put in place measures to include women who cannot travel alone to participatory forums for cultural or security reasons, and expecting participants to arrange transport when availability can be erratic or non-existent can all limit the participation of women's rights organisations. The resultant lack of representation and diversity of participants limits in turn the range of experience, insight, and knowledge available to inform the process at hand.

Even where smaller organisations are included, they can have difficulties getting their voices heard because they are not familiar with the international development discourse employed by donors, which can operate as an exclusive and exclusionary language among development practitioners.[4]

It must be acknowledged that some 'barriers', such as travel restrictions due to security concerns, cannot nor should not be controlled by the donor governments. However, they are often able to put in place reasonable measures to overcome these barriers – if the will and resources to do so are made available. Taking such concrete steps not only contributes to the implementation of full, meaningful, inclusive participatory processes, but can impact positively on several other key areas, including the mutual accountability of donor initiatives along the policy or programme cycle.

Participation in practice: recent UK government actions

In this section, we explore initiatives involving the UK government to provide analytical examples of the extent to which it has been able to respond to the issues raised thus far in the chapter. The UK government has recently made high-level commitments to women's participation and recognised the importance of women's voices to peace, security, and stability, for example by offering some support to Syrian women aimed at increasing their participation in the Geneva II peace negotiations (Foreign and Commonwealth Office and The Rt Hon William Hague 2013). It also reaffirmed commitments in this area before and during the launch of the UK National Action Plan on Women, Peace and Security 2014–2017 in June 2014. Following this, the then-UK Foreign Secretary, William Hague, made a clear statement at the Global Summit to End Sexual Violence in Conflict, hosted by the UK government in June 2014:

> *I am saddened that women and women's groups still have to ask to be included at the negotiating table, as if it were a concession to be granted, or a right to be begrudgingly accorded, when in fact it is the only route to better decisions and stronger and safer societies. We should not have to be reminded, as governments, that women must have a seat in every forum of decision-making.*

(Rt. Hon William Hague, Closing Speech at the Global Summit to End Sexual Violence in Conflict, London, 13 June 2014. Full speech online at: https:// www.gov.uk/ government/speeches/foreign-secretary-closes-global-summit-to-end-sexual-violence-in-conflict, last checked by the authors 14 May 2015)

Development of the UK National Action Plan (NAP) on Women, Peace and Security 2014–2017

As the main UK-based co-ordinating body of civil society liaison with government and parliament on issues relating to Women, Peace and Security since 2007, GAPS can confirm that there was an improvement in civil society participation during the review of the last UK NAP on Women, Peace and Security (2011–2013) and the development of the current NAP (2014–2017). The UK NAP is a strategic document outlining the UK government's commitments in the area of Women, Peace and Security, with ongoing practice collated in a separate Implementation Plan.

The review of the previous NAP included an independent unpublished evaluation, and a questionnaire provided by the Foreign and Commonwealth Office to UK-based civil society organisations focusing on this area. In addition consultations in London jointly hosted by civil society and government, and three in-country workshops organised by civil society and supported by the UK government, took place during the development of the new NAP. This degree of consultation went further than the external review processes of previous NAPs, which were entirely civil-society organised, with GAPS acting as the co-ordinating body and GAPS member organisations independently leading the organisation of in-country workshops. However, despite this progress, the consultations did not take place in all six UK NAP focus countries; they were limited to three – Afghanistan, Burma, and Somalia (including Somaliland).

In our view, it is important that planned and funded participation across all NAP focus countries for the full life of the NAP is outlined in the NAP itself, which is not currently the case; annual reviews are undertaken in consultation with women's rights organisations; and a final evaluation used to develop future NAPs. These processes are central to full and meaningful participation in NAP development, and therefore to the sustainability and impact of Women, Peace and Security policy. The experience of GAPS as the main point of liaison between the UK government and civil society on the NAP is that it is difficult for women's rights organisations or the consultations themselves to inform the work programme linked to the NAP.

Global Summit to End Sexual Violence in Conflict and International Protocol on the Documentation and Investigation of Sexual Violence in Conflict

In June 2014, the UK government and the actor Angelina Jolie co-hosted a Global Summit to End Sexual Violence in Conflict. The Summit brought together over 900 experts from across the world in an aim to turn high-level commitments into practical action, including the United Nations General Assembly Declaration of Commitment to End Sexual Violence in Conflict signed by 155 states and other high level commitments (UK Government 2014). The International Protocol on the Documentation and Investigation of Sexual Violence in Conflict was launched at the Summit, and was the culmination of two years' work by the UK government aimed at removing the culture of impunity around sexual violence.

The development of the protocol was led by the UK, and had an Advisory Board of international NGOs. The protocol was field-tested close to its final completion in Colombia and the Democratic Republic of Congo. In some conflict-affected countries a few organisations were asked to review the draft, including some women's rights organisations, such as Isis-WICCE in Uganda. However, as organisations based in the UK and Uganda, and with close partnerships with women's rights organisations globally, we know that the document was not systematically consulted on with women and women's rights organisations across conflict-affected countries, nor was the participation of women and women's rights organisations fully integrated into the development process from its initiation. While field-testing and consultation are important steps in developing a protocol designed for use primarily by women in conflict-affected countries, it is imperative that women are able to fully participate from the initial design phase to ensure that it fully reflects the contextual needs of survivors of sexual violence.

UK-hosted 2014 NATO Summit

At the UK-hosted Global Summit to End Sexual Violence in Conflict in 2014, the UK, NATO, and other states and multilateral organisations made statements on the importance of women's participation in international summits, and the UK NAP, launched during this event, makes a specific commitment to 'Ensure that women are fully and meaningfully represented at an international peace-building event or summit hosted by the UK, by encouraging government delegations to fully include women representatives' (Foreign and Commonwealth Office 2014, 11). In addition, commitments were outlined in the current NATO Action Plan on UNSCR 1325 to include Women, Peace and Security in the September 2014 NATO Summit, held in Wales.

However, women were not fully included and consulted in advance of this UK-hosted NATO Summit (Taylor 2014). Women, Peace and Security was not an agenda item, as it had been in Chicago two years before. Despite previous commitments, women from conflict-affected countries were not present at the NATO Summit and as a result the voices and experiences of women not addressed. Samira Hamidi of the Afghan Women's Network commented:

> *How can we be expected to be taken seriously at home when we are being side-lined in the very places where we should be championed? The absence of women sends a dangerous message to Afghanistan and beyond that the rights*

and roles of women are not important. (See: http://gaps-uk.org/at-the-nato-summit-where-are-the-women/ (last checked by the authors 20 April 2015)

Ways forward

Significant progress has been made in international donor efforts to improve the participatory processes which will increase the accountability, sustainability, and impact of interventions that are meaningful to women's security and stability. However, implementation of those commitments has not led to the systematic full and meaningful participation of women across the four 'pillars' of UNSCR 1325. Recognising that women's rights organisations are critical in bringing the voices of women from conflict-affected countries to policy-making and resulting programming would significantly increase the impact of the next phase of the UK government's Women, Peace and Security work. Identifying best practice and gaps to be addressed in full collaboration with these organisations will ensure that UK government policy and practice best meets the needs and priorities of women in conflict-affected countries.

We have not attempted to provide a 'one-size-fits-all' approach to address the issues, and as we argued earlier, this is all to the good, as it would not be possible to find one. Although participatory processes will inevitably be varied and context-specific, they will ideally be backed up by strong political support, be systematically planned and funded, adhere to local realities, and be based on certain core principles. In some cases, donors would be required to re-examine their established approaches. For example, the notion of needing to 'develop capacity' of Southern partners to engage in donor-led processes assumes an inherent deficiency of the partner, when 'sometimes it is the [policy] forum that lacks "capacity" to reach out to grassroots groups, whether capacity is technical, linguistic, or otherwise' (Kiai 2014, 13).

Policy spaces must be inhabited by the women directly affected by conflict, and with careful planning and dialogue in-country contributing to diversity in participants' perspectives and geographical base. It is crucial to engage self-led women's rights organisations, for example of rural women, indigenous women, women living with HIV or disabilities, or more specific issue groups such as market trader women, and finding ways to find consensus and direction amidst myriad viewpoints. Establishing mechanisms and resources to support women to organise collectively, discuss and develop shared responses to donor initiatives can be extremely productive. However, donors must be prepared for the ensuing conversations – truly embracing women's understandings and priorities may lead them in new and challenging directions.

A sensible starting point would be for donors to collaborate with networks and platforms already established in-country, in which women's rights organisations are frequently active. These bodies operate at many levels and with different focus themes. In Uganda, at the national level, women's rights organisations are organised based on their thematic niche. For example, Isis-WICCE is part of the Civil Society Budgetary Group (CSBG) which focuses on financing, and is also involved in a group co-ordinating advocacy for gender responsive policies, as well as the aforementioned mobilising platform handling Women, Peace and Security-related issues. Additionally, the International Conference of the Great Lakes Region (ICGLR), through its civil society forum, also monitors member state implementation of the December 2011 'Kampala Declaration on the Fight Against Sexual and Gender Based Violence in the Great Lakes Region' (Isis-WICCE 2014b).

Although donor governments must ensure close collaboration with their recipient counterparts, finding ways to reach out to women-led spaces will enable nuanced and insightful exchanges not offered within 'mainstream' fora. Although potentially more challenging at the outset, moving away from technocratic, structured spaces is likely to provide donors with realistic, impactful, and sustainable solutions to the challenges faced by women survivors of conflict.

It is important for documents to clearly commit to and outline participatory processes which will be engaged in throughout the life of the policy or programme. Establishing internal guidance for the facilitation of participatory processes can be useful, particularly where regular reviews to incorporate learning and experience take place. Minimum standard procedures could include *inter alia*, ensuring that financial and logistical support is provided to participants, ideally drawing on internal funds earmarked for this purpose; risk analysis and mitigation, focusing on the safety of participants; working with women to establish how the donor can provide an 'enabling environment' within consultative forums, for example by providing translators, employing accessible and non-technical language, and measures to establish speaking rights for all participants in any meetings. A comprehensive, long-term approach would also ensure the establishment of post-project review systems to assess efficacy of the process and to inform future efforts, with inbuilt and accessible feedback mechanisms for partners to input into this process. However, establishing a set of procedures is not enough; implementation must follow.

These approaches offer the potential to shift the power relations between international government donors and women in conflict-affected countries. They would also ensure that donor policy and practice is sustainable, impactful, and responds fully to the needs of the poorest and most marginalised women in the global South, and that the policymaking process itself is empowering to the women involved.

Notes

1. The donor community which supports initiatives relating to ending conflict, post-conflict reconstruction, and peace-building includes a wide range of different actors. These range from national governments, NGOs, UN agencies, and other multilateral international development institutions, international, national, and local organisations including NGOs. In

this chapter we refer throughout to 'donors', by which we mean official agencies, including state and local governments, or their executive agencies, which provide financial flows in the form of official development assistance (ODA) to countries and territories on the OECD-DAC list of recipient countries and which 'is administered with the promotion of the economic development and welfare of developing countries as its main objective' (OECD 2008, 1).

2. By the 'participatory approach', we mean initiatives which involve citizens in statutory decision-making, and are based on 'a conviction that participatory fora that open up more effective channels of communication and negotiation between the state and citizens serve to enhance democracy, create new forms of citizenship and improve the effectiveness and equity of public policy' (Cornwall and Schattan Coelho 2006, 6–7).

3. The other three 'pillars' are Protection, Prevention, and Relief and Recovery.

4. For an examination of language and terminology in international development, see Cornwall and Eade (2010).

References

ActionAid, Institute of Development Studies, and Womankind Worldwide (2012) 'From the Ground Up: Women's Roles in Local Peacebuilding in Afghanistan, Liberia, Nepal, Pakistan and Sierra Leone', http://www.womankind.org.uk/wp-content/uploads/down loads/2012/09/From-The-Ground-Up-FINAL.pdf (last checked by the authors 20 May 2015)

Alemany, Cecilia, Nerea Craviotto, Fernanda Hopenhaym, Ana Lidia Fernández-Layos, Cindy Clark, and Sarah Rosenhek (2008) 'Implementing the Paris Declaration: Implications for the Promotion of Women's Rights and Gender Equality', Paper commissioned by the Canadian Council on International Cooperation (CCIC) and developed by AWID and WIDE. http://www.iwtc.org/cd_finance/28_ca.pdf (last checked by the authors 20 May 2015)

Bell, Christine and Catherine O'Rourke (2010) 'Peace Agreements or Pieces of Paper? The Impact of UNSC Resolution 1325 on Peace Processes and their Agreements', International and Comparative Law Quarterly, p. 59

CARE International (2014) *A Call to Action on Gender and Humanitarian Reform', From the Call to Action on Violence against Women and Girls in Emergencies to the World Humanitarian Summit*, http://humanitariancoalition.ca/sites/default/files/basic-page/care_call_to_action_vawg_emergencies_brief_160914.pdf (last checked by the authors 20 May 2015)

Chambers, Robert (1997) *Whose Reality Counts? Putting the First Last*, London: Intermediate Technology Publications.

Chigudu, Hope (2014) *Politics of the Body: The Social Imaginaries of Women's Peace Activists in Eastern and Northern Uganda*, Dissertation submitted in partial fulfilment of the requirements for the degree of Master of Science in African Studies, 2013–2014

Cornwall, Andrea and Deborah Eade (eds.) (2010) *Deconstructing Development Discourse: Buzzword and Fuzzwords*, Rugby: Practical Action Publishing

Cornwall, Andrea and Vera Schattan Coelho (eds.) (2006) 'Spaces for Change? The Politics of Citizen Participation in New Democratic Arenas Zed Books: London', http://ww.drc-citizenship.org/system/assets/1052734500/original/1052734500-cornwall_etal.2007-spaces.pdf?1289508570 (last checked by the authors 20 May 2015)

Englebert, Pierre and Denis M. Tull (2008) 'Postconflict reconstruction in Africa: flawed ideas about failed states', *International Security* 32(4): 106–39

Esplen, Emily (2013) 'Leaders for Change: Why Support Women's Rights Organisations? Womankind Worldwide', http://www.womankind.org.uk/wp-content/uploads/downloads/2013/03/LeadersForChange-FINAL.pdf (last checked by the authors 20 May 2015)

Foreign and Commonwealth Office (2014) 'United Kingdom National Action Plan on Women, Peace & Security 2014–2017', https://www.gov.uk/government/publications/uk-national-action-plan-on-women-peace-and-security (last checked by the authors 20 May 2015)

Foreign and Commonwealth Office and the Rt Hon William Hague (2013) 'Written statement to Parliament – Geneva II negotiations on Syria: women's participation. Delivered on 19th December 2013', https://www.gov.uk/government/speeches/geneva-ii-negotiations-on-syria-womens-participation (last checked by the authors 20 May 2015)

Gaventa, John (2003) 'Towards Participatory Local Governance: Assessing the Transformative Possibilities', paper presented at the conference on Participation: From Tyranny to Transformation, Manchester, 27–28 February, 2003

Hunt, Abigail and Bethan Cansfield (2014) 'Moving Forward: Recommendations for the UK National Action Plan on Women, Peace and Security', London: Womankind Worldwide. http://www.womankind.org.uk/2014/02/moving-forward-on-women-peace-and-security-next-steps-for-the-uk-government/ (last checked by the authors 20 May 2015)

Htun, Mala and S. Laurel Weldon (2012) 'The civic origins of progressive policy change: combating violence against women in global perspective 1975–2005', *American Political Science Review* 106 (3):548–563

Isis-WICCE (2014a) The Harare Conversation: Isis-WICCE Think Tank III, Report of Think Tank event of feminist thinkers from different parts of Africa to discuss the situation of women, peace and security in Africa, February 2014. http://www.isis-wicce.org/resource/harare-conversation-isis-wicce-think-tank-iii (last checked by the authors 20 May 2015)

Isis-WICCE (2014b) *Towards an Anti-Sexual and Gender–Based Violence Norm in the Great Lakes Region of Africa: A review of the Implementation of the 2011 ICGLR*, Kampala: Isis-WICCE

Jad, Islah (2007) 'The NGO-ization of Arab women's movements', in Andrea Cornwall, Elizabeth Harrison, and Ann Whitehead (eds.) *Feminisms in Development: Contradictions, Contestations & Challenges*, London: Zed Books, pp. 177–190

Jones, Harry, Nicola Jones, Louise Shaxson, and David Walker (2012) *Knowledge, Policy and Power in International Development: A Practical Guide*, Bristol: The Policy Press

Kiai, Maina (2014) 'Report of the Special Rapporteur on the Rights to Freedom of Peaceful Assembly and of Association', A/69/365, Thematic report submitted to the Sixty-ninth session of the United Nations General Assembly, 1 September 2014. http://www.ohchr.org/EN/newyork/Pages/HRreportstothe69thsessionGA.aspx (last checked by the authors 20 May 2015)

Knight, Michelle (2000) 'Ethics in qualitative research: multicultural feminist activist research', *Theory into Practice* 39(3): 170–76

Nunnenkamp, Peter (1995) 'What donors mean by good governance: heroic ends, limited means, and traditional dilemmas of development cooperations', *IDS Bulletin* 26(2): 9–16.

O'Connell, Helen (2012) *What Added Value Do Organizations that Are Led and Managed by Women and Girls Bring to the Work Addressing the Rights, Needs and Priorities of Women and Girls*, London: Comic Relief

OECD (2008) Factsheet: Is it ODA? http://www.oecd.org/dac/stats/documentupload/IsitODA.pdf (last checked by the authors 20 May 2015)

Stone, Diane (2004) 'Transfer agents and global networks in the "transnationalisation" of policy', *Journal of Eurpoean Public Policy* 11(3): 545–66

Taylor, Leonie (2014) *At the NATO summit – where are the women?* Gender Action for Peace and Security. http://gaps-uk.org/at-the-nato-summit-where-are-the-women/ (last checked by the authors 20 May 2015)

Tembo, Fletcher and Adrian Wells (2007) *Multi-donor Support to Civil Society and Engaging with 'Non-traditional' Civil Society: A Light-touch Review of DFID's Portfolio*, London: ODI

UK Government (2014) 'About the Global Summit to End Sexual Violence in Conflict', https://www.gov.uk/government/topical-events/sexual-violence-in-conflict/about (last checked by the authors 20 May 2015)

Wallace, Tina, Fenella Porter, and Mark Ralph-Bowman (2013) *Aid, NGOs and the Realities of Women's Lives: A Perfect Storm*, Rugby: Practical Action Publishing

About the Authors

Abigail Hunt is Policy & Advocacy Manager at Womankind Worldwide, UK, and Co-chair of the UK Gender and Development Network Working Group on Women's Participation and Leadership. Email: abigail@womankind.org.uk

Hannah Bond is Director of Gender Action for Peace and Security UK (GAPS). Email: hannah.bond@gaps-uk.org

Ruth Ojiambo Ochieng is Executive Director of Isis Women's International Cross-Cultural Exchange (Isis-WICCE), Uganda. Email: oruth@isis.or.ug

CHAPTER 12
Resources for gender and inequalities

Liz Cooke

Combating Poverty and Inequality: Structural Change, Social Policy and Politics (2010) Geneva: UNRISD, http://www.unrisd.org/unrisd/website/ document.nsf/(httpPublications)/BBA20D83E347DBAFC125778200440AA7? OpenDocument (last accessed May 2018), 380 pp.

Arguing that 'poverty and inequality must be considered as interconnected parts of the same problem' (p. 5) this major report published by the UN Research Institute for Social Development in 2010 finds that for countries that have been successful in increasing the well-being of the majority of their populations over relatively short periods of time, progress has occurred largely through state-directed strategies that combine economic development objectives with active social policies and forms of politics that promote the interests of the poor in public policy. The report is structured around three main issues, which, it argues, are the crucial elements of a sustainable and inclusive development strategy: patterns of growth and structural change; comprehensive social policies; and protection of civic rights, activism, and political arrangements. Two chapters focus specifically on inequalities between women and men. Chapter 4 – Gender Inequalities at Home and in the Market – examines women and the labour market, making the important point that while women's access to paid work has increased in most countries, at the same time a deterioration has occurred in the terms and conditions of much of that work, with livelihoods becoming increasingly insecure and precarious: 'Economic growth does not necessarily reduce gender gaps in earnings or enhance women's economic autonomy' (p. 107). The report also makes the worrying point that sex-ratio imbalances are deepening in China and India, two countries that have seen rapid rates of economic growth over the past decade, along with a rise in sex-selective abortions. Chapter 7 – Care and Well-Being in a Development Context – argues for the urgency of addressing unpaid care – which while invisible and undervalued, underpins economic growth and social development and is undertaken predominantly by women across all economies and cultures – through public policy.

Strengthening Social Justice to Address Intersecting Inequalities Post-2015 (2014) Veronica Paz Arauco, Haris Gazdar, Paula Hevia-Pacheco, Naila Kabeer, Amanda Lenhardt, Syeda Quratulain Masood, Haider Naqvi, Nandini Nayak, Andrew Shepherd, Deepak Thapa, Sukhadeo Thorat, and D. Hien Tran,

http://dx.doi.org/10.3362/9781780447278.012

London: ODI, http://www.odi.org/publications/8909-strengthening-social-justice-address-intersecting-inequalities (last accessed May 2018), 76 pp.

Taking as its starting point Naila Kabeer's 2010 report Can the MDGs Provide a Pathway to Social Justice? The Challenge of Intersecting Inequalities (https://www.ids.ac.uk/publication/can-the-mdgs-provide-a-pathway-to-social-justice-the-challenges-of-intersecting-inequalities, last accessed May 2018) this scholarly paper argues that the people most likely to be left out of development progress are those who experience 'intersecting inequalities' that is, economic disadvantage which intersects with discrimination and exclusion on the grounds of identity (often ascribed from birth; such as race, caste, and ethnicity and which can include religion, disability, and sexuality) and locational disadvantage. The authors state that 'Gender cuts across these different identities so that within most groups women and girls are positioned as subordinate to men. Unlike most socially subordinate groups, however, women and girls are distributed fairly evenly across different economic classes so that gender on its own does not constitute a marker of poverty. It is the intersection of gender with economic and other inequalities that explains the intensified nature of disadvantage often faced by poorer women and girls' (p. 10). However, they provide the important qualification that most poverty data only assess income and consumption levels at the household level, so that intra-family economic inequalities often remain hidden (p. 10). Focusing on the experience of seven countries, the report finds that the key ingredients for addressing intersecting inequalities are: social movements demanding change; political projects with a goal of enhancing social justice; the potential of constitutional change; frameworks of rights and guarantees; and commitment to long-term approaches and policies to reduce intersecting equalities over time. Of particular interest to readers of G& D may be the data on gender and social marginalisation in South Africa (taken from Kabeer 2010) on p. 2; life expectancy rates of Dalit women in India (p. 42); the section on women's land rights on p. 47; and the section on targeted versus universalist policies and programmes, which includes assessments of cash transfer programmes focusing on women in Brazil and Pakistan and the gender-blind Pluri-national Plan in Ecuador (pp. 52–7).

Gender, Poverty and Development (2015) Sylvia Chant and Gwendolyn Beetham (eds.), London and New York: Routledge, ISBN: 978-0-415-71195-1, 1,924 pp., website: www.routledge.com

This multi-volume compendium, probably likely to be found only in major or academic libraries, includes groundbreaking, classic texts alongside new research. It forms a hugely valuable resource that seeks to provide what is essentially a stand-alone 'library' for understanding the gendered dimensions of the contexts, causes, and effects of poverty, internationally. Each volume opens with an introductory essay by the editors, and given the exhaustive scope of the compendium, it is worth providing a full breakdown of how the contents are organised here: Volume I, Key Approaches and Concepts – Part 1: Conceptual Approaches to Gender and Poverty in Relation to Household Dynamics, Divisions of Labour, and Sexuality. Part 2: Feminization of Poverty. Part 3: Gender, Structural Adjustment, and Economic Crisis. Part 4: Quantifying Gendered Poverty and Inequality: Measures and Indicators. Volume II, Gender and Poverty in the Domestic Domain – Part 1: Gender, Households, and Poverty. Part 2: Femaleheaded Households and Poverty. Part 3: Reproductive Rights and Gender Discrimination. Volume III, Gendered Poverties in Relation to Health, Labour Markets, and Assets – Part 1: Health. Part 2: Employment and Labour Markets. Part 3: Assets and Social Capital. Volume IV, Gender, Poverty, and Policy Interventions – Part 1: Policy Approaches: Development 'Goals', Gender Mainstreaming, and 'Women's Empowerment'. Part 2: Poverty Reduction Programmes: PRSPs, CCTs, and Microfinance.

'Gender, poverty and inequality: the role of markets, states and households' (2010) Shahra Razavi and Silke Staab, in Sylvia Chant (ed.), *The International Handbook of Gender and Poverty: Concepts, Research, Policy*, Cheltenham, UK: Edward Elgar, pp. 427–33

This short article analyses income poverty from a gender perspective, examining the interplay between the labour market – characterised everywhere by the concentration of more women than men in sectors with lower pay, poorer working conditions, and limited prospects – the welfare policies pursued by governments that serve to mitigate women's disadvantages; and the household, where, in all societies, the labour force is itself 'produced' by the unpaid care work performed disproportionately by women and girls, and where although income pooling, for example, might mean a household qualifies as non-poor, a woman herself may experience poverty at an individual level, and/or be rendered dependent on a male breadwinner. Using this framework, and with selected country examples, the authors compare and contrast the situation in advanced industrialised countries; middle-income and 'highly unequal' Brazil and South Africa; and the agrarian contexts of India and Kenya. Conclusions include that gender norms are embedded within labour markets and operate as a form of social regulation, and that the state has an essential role to play in countering market-based discrimination and in creating decent employment for women, along with providing income support to expand women's options.

The International Handbook of Gender and Poverty: Concepts, Research, Policy (2010) Sylvia Chant (ed.), Cheltenham, UK: Edward Elgar, ISBN: 978 1 84980 095 2, 736 pp., website: www.e-elgar.com

Another key reference work, this edited volume incorporates conceptual, methodological, and practical contributions, which taken together provide a comprehensive guide to understanding poverty and inequality as processes that are gendered. The thematic range is wide, as is the geographical coverage, with authors offering learning from across the world. The book is organised into the following ten sections: Concepts and Methodologies for Gendered Poverty; Debates on the 'Feminisation of Poverty', and Female-headed Households; Gender, Family and Lifecourse; Gender, 'Race' and Migration; Gender, Health and Poverty; Gender, Poverty and Assets; Gender, Poverty and Work; Gendered Poverty and Policy Interventions; Microfinance and Women's Empowerment; and New Frontiers in Gendered Poverty Research. Particularly welcome is the accessibility of the contributions in what might be regarded at first glance, at least, as a book aimed primarily at a scholarly/ academic audience.

Even it Up: Time to End Extreme Inequality (2014) Emma Seery and Ana Caistor Arendar, Oxford: Oxfam International, http://policy-practice.oxfam.org.uk/ publications/even-itup-time-to-end-extreme-inequality-333012 (last accessed May 2018), 138 pp.

Oxfam's recent flagship report on extreme inequality is an informative and accessible primer on the increasing levels of economic inequality, both between and within countries. Reflecting the 'very strong link between gender inequality and economic inequality' (p. 10), and the fact that 'women are worst affected by market fundamentalist policies' (p. 13), the report includes a chapter on achieving economic equality for women, and a set of policy prescriptions (pp. 114–5) for promoting women's economic equality and women's rights.

Progress of the World's Women: Transforming Economies, Realizing Rights (2015) New York: UN Women, http://progress.unwomen.org/en/2015/pdf/unw_ progressreport.pdf (last accessed May 2018), 339 pp.

UN Women's flagship report concentrates on the need to redress the socioeco-nomic inequalities faced by women while at the same time addressing factors – 'stereotyping, stigma and violence' – that reinforce women's disadvantage, and the need to strengthen women's 'agency, voice and participation'. The aim is substantive equality for women – that is, a situation where the formal laws and policies guaranteeing the equal rights of women and girls around the world become a reality on the ground, and the creation of an economic model that works for women. Central to this is the recognition, reduction, and redistribu-tion of unpaid care work. The report is a hugely impressive survey of where we are now, and what needs to change, incorporating large amounts of new research and contributions from many experts in the field, along with case studies documenting positive change. The four main sections focus on public policy, in the form of the law and human rights; the transformation necessary in paid and unpaid work; social policy; and macro-economic policies.

'Advancing the scope of gender and poverty indices: an agenda and work in progress' (2010) Thomas Pogge, in Sylvia Chant (ed.), *The International*

Handbook of Gender and Poverty: Concepts, Research, Policy, Cheltenham, UK: Edward Elgar, pp. 53–8

In this chapter the author critiques leading indices of development, poverty, and gender equity, such as the UN's Human Development Index and Gender Development Index, highlighting what for him are crucial flaws in methodology, particularly in regard to the shift in focus from individual to country level assessment – for example, life expectancy being averaged across a national population (or across a female and male population), with differences between class or ethnic groups rendered invisible. Another problem highlighted is the bias towards the better off, for example, the inclusion indicators that are relevant to the more privileged, such as women in parliament or women in higher education, which the author argues matter, but 'are less important than the gender inequities burdening much larger numbers of more disadvantaged women and girls …' (p. 57). With flawed indices providing misleading information to policymakers, the author argues for the importance of constructing better measures of deprivation.

Measuring Key Disparities in Human Development: The Gender Inequality Index. Human Development Research Paper 2010/46 (2010) Amie Gaye, Jeni Klugman, Milorad Dovacevic, Sarah Twigg, and Eduardo Zambrano, New York: UNDP, http://hdr.undp.org/sites/default/files/hdrp_2010_46.pdf (last accessed 8 May 2015), 41 pp.

Arguing that gender inequality remains a major barrier to human development, this paper, published in 2010, introduces the UN Development Programme's Gender Inequality Index (GEI), which first appeared as part of the 2010 UN Human Development Report. The paper helpfully outlines the difficulties involved in measuring and monitoring gender inequality, and sets out the limitations of previous indices developed by UNDP. It goes on to explain the choice of indicators, which include economic and political participation, educational attainment, and reproductive health issues, and outlines the methodology for calculating a country's rating. The final section outlines the results as contained in the 2010 Human Development Report (with the Netherlands ranking highest – that is being the country closest to gender equality – and Yemen lowest) and compares them with results of a selection of other gender indices. (In the 2014 Human Development Report, the GEI ranks Slovenia highest, and Yemen lowest – see http://hdr.undp.org/sites/default/files/hdr14-report-en-1.pdf (last accessed 11 May 2015).

'Transcending the impact of the financial crisis in the United Kingdom: towards plan F – a feminist economic strategy' (2015) Ruth Pearson and Diane Elson, *Feminist Review* 109(1): 8–30

Arguing that it is women who have borne the brunt of austerity policies in the UK, through the impact on unemployment, employment protection and security, public sector services, social security benefits, pensions, and the real value of wages and living standards, this excellent paper by two world-renowned feminist economists calls for the recognition of the gendered nature and operation of the economy – which the authors divide into three spheres – finance, production, and reproduction, the latter being historically neglected in economic policymaking. The paper provides valuable statistical evidence on the gendered impact of austerity in the UK, and sets out measures that would see governments investing in the social infrastructure associated with the reproductive sphere of the economy, along with proposals for financing such a feminist economic policy.

The Price of Austerity: The Impact on Women's Rights and Gender Equality in Europe (2012) Anna Elomäki, Brussels: European Women's Lobby, http://www. womenlobby.org/spip.php?article4257(last accessed May 2018), 18 pp.

This paper argues that the austerity policies implemented by European governments in response to the global recession are having specific, gendered effects, and run the risk of rolling back years of progress made towards the achievement of gender equality. The paper focuses on three areas: cuts in public sector jobs (which have often provided secure and relatively well-paid employment for women) and wages; cuts in services and benefits (which result in women, in their traditional role of 'carer', having to fill the void); and cuts in funding for women's rights and gender equality, with women's voices silenced through lack of funding for women's NGOs, along with their capacity to respond in terms of service delivery, and deprioritisation of gender equality as an issue at the national level.

'Women's Economic Independence in Times of Austerity'. *European Women's Voice* (2015) Brussels: European Women's Lobby, http://www.womenlobby. org/spip.php?article7102&lang=en (last accessed May 2018), 46 pp.

In what serves as a follow up to The Price of Austerity (see above), this edition of European Women's Voice seeks to demonstrate that ongoing austerity measures across the European Union are undermining women's economic independence. The paper is divided into two parts. Part 1 outlines the situation in five different countries – Scotland, Slovenia, Sweden, Greece, and Italy – noting the consequences of gender-blind and austerity policies (carried out with little or no social impact assessments) which in the case of Greece, the authors argue, have led to a loss of trust in democratic systems. Part II is a call for new economic models that 'truly tackle the current inequalities in terms of gender pay and pension gaps [and] the imbalance of unpaid work and care responsibilities' (p. 3), and includes 'Lessons from Feminists & Women in the Global South' (p. 34) on the damage wrought by the structural adjustment policies of the 1980s and 1990s, and gender pension inequality in the EU (pp. 32–3).

End of Equality: The Only Way is Women's Liberation (2014) Beatrix Campbell, London: Seagull Books, ISBN: 9780857421135, 96 pp. website: www. seagullbooks.org

This short book by British feminist and author Bea Campbell is aimed at a general, non-academic audience, but is nonetheless solidly grounded in academic debates and contains large amounts of information from around the world (for which see the many references included). In the book, Bea Campbell argues that we are living under a 'neoliberal neopatriarchy', in which many feminist advances have not only stalled, but are going backwards. For the author, the detrimental effects of global neo-liberal economic policies on women, along with the high levels of violence experienced by women, in peace time and conflict, represent a crisis for women and for societies as a whole, with welfare states and social solidarity under threat and impunity for perpetrators of sexual violence. In the face of this 'new sexual settlement', she calls for a revolution, to bring about a world free from male violence and where collective responsibility is taken for the care of others.

Oxfam GB is a development, relief, and campaigning organization that works with others to find lasting solutions to poverty and suffering around the world. Oxfam GB is a member of Oxfam International.

As part of its programme work, Oxfam undertakes research and documents its programme and humanitarian experience. This is disseminated through books, journals, policy papers, research reports, campaign reports, and other online products which are available for free download at: www.oxfam.org.uk/ publications

www.oxfam.org.uk
Email: publish@oxfam.org.uk
Tel: +44 (0) 1865 473727

Oxfam House
John Smith Drive
Cowley
Oxford
OX4 2JY

The chapters in this book are available to download from the website: www.oxfam.org.uk/publications